21st Century Journalism in India

21st Century Journalism in India

Edited by

Nalini Rajan

SAGE Publications
New Delhi ■ Thousand Oaks ■ London

84110

Copyright © Nalini Rajan, 2007

First published in 2007 by

Sage Publications India Pvt Ltd
B1/I1, Mohan Cooperative Industrial Area
Mathura Road
New Delhi 110 044
www.sagepub.in

Sage Publications Inc
2455 Teller Road
Thousand Oaks, California 91320

Sage Publications Ltd
1 Oliver's Yard, 55 City Road
London EC1Y 1SP

Published by Vivek Mehra for Sage Publications India Pvt Ltd, typeset in 10/12 Concorde BE Regular by Star Compugraphics Private Limited, Delhi and printed at Chaman Enterprises, New Delhi.

Library of Congress Cataloging-in-Publication Data

21st century journalism in India / edited by Nalini Rajan.
    p. cm.
  1. Journalism—India. I. Rajan, Nalini, 1954– II. Title: Twenty first century jouralism in India.

PN5374.A14   079'.54–dc22   2007   2007001005

ISBN: 978-0-7619-3561-2 (Hb)   978-81-7829-721-7 (India-Hb)
        978-0-7619-3562-9 (Pb)   978-81-7829-722-4 (India-Pb)

Sage Production Team: Vidyadhar Gadgil, Roopa Sharma, and
                             Santosh Rawat

Contents

Acknowledgements

I am very grateful to Mr Tejeshwar Singh of Sage Publications for giving me the opportunity to edit this volume, close on the heels of my previous publication, *Practising Journalism: Values, Constraints, Implications* (2005). Working on a sequel is always a boon as far as an editor is concerned, because it gives her the opportunity to make up for the 'shortcomings' in the previous edited volume. In this book, I have included articles on broadcast journalism, covering the arts and the sciences, photojournalism, and so on, apart from those on emerging genres in journalism. In short, I have tried to bring into this volume much of what I had hoped to include in the earlier volume but could not, owing to various constraints. For this, I am extremely grateful to all the contributors to this book. Special thanks to Sashi Kumar for giving me permission to use a slightly modified version of his article, earlier published under the title 'In the Melting Pot' in *Frontline*, Volume 22, Issue 22, 22 October–4 November 2005.

I would also like to thank the the anonymous reader of this manuscript, who illuminated the flaws in the first draft; my colleagues and friends; and my students at the Asian College of Journalism, who teach me more than they can imagine.

Nalini Rajan
February 2007

Introduction

Nalini Rajan

Journalists are generally on the side of progress and reform; yet they are deeply sceptical about all the major institutions of society except their own. The very notion of self-criticism has become taboo to journalists, and the word itself has become a semantic flame, which attracts outraged moths, both legitimate and illegitimate. For every hundred exemplary works of literary criticism, there is probably just one on journalism. There is, quite simply, little or no important critical literature concerning journalism, especially within the Indian sub-continent. The newspaper or broadcast channel may foster such literature in every other field; it does not foster it in its own domain. Unusually enough, many chapters in this volume—the majority of which are written by practising journalists—attempt to turn the spotlight on the journalistic profession itself.

Ideally, a media system suitable for a democracy ought to provide its readers with some coherent sense of the broader social forces that affect the conditions of their everyday lives—but that is hardly the case. Dramatic changes in the technology of reproduction within the media have led to the implosion of representation and reality. As we know from Marshall McLuhan, the medium is the message, and as Jean Baudrillard often reminds us, media practitioners live in a world of pure simulations with no corresponding substance or reality beneath them.[1] Increasingly, representation becomes dominant, as 'simulacra' or hyperreal representations are substituted for a reality that has no foundation in experience.[2] This is true not only of journalism, but also of the other media. An advertisement, for example, may be intended merely to sell a car to women, but it may incidentally encode a message about gender relations and what it means to be a 'woman'.

Reading media imagery is an active process in which context, social location and prior experience can lead to quite different interpretations. Much of media discourse does involve struggles over meaning. Furthermore, it is frequently interactive, taking place in conversation with other readers who may see different meanings, as the chapters in the last section in this volume inform us. On the one hand, events and experiences are framed by external circumstances; on the other, journalists themselves frame events and experiences. But journalists are supposed to be active processors and, however encoded their received reality, they may decode it in different ways. The very vulnerability of the framing process makes it a locus of potential struggle, not a leaden reality to which scribes must inevitably yield.

According to many writers in Part I of this volume–not all of whom are journalists–communication in the public realm oscillates between struggle and submission, as the media witnesses the encounters between the government and the community, or their representatives. The media constitutes a third voice and does not always substitute for the people. In general, the media traffics in representations, and its audience consumes those words, symbols and images. For this very reason, the media has a duty and responsibility towards its audience, that of fulfilling its various roles of information disseminator, watchdog and educator. The media sometimes amplifies the critical process, adding information to it in the form of reports and analyses, and at other times, owing to media ownership affiliations, merely represents the interests of political or commercial groups. In the former case, the media operates in a critical way only in order to defend its own values and to supply information. In the latter case, the media does not–for its most important stories–observe the events. It reports what spokespersons, sources and authorities of different stripes say about the events. The media becomes the conveyor, rather than the originator, of observations.

New information technologies appear to enhance and reinforce the same general ownership patterns and increase the range and power of the production of imagery by large corporations with many shared ideological and cultural interests. The net result is a homogenization of imagery that celebrates existing power relationships—separating 'us' from 'them'—and makes these seem a normal and acceptable part of the natural order.

The 'us' and 'them' dichotomy constitutes a throwback to the discipline of anthropology and is also responsible for several exclusions within the media itself. Whether a journalist struggles against these power relationships or submits to them as part of a 'leaden reality' will depend largely on her social location in terms of gender, caste, community or class. Indeed the mass media has contributed to the processes of cultural and disciplinary displacement. Analyses of orientalism and 'the objectifying gaze' in art, photography, travel literature, tourism, world fairs and museums apply equally to the construction of otherness, the primitive and the exotic in news reporting and photojournalism.[3] Part I, 'Representing the Unrepresented', with contributions from 'insiders' and 'outsiders' of the journalistic profession, discusses the way the media looks at women, queers, untouchables and children.

The struggle for representation is multifaceted, plural and complex. The questions we face include the ethics of representation, the composition and institutions of representation, and the manner of representation. Classic liberal theory begins with the individual as its primary unit, whereas the current crisis of representation stems from the claim that groups also have a right to representation.

In her well-researched chapter in this volume, Ammu Joseph lays bare the specific problems of economically deprived women in disaster zones, like in the aftermath of the Asian tsunami. Wherever disasters strike, women usually pay a high price, owing to pre-existing patriarchal structures and unequal social conditions. Again, in crisis situations, women's bodies become the site of violence in the form of rape and sexual harassment. The problem, however, is that gender issues often become a domain of potential struggle within the media, with some women journalists becoming increasingly defensive about the need to focus on gender. Others—mainly men—become increasingly (and worryingly) gender-blind in their observations, in the name of maintaining standards of 'objectivity'.

There is, however, one area of gender politics that is better represented in advertising than in journalism per se. There is the much-quoted instance of Western advertisements for Calvin Klein products, which depict men in provocative poses that sexualize the male body. The queering, or feminization, of male representations, even if largely confined to the realm of advertising in Western media, reflects its ever-changing ideas about masculinity. English-language journalism in India occasionally makes a gesture towards liberalism, especially in the opinion pieces, and calls for the abolition of Section 377 of the Indian Penal Code, which criminalizes homosexuality. Nevertheless the reports on homosexuality that appear in the same media are unabashedly homophobic, and deny the politics of difference.

The truth is that 'objective reporting' is usually a euphemism for perpetrating the existing patriarchal power structure and the status quo. As Siddharth Narrain explains in Chapter 2,

> Media reporting around queer issues cannot be divorced from the reality of queer people's lives. If the Indian media has to address the issue of homophobic reportage, it has to stop clinging to the canon of objectivity. What the media needs are standards that will ensure that journalists recognize, and take into account, the ways in which queer persons and communities negotiate existing discrimination against them, in place of the 'objective' standards that reinforce such prejudices.

Compared to children's issues, perhaps gender-related issues have a better equation with the media. Feminists and 'queer' theorists have established a body of reading strategies, analytical frameworks and theoretical models for understanding better the crucial role that media perform in the reproduction of gender inequality. Sandhya Rao illustrates Chapter 3 with the voices of children to convince us of the crying need for greater representation for children's issues in the form of more children's magazines in India.

Affirming the politics of difference, however, could give rise to broader vistas of self-expression. More importantly, identity politics forces journalists from marginalized groups to become activists as well. (So much for the need for objectivity or neutrality in the media!) On the one hand, marginalized groups, like women, queers and children, are finding new outlets for expressing identity through the mainstream news media and gaining access to cheaper and more accessible media, like film and video, to serve their own ends. On the other hand, the spread of communications technology with its homogenized messages tends to erode the plurality of cultures. Should the marginalized groups therefore run their own newspapers, magazines, broadcast channels and online Websites?

V Geetha's illuminating interview with Punitha Pandian, editor of *Dalit Murasu*, illustrates the new trend of self-conscious, even activist, journalism, especially on the part of the hitherto oppressed. In south India, its lineage goes back to the mid-19th century, to the early decades of anti-caste publishing, and is concerned with persuading the public of the virtues of anti-caste radicalism. As Geetha points out, this trend

> seeks to universalize a point of view that is usually considered subaltern or marginal and thereby urges its claims to speak on behalf of a decent, civic humanity, and one committed to social and economic justice. The 'Dalit' in *Dalit Murasu* is both an invocation of an oppressed condition that has to be remembered, as well as an invitation to a future, where the oppressed become the measure of all that is to be human and imagine and build a brave new world.

D Ravikumar elaborates on the lineage of anti-caste and Dalit publishing referred to by V Geetha. Work being produced by oppressed minorities about themselves is also concerned with mediating across boundaries, to heal disruptions in cultural knowledge, historical memory and identity between generations, due to the tragic but familiar litany of assaults—expropriation of lands, destruction of houses, political violence, bodily harm, expansion of capitalist interests, and unemployment. Unfortunately, such work has been ghettoized and does not appear in the mainstream media—and consequently does not become a part of our common heritage and history. As Ravikumar succinctly puts it, '[The Dalit newspaper] *Parayan*'s defeat is a mere story, whereas the success of the *Hindu* becomes history.'

Social conflicts—as well as misrepresentation by the media—are compounded when it comes to the interaction of different religious and cultural communities, owing to their global reach. Subarno Chattarji examines four articles by American writers in the *New York Times* on the Madrid bombings of March 2004 and the Socialist victory in the Spanish elections that followed, in order to study the complex interface of democracy and journalistic reporting. Chattarji reaches the conclusion that the articles simplistically reflect the US anxieties about the spectacle of Spanish democracy rather than its content, by suggesting that the Socialist victory in Spain implied appeasement of Islamic terrorists. After all, the Spanish Socialists had opposed the US invasion of Iraq; therefore, they had to be on the side of the terrorists, according to the 'objective' reasoning of the *New York Times* opinion writers. Even in the best of cases, a certain 'us' and 'them' dichotomy seems to operate when Anglo-Saxon writers express themselves on global issues.

Anjali Kamat makes a similar point about the growing inability of the Western media to turn the spotlight on itself, particularly in the context of the 2005 publication of Danish cartoons that caricatured the revered Prophet of Islam. To frame the issue as a battle between freedom of expression in Western secular democracies and the narrow religious orthodoxies of a humourless Islamic world is to revive Samuel Huntington's simplistic 'clash of civilizations' theory and demonstrate an unwillingness to see the cartoons for what they are: hateful and racist.

Turning the spotlight on Western journalists leads us to examine our own journalistic practices in the developing world. The tasks of the future, then, include representing and institutionalizing truth, democracy, justice and liberty differently, and in ways that better accommodate the claims of social and cultural difference. That the first four chapters in Part II are written by 'outsiders' is an indication of the wide interest that such ethical issues arouse even among non-journalists. V K Natraj alerts us to the educational role of the media by pointing out that the real difference between the rich and the poor is not merely in respect of wealth and resources but in terms of access to information. Lack of information, in the case of the economically and socially deprived, restricts choice and adversely affects their participation in state and society. This, then, is the motivating force behind what has come to be called development communication.

However, lack of information can affect both the sender and receiver in the communication network. It is not that the mainstream media avoids covering the deprived sections of society. The point is that it does cover issues of deprivation and oppression, but in a manner that leaves much to be desired, mainly because of insensitivity, ignorance and laziness on the part of journalists. Geeta Ramaseshan informs media practitioners of the problem of violating the right to privacy of the most vulnerable groups in society, like physically and psychologically traumatized children, sex workers and HIV-positive persons.

K Kalpana, for her part, focuses on the largely 'feel-good' journalistic coverage of self-help groups involving Indian rural women. According to her, journalism that celebrates the 'success' of micro-credit in the countryside invariably ends up obfuscating as much as it reveals. The reason is that such coverage is under-taken mostly by upper-caste, upper- and middle-class journalists, who fail to acknowledge the caste and class differences between women. If only these media practitioners probed a little deeper, they would become aware of the multi-layered complexities of caste-based stratification, class hierarchies and family relation-ships—which operate within self-help rural groups.

The question is: how does one effectively tell the truth about different sections of society? Truth-telling is no longer fixed and set in tradition, revealed in sacred texts and authoritatively inter-preted by the monarch and the head priest. The positive fallout of this shift from sacred authority to popular will is the growth of democracy, but central to the growth of democracy is the growth of criticism. The first arena in which this liberation was experienced is in the essential critical discipline of science. In a world with no fixed and final truths, without authoritative texts, how are truth and knowledge derived? The answer is somewhat Kantian in nature—by turning to experience itself, i.e., by exam-ining nature and thereby one's own self. Following the work of the 18th-century philosopher Immanuel Kant, this novel idea of directly observing nature gave rise to the notion of a scientific report: i.e., rendering through language one's own observations of the particularity of nature. In order to accomplish this novel task, at least three things were needed: a clear and rigorous set of procedures for observation, a language of description that was factual rather than emotional, and a forum of criticism that would verify recorded observations.[4]

Journalists' requirements are not too different from the scien-tists', namely, some clear description of observations, a relatively neutral language, and a forum of response to recorded obser-vations. Curiously enough, as Vijaya Swaminath points out, when the journalist begins writing on science, she ought to break all these rules and consciously become more of a storyteller, using catchy headlines and seductive prose, rather than a mere functional writer trained in scientific knowledge. The reason is that very few people understand the specialized jargon of science. It behoves the science writer to not only make it accessible to laypersons but also irrevocably grab their attention.

Originally, it was believed that only the industrious, property-holding middle classes possessed communicative abilities. But in the 19th century the democratic impulse all over the world was too strong, and all barriers to participation in the media were inexorably overcome. No doubt there is a persistent danger in this process: if the critical process in democracy depends upon precise information and the requirements enumerated above, then how can the sources of information be protected from state or societal censorship and, at the same time, escape the vulgarity and irresponsibility that mass participation presumably portends?

With all these caveats in place, is there any possibility that humour could make greater inroads into journalism? Baradwaj Rangan laments the fact that humour in journalism could be a non-starter, given the reiteration of the lofty ideals of the profession in every public forum. Considering the additional constraints imposed on Indian media practitioners, namely, the need to respect elders, and the fear of offending politicians and people in high places, there is little chance of journalists here engaging with the lighter side of life.

Apart from the serious journalist's sense of panic that entertainment in news could easily spill over into the dreaded realm of tabloidization, there is the persistent bogey of commercialization confronting the media. Indeed, it is commercialization of the media, claims Aditi De, that has led to the shrinking of space for the arts in the Indian media since the year 2000. Journalists must ponder over the reasons for this phenomenon. Does this reflect a lack of public interest in art or a decision by business interests that culture does not pay its way as journalism as commerce rears its head? If the arts writer bravely persists in working on her beat, it is because the rewards of spending time with the most creative personalities of our age more than make up for the many constraints of rampant media commercialization.

This is why Geeta Doctor says that writing about art can be as exhilarating an adventure as skydiving or as prosaic as brushing and flossing one's teeth at night, or as demanding as a love affair.

Experiencing art may be heady, but the journalist is also a communicator. She must therefore write about it in order to share her sense of pleasure with the reader. This is the imperative of covering the arts in the print media.

There is, however, an art form that is not 'covered' in a newspaper, but is an integral part of it. In the early days of the press, newspaper design did not exist independent of the routines and practices of journalism, as it does today.[5] An integral part of newspaper design is photography. Modern photojournalism complements that primary task of professional reporting, providing a state of visual immediacy to go with the formally structured text. In the text and image, the modern newspaper sometimes requires the effacing of the persona of the journalist, i.e., both the text writer and the photo-taker. From this perspective, the journalist and photojournalist are seen as experts, not authors. In India, as Desikan Krishnan explains in Part III, the journey of the photojournalist has been a long one—from being an underpaid, disreputable hack mainly hanging around weddings and other functions, he has today metamorphosed into the glamorous persona of a trendy artist or a 'breaking news' reporter. Equally, the Indian newspaper tends to give more and more space to visuals, partly to enhance its aesthetic design component, and partly for commercial reasons, in order to attract more subscribers.

The spectre of commercialization is ever present in the media, especially in the realms of politics and culture. Journalists therefore face a dilemma from which there is no easy escape. In their eagerness to involve the entire community into the media process—after all, newspaper circulation and television ratings do count—journalists have often succumbed to the temptation to pander to the tastes and self-deceptions of large audiences. Such a situation could attract censorship or some deliberate political control. In the context of democracy, there is only one alternative to censorship: the same critical analysis must be turned inwards—upon the sources of information and their operation. The question here is not a matter of 'shooting the messenger' but of subjecting her to systematic, critical public analysis, lest she be controlled by censorship or corrupted by her own power and illusions.

Throughout the last quarter of the 20th century in India, government at all levels had begun to be increasingly distanced from the people. It became more professionalized, less subject to direct control by the people, more mysterious in its operations, and less bound by common language, ties and encounters. The more socially committed media has moved into this vacuum and seen itself in a new role, along with other forces in civil society, as a voice of the community, as a shaper and expositor of community opinion (see the chapter by Subramaniam Vincent and Ashwin Mahesh in Part IV). These committed institutions, more as representatives of the community than as independent critics, rationalize their position not in terms of the rights of the media but in terms of the needs and rights of the community—a view which has since passed into our common language as the 'people's right to know'.[6]

Nevertheless different countries take different positions on people's right to information. Mustafa K Anuar's 'Media in Perspective', a courageous article on this subject in Part III, elaborates on how the Malaysian government sees media freedoms as privileges rather than as rights. Although the Malaysian Constitution grants freedom of expression, it also slaps a whole range of restrictions on this freedom—many of them in the name of defending the interests of cultural pluralism and diversity—so as to render media operations like truthful reporting and in-depth analysis virtually ineffective. Although this article is not directly connected to Indian journalistic practice, it holds many lessons for journalists who have been working in oppressive conditions in certain parts of India.

In countries where there is greater freedom of expression, how do journalists go about their job? For several decades, straightforward reporting used to be the dominant style in newspaper offices the world over, guided by the journalist's five 'W's—'who', 'what', 'where', 'why' and 'when'. Since the facts were often based on what public figures had said or done, they greatly influenced the tone of the coverage. A standard formula for a news story was a descriptive account of what a public figure said and to whom she said it. News accounts did not ordinarily delve into why she said it, for that would venture into the realm of subjectivity. At the very least, journalists took pains to separate the facts of an event from their interpretations of it.

Nevertheless there has been a quiet revolution in news reporting during the past few decades. The traditional descriptive style of reporting has given way to an interpretive style that empowers journalists by giving them more control over content. Today, facts and interpretation intermix freely in news reporting— and this is probably more true of broadcast journalism. Interpretation provides the theme, which is of primary importance, and the facts merely illustrate it.

On the whole, whereas descriptive reporting is driven by facts, the interpretive form is driven by the theme around which the story is built. The descriptive style casts the journalist in the role of a reporter. The interpretative style requires the journalist to act also as an analyst; the journalist is thus positioned to give shape to the news in a way that the descriptive style does not allow. It raises the journalist's voice above that of the newsmaker. The broadcast journalist, for one, is always at the centre of the story as narrator, and ends up speaking much more than public figures on television. Interestingly though, what the public consumes is mainly the journalist's view of politics.

Subhashini Dinesh informs us that the interpretative style is not solely the prerogative of the reporter. In many cases, the news desk acts as a filter of news; in a few cases, it even *makes* the news. After all, the editor on the news desk has to exercise her judgement every working day whether or not to carry a story, whether or not to play it up, whether or not to use an illustration or photograph with it, on which page to allot the story, what kind of headline to use, and so on. In each of these cases, the newsdesk can, as much as the reporting desk, make or break the news. Equally, in every case, the news desk creates and establishes the ideological tone of the newspaper or broadcast channel.

Both Sashi Kumar and Amanda Harper, in their respective articles, provide a sharp critique of the broadcast media. If in the print media the news is divided in terms of position and space, then in television the division is made in terms of position and time allotted. The inverted pyramid form of the traditional newspaper story is less suited to television. This form consists of proceeding from the most salient fact of an event to the least important in a news report, allowing the newspaper editor to cut the story almost anywhere in order to fit it into the available space. The reader's eye is expected to anticipate the concluding line. On television, however, this form gives the appearance of a news story that has been abruptly terminated, ending with a whimper rather than a bang. Accordingly, network executives devise a more punchy style of reporting, built around storylines and time slots. This, then, involves a heady torrent of fiction and drama, conflict and denouement: a beginning, middle and end, not necessarily in that order. As Sashi Kumar points out in his article in this collection, 'the look of the new age TV screen ... demands fairly developed multitasking and non-linear ingestion capabilities of the viewer.'

No wonder, then, that the media–especially broadcast media–has a poor opinion of the representational skills of academics. Universities must increasingly compete with private corporations and foundations, with the media, and with various publicly organized activist groups that lay claim to representation in these arenas. 'Education' comes through MTV, advertising, the talk shows, and cinema; 'ideology' and 'subject positions' are produced by organizations through their texts, television shows and other public events. Academics, who may be experts in the university culture of the definitive footnote and the dazzling demolition of established theses, could find themselves incompetent, even marginalized, when pulled into the arenas of the op-ed page, the Prime Time News Hour, or the sound bite worlds of Star News and NDTV. The academic crisis in representation in the public sphere stems from a lack of time, training and experience in the art of communication. This may have changed over the last decade or so, with a few media-savvy academics adapting themselves to the sound-bite television culture, in place of the older, more tedious and demanding Gutenberg technology.[7]

Media texts, especially in television, are 'open' when they do not attempt to shut off alternative meanings and narrow their focus to one easily attainable meaning, and hence permit a richness and complexity of readings. This, of course, is the ideal to which we aspire. Sadly, these days, between wannabe journalists and dumbed-down audiences, there is little chance of such an enriching process taking place, as Amanda Harper's engaging chapter on teaching broadcast journalism reminds us. Live television coverage of the Kashmir conflict or of students demonstrating in France does provide viewers with real-time access to events on the other side of the globe. Nevertheless the compression of time in broadcast news leads to a preoccupation with the immediacy of surface meaning and the absence of depth. News comes in quotations with ever shorter sound bites. Distinctions between entertainment and news are artificial because they are all part of the same media spectacle, interspersed with the same advertisements in a seamless, all-prevalent montage. The primary effect, regardless of content, is to substitute hyperreal representations or 'simulacra' for the 'real' world. The result is that we have become a shallow society, concerned with spectacle rather than news or information. This is reiterated by Sashi Kumar: 'Depth has yielded to breadth and we "surf" TV channels across a shallow expanse.'

Today, while pepping up a story, some reporters tend to blur the distinction between subjectivity and objectivity. As a result, they have begun to question the actions of public figures and commonly attribute strategic intentions to them. In some extreme cases, journalists' reports may teeter dangerously on the brink of idle gossip, which often goes under the more respectable garb of 'Page 3 news' or the 'Metro section'.

Against the grain of conventional ideas on the media, Shonali Muthalaly makes a spirited defence for the Metro section of the newspaper, by claiming that its content need not be trivial or 'lowly', but could focus instead on creative writing or on providing useful information to local urban communities. Quite simply, the important news items that do not fit comfortably into the political, business or sports pages could easily find a place in the Metro section. This is why the Metro section is a crucial part of the newspaper.

One of the paradoxes of the power of interpretation is that journalists, who tend towards liberal beliefs, have become the unwitting handmaidens of the conservatives. One consequence is a form of news coverage that focuses on the negative aspects of politics. Excessive liberalism fails because it ignores the checks and balances within the news system. The problem would be attenuated by a model of reporting that subordinates the voice of the journalist and aims for a more balanced portrayal of the workings of the political system. 'Balance' in reporting does not imply 'neutrality' or 'objectivity, according to A S Panneerselvan. In his contribution to this volume, Panneerselvan raises admittedly controversial, albeit politically pertinent, points on the rationale of working for an openly partisan media organization.

He considers the five challenges of being a journalist in a politically affiliated news channel like Sun TV, which is the media organ of the Dravida Munnetra Kazhagam of M Karunanidhi in Tamil Nadu. The first is the question of dealing with an adverse government—in this case, it was the erstwhile ruling All India Anna Dravida Munnetra Kazhagam government of J Jayalalithaa—and using the network as a platform to protect the rights of journalists. The second is the question of protecting the integrity of news in the era of corporate sponsorship. The third concerns the political affiliations of the owners of the news channel, while the fourth is connected to devising the right mix of local, national regional and international news for an essentially south-Indian network. The fifth is linked to the economics of news. According to Panneerselvan, Sun Network's success is a result of effectively meeting all these challenges.

The last point on the economics of news is related to the emergence of media conglomerates within a global market, which has led to an unprecedented integration of multiple media. These can simultaneously market the same message in multiple forms through an array of new technologies. As a result, the media is perceived to have a credibility gap in the present day. So what can be done about it? Part IV, 'Future Trends', discusses the ways and means by which this credibility gap may be filled in the 21st century.

One solution is the creation of a tradition of media criticism that will reconnect the newspaper to the community it serves. But how does a newspaper connect with its community? In effect, the entire system of communication has become one of address—the people are spoken to, are informed, are often propagandized, but in no sense are their own perceptions, understandings and judgements fed back into the process, apart from the 'letters to the editor' column. Subramaniam Vincent and Ashwin Mahesh describe the English-language media in India as concentrating on urban and Delhi-centric issues, except when it comes to 'juicy' subjects like crime or natural or man-made disasters.

In the case of the latter, the press is even capable of expanding the notion of the 'journalist', as revealed by the media experience during the aftermath of the Asian tsunami. Photographs, SMS texts and video clippings are now openly solicited by some media organizations from ordinary citizens who happen to be at the spot of the tragedy in question. This has given rise to a new phenomenon called 'citizen journalism', according to Ethirajan Anbarasan. In a sense, online journalism provides a much wider and interactive forum than the more traditional media like the press and television. This point is illustrated by Subhash Rai's contribution, which focuses on the growing popularity of blogging, and expands the meaning of the 'independent media' by making greater inroads into the community.

In the past, verbal language alone has been the most important aspect of our educational system, as it was the language tool used for carrying on most of the formal learning in our culture. But now people can acquire their information for cultural functioning through a more comprehensive multi-media language.

Sunil Saxena, for one, believes that the future of the community is clearly on the side of the new media in India, with phenomena like e-journals, news portals, blogging and value-added news services in mobile phones gaining ground every day. Frederick Noronha, for his part, takes this idea further and discusses the democratic potential of the new media, with constant technology innovation and the increasing participation of civil society in the dissemination of information. The liberating potential of the Internet, referred to by Saxena and Noronha, is also reiterated by Anuar in the Malaysian context (in Part III of this volume).

While Jurgen Habermas's work has done much to revive the notion of the public sphere and the importance of community, his failure to consider how the hegemonic operations of the public sphere exclude unwanted voices cautions us against too readily returning to an unquestioned idea of public representation. For instance, language—which is a crucial part of cultural representation—was not a common resource until the 18th century, even in England. It was not until 1755 that the first dictionary was produced in English and, therefore, it was not until the end of the 18th century that a set of stable, uncoloured denotative terms was available for general use. In England, the conflict over language continued throughout the 19th century between the Benthamites or Utilitarians on one side and an older, conservative tradition of language represented by Coleridge and Cardinal Newman that was essentially religious and poetic in inspiration on the other.

A recent form of feature writing in India heralds the media avatar of poetic language. Robin Reisig provides a fascinating account of narrative journalism–that genre-blurred heady mix of investigative reportage and fiction.[8] This new form of journalism styles itself as an alternative to more standard media renderings of social reality, promising to reflect a 'more real' reality, to tell the 'truer' story of the many social crises splitting our society. It was not only a loss of interest in fiction that engendered the search for a new narrative style in journalistic reporting. It was, probably even more significantly, the realization that the media's claim to be 'objective' is often a smokescreen for bias. Narrative journalism offers its audience an opportunity to read news reportage by journalists who could write with empathy on every subject. Only through a dramatic novelistic method could reporters openly communicate (rather than mask) their own direct engagement with the experiences they reported.

Narrative journalism is believed to seek a larger truth than is possible through the mere compilation of verifiable facts. Robert Brown discusses the immense potential for literary reportage in the Indian sub-continent in the 21st century. At the same time, he alerts us to some of the potential dangers in pursuing this demanding genre of writing. After all, the journalist's imitation of fiction writing may well lead her to disregard the facts and eschew the principle of truth-telling which is the mainstay of her profession.

Journalism, then, holds many promises for journalists, especially for those about to embark on a career. However, behind every promise there lurk dangers and temptations, which must be scrupulously avoided if the basic values of the profession are to be safeguarded. Otherwise, the relentless spotlight of criticism will turn once more on journalism and its practitioners.

Notes

1. Gregory S Jay, *Knowledge, Power, and the Struggle for Representation College English*, 56:1, January 1994, pp. 9–29.
2. See Jean Baudrillard, 'Simulacra and Simulations', in Mark Poster (ed.), *Jean Baudrillard: Selected Writings* (Stanford, Stanford University Press, 1988), pp. 166–84.

3. See Debra Spitulnik, 'Anthropology and Mass Media', *Annual Review of Anthropology*, 1993, Vol. 22, pp. 293–315.

4. James W Carey, 'Journalism and Criticism: The Case of an Undeveloped Profession', *The Review of Politics*, 36:2, April 1974, pp. 227–49.

5. See Kevin G Barnhurst and John Nerone, 'Civic Picturing vs. Realist Photojournalism–The Regime of Illustrated News 1856–1901', *Design Issues*, 16:1, Spring 2000, pp. 59–79.

6. An excellent example in the Indian context is the Right to Information Act, 2005, which covers the whole of India, except the state of Jammu and Kashmir. It includes the right to inspect works, documents, records; take notes, extracts or certified copies of documents or records; take certified samples of material; and obtain information in the form of printouts, diskettes, floppies, tapes, video cassettes or in any other electronic mode or through printouts.

7. The implicit reference here is to the print medium and Herbert Marshall McLuhan's *Gutenberg Galaxy: The Making of the Typographic Man* (University of Toronto Press, 1962).

8. For more information on the subject, see by Michael E Staub, 'Black Panthers, New Journalism, and the Rewriting of the Sixties', *Representations*, 57, Winter 1997, pp. 52–72.

Part I

REPRESENTING THE UNREPRESENTED

1

The Gender Factor

Ammu Joseph

At an international conference on the media's role in the post-tsunami scenario in April 2005, a journalist who questioned the scant coverage of women's concerns in the aftermath of the December disaster was told off by a male resource person for being 'too gender sensitive' and advised by a fellow female participant to shed her 'women's ghetto mentality'. 'This sort of thinking isn't going to get you anywhere,' the latter cautioned her. 'People died, not just women. Why should the media concentrate on the women?'[1]

Anticipating just such a reaction to my presentation on some of the missing links in media coverage of the tsunami at a workshop in January 2005, I had flagged the doubt myself: 'It may seem irrelevant to raise the question of gender awareness in the context of media coverage of a natural disaster such as this one, which obviously affected those who happened to be in the path of the massive waves–men, women and children. Can there possibly be a gender angle to the tsunami story? Is it at all reasonable to call for a gender perspective while covering the post-tsunami situation?'[2]

It was not long before it became abundantly clear that gender was indeed a critical factor in the tragedy, as well as in the relief, recovery and rehabilitation process that followed.[3] For example, there is substantial evidence that more women than men died when the killer waves engulfed the shores. Most of the reasons cited for the apparently higher female death toll have everything to do with gender as manifested in many of the affected countries, such as women's restrictive clothes, their customary inability to swim or climb trees, and their conventional roles as mothers and care-givers. There were also early reports of molestation and rape at some relief camps, of trafficking in women and girls, and of adolescent girls being made to marry older men who had lost their wives in the calamity.

At another level, the special needs and concerns of women and girls—such as inner wear and sanitary napkins, accessible toilets with adequate water, reproductive and maternal health care, female health workers, safety and privacy—were often forgotten in relief efforts. Many women also found themselves left out in the distribution of relief money and material, thanks to traditional notions about heads of families and/or breadwinners. Single women—including female heads of households—were particularly vulnerable, especially if they did not have adult sons.

In the rehabilitation and reconstruction phase too, women were disadvantaged, especially with regard to the restoration of means of livelihood. With the plight of fishermen and their losses in terms of assets like boats and nets occupying centre stage, little attention was paid to other economic activities in coastal areas, including those involving women. In addition, the 'property owner-centric' approach that generally characterized rehabilitation packages came under criticism for ignoring the needs of people from the fishing and farming communities who do not own boats, nets, land or shops but do contribute their labour and skills to the coastal economy. Under the circumstances, women—who traditionally form a major section of the informal or unorganized sector of labour and who rarely own property—were rendered doubly invisible, with their economic activities, losses and needs by and large unaccounted for.

The consequent neglect of women's livelihood needs was obviously catastrophic for a large number of families, especially among the poor, because women are often their sole earners and/or sources of support. Besides, in any case, women's earnings tend to go directly towards meeting the basic needs of their families, while a significant portion of many men's earnings is frequently spent on personal habits such as drinking, smoking and gambling. There have, in fact, been reports of relief money being wasted in this way and then serving as a trigger for domestic violence.

To make matters worse, in the process of post-tsunami planning and decision-making, women and local women's collectives–including self-help or savings and credit groups–were often ignored by the government, other agencies, and also the *gram panchayats*. This was clearly a widespread problem across the affected region, highlighted at several meetings in July 2005.

For example, a statement issued by participants in an Asian women's consultation on post-tsunami challenges in Banda Aceh (Indonesia) began by asserting, 'Seven months after the December 2004 Indian Ocean Tsunami, affected women continue to be marginalised, discriminated against and excluded from the process of rebuilding on all levels: the family, the community and the nation.'[4] A South Asian conference on gender concerns in post-tsunami reconstruction in Batticaloa (Sri Lanka) also highlighted the lack of women's representation and decision making powers for women in rebuilding activities, apart from land rights and livelihood issues.[5] And a meeting called by the Tamil Nadu Dalit Women's Movement in Tharangambadi focused attention on the continuing plight of Dalit women survivors in different parts of the worst affected state in India.[6]

At the same time, tsunami-affected women were not merely victims. In fact, many played active roles in rescue, relief, rehabilitation and reconstruction. What is more, as 'first responders' they often took on the challenging task of restoring a semblance of normalcy to life after the disaster: cooking; cleaning; taking care of the sick and the injured, the young and the old; sending children to school; salvaging belongings; helping to repair homes; and trying to make ends meet and regain livelihoods under extremely difficult circumstances.

Many women survivors also grew in strength and confidence in the wake of their experience of devastation and tragedy. They approached both government officials and non-governmental organizations for assistance in rebuilding their lives and livelihoods. Recognizing the multiple benefits of collective action, they formed, joined or reactivated self-help groups, some learning from the experiences of earthquake-affected rural women from Gujarat and Maharashtra who had turned disaster into opportunity by working together to re-establish themselves and their communities.[7] In the process they managed to overcome prior restraints on their mobility, to become more assertive and ambitious in claiming their rights, and to compel families and communities to recognize their personhood and capabilities.

So, yes, people died–not just women. People–not just women–suffered, succumbed, survived, recovered and rebuilt. Nobody would be stupid enough to suggest that the media should focus exclusively on women. But it is surely not unfair to propose that the media–in their vital role as the Fourth Estate, the watchdog of society, defenders of the public interest–must attempt to reflect the experiences, concerns and opinions of diverse sections of the population, including the female half of the human race? Yet, despite the well-documented gender differences in the impact of disasters, and despite the fact that women and children constitute the majority of victims seen in the media's representation of disasters–natural and otherwise–media coverage of recurring disasters across the world continues to be, by and large, gender-blind.

As Oxfam's March 2005 briefing note, 'The Tsunami's Impact on Women', put it, 'There is no scarcity of reflections and commentary on the impact of the disaster that shook the coasts of several Asian countries on 26 December 2004. The media have ... looked into almost every conceivable angle–the impact on tourism, the impact on the environment, revealed underwater villages, even the impact on animals. One area that has ... received less attention is the gender impact of the tsunami, and its impact on women in particular.'[8]

Months later, media coverage of Hurricane Katrina, which devastated New Orleans and neighbouring areas in the United States of America, was little better. As Joni Seager pointed out, while the mainstream media 'started asking tough, targeted questions about why this disaster fell so hard on one side of the race line'–at least a few days after the event–they were not so quick to notice and highlight the fact that the disaster 'fell hard on one side of the gender line, too.'[9] According to her, 'The "not-noticing" of the gendered dimensions of this disaster by the American media and by the panoply of experts who interpreted the disaster to the public through the media is alarming and warrants attention in itself.'

Gender-blindness also characterized much of the reporting on the massive earthquake that struck parts of Pakistan and India, particularly Kashmir, in October 2005. Yet there are many

indications that gender played a crucial role in the dispropor-
tionate number of female casualties, as well as in women's access
to aid and health care, and that it will continue to determine the
lives of many survivors.

For example, an early Reuters report quoted Pakistani officials
who acknowledged that the majority of the victims were women
and children but that much of the aid, including relief material,
was being intercepted by and distributed through the men of the
affected communities.[10] According to Aditi Kapoor, 'Most aid
workers arriving in the affected areas are usually greeted first by
groups of men. Women from the affected communities usually
stand some distance away.'[11] As one woman told her, 'It is easier
for men to voice their concerns. But whom can we go to for
[our] issues?'

UN estimates suggest that there were 40,000 pregnant women
among the four million people affected by the deadly quake.[12]
Health officials warned that the tremors could have triggered
miscarriages and premature labour, which would entail more risk
than normal in view of the destruction of many of the clinics and
hospitals that constituted the limited healthcare facilities available
in the worst-affected areas at the best of times. According to
Prakriiti Gupta,[13] even on the Indian side of Kashmir, which was
relatively less devastated, over 300 cases of miscarriage were registered in the weeks after the disaster, emergency obstetric care
was inaccessible, and trauma counselling negligible.

One of the most widely reported post-earthquake 'gender'
stories, versions of which appeared in a number of mainstream
international news outlets, was the Melody Cinema one about
the conversion of an abandoned movie theatre in Islamabad into
a women's hospital catering to the needs of the large number of
women who sustained spinal injuries in the disaster. A doctor
attending to the severely injured in the makeshift medical centre
said that 90 per cent of the patients he had seen were girls and
women. Most were paraplegics.[14] The fact that most of the patients
with spinal injuries were women is attributed primarily to gender-
related roles and restrictions.

The future of these women too will in all likelihood be determined by gender. Unable to walk and, in many cases, to control
their bladders or bowels, they may require constant care for the
rest of their lives. Under the circumstances, the married ones

lived in fear of being abandoned by their husbands and the single ones knew their chances of marriage were virtually non-existent. The attending doctor was obviously concerned about what would happen to his patients after they left the hospital. 'This society is cruel,' he said. 'They will be out on the streets unless they can get a skill and become independent. A young woman who does not walk, who has no control over her bladder, has no real chance in this society.'[15]

Paraplegics were not the only ones facing a bleak future. There were reports of women survivors—especially widows without adult sons—losing property to male relatives after moving out of their broken homes in shattered mountain villages in the immediate aftermath of the disaster.[16] Most of them have no papers to prove their ownership and, according to customary law, a dead man's property reverts to his brothers rather than his wife. Although daughters do have a right to a share in the property, this is generally denied to them. As a result, a large number of quake-affected women and girls could be left with no home to call their own.

Still, several women have also been able to turn the disaster into an opportunity to restructure their lives for the better. With so many families having lost homes, assets and means of livelihood in the rubble, these women faced less opposition to their efforts to find work outside the confines of their houses. Some set up petty shops, others found employment in non-governmental organizations. Encouraged by humanitarian organizations, some of them set up women's committees to assess their communities' rehabilitation and reconstruction needs.[17]

One unfortunate constant across the many disasters that took place in several parts of the world through 2005 was the huge toll they took on women. After a trip to tsunami-ravaged Sri Lanka in November 2005, Ritu Sharma noted, 'I am [now] more cognizant than ever of how natural disasters impact women severely and in specific ways that are often not recognized, especially during reconstruction phases after the crises have faded from the news.'[18]

Clearly, then, gender *is* an angle that needs to be explored in media coverage of disasters and their aftermath. As the Oxfam briefing note put it, 'Disasters, however "natural", are profoundly discriminatory. Wherever they hit, pre-existing structures and social conditions determine that some members of the community will be less affected while others will pay a higher price. Among the differences that determine how people are affected by such disasters is that of gender.'[19]

The media need to recognize more fully that even 'hard news' coverage, including the reporting of disasters, can actually benefit from gender consciousness. By focusing attention on the inevitable social consequences of 'natural' calamities, the media can alert both communities and the authorities to the impact of the event on different sections of the affected population (including various categories of women), and highlight the importance of taking their experiences, opinions, needs and resources into account in the relief, rehabilitation and reconstruction process. The bonus is that the special stories that can result from gender awareness not only serve a valuable purpose in the aftermath of such events but are also likely to stand out as more memorable than others in the customary media blitz that generally follows.

The same is true of violent conflict, that other staple of media fare. But here, too, 'gender' coverage, if any, tends to be restricted to reports on the sexual violence against women that is all too often a weapon of war, both external and internal.

For example, the media did report—albeit belatedly—on the rapes suffered by Muslim women in Gujarat during the prolonged communal conflagration in the state in 2002, with some follow-up thanks to the few cases that went to trial.[20] However, there has been little reporting or comment on the effects on women of the long-term repercussions of the violence, including destruction and confiscation of homes and other assets, stoppage of means of livelihood, and so on, let alone the continuing deprivation and tension under which many survivors continue to live.

To take another example, despite the carpet coverage given to the war in Iraq since 2003, little of it has shed light on the situation of women in the ongoing conflict: the large number of female casualties among the non-combatants caught in the cross-fire; those who died because they could not access medical care in the tense and violent environment; the girls who have dropped out of school because their parents cannot risk sending them out in such unsafe conditions; the rise in sex work to compensate for increased unemployment and decreased social welfare; the related growth in human trafficking; the detention and abuse of female relatives of former Baath Party officials and/or suspected militants; the hurdles in the path of women's political participation; their continuing struggle for food, water, sanitation and health care; the growing incidence of various forms of violence against women (including the sexual harassment and rape experienced by female soldiers within the 'coalition forces'); the resurgence of religious fundamentalism and its impact on women, and so on.[21]

Similarly, the conflict in and over Kashmir has produced reams of media copy over the past couple of decades but there has been, barring a few notable examples, little focus on the impact of the continuous, ongoing tension and violence on women.[22] According to Urvashi Butalia,

> The Kashmir conflict ... has generated a vast amount of analytical and historical literature; very little of it actually mentions women. Yet today, in Kashmir, there are large numbers of women who are identified as 'half-widows' [women whose husbands are assumed dead but there is no proof to show they actually are], widows, mothers who have lost their sons, or those whose daughters have been raped, young women who dare not step out of the house, women who have been pushed out of employment by the fear and uncertainty created by conflict, and those who are suffering from medical and psychological conditions related to stress and trauma.[23]

Many Kashmiri women have also become active in the public sphere, whether in the Association of the Parents of Disappeared Persons (set up to track down the thousands of people who have gone missing since the conflict began), which has a predominantly female membership, or in the Dukhtaran-e-Millat, the state's sole all-women separatist group. Others have defied the diktats of fundamentalist organizations in order to continue their education and live their lives as normally as possible. Kashmiri Pandit women have had to deal with displacement, with many having to cope with life in cramped refugee camps, economic hardship, disruption of children's education, insecurity, loss of identity, and so on.

Yet few of these women (Muslim or Hindu), their struggles or their opinions make it to the media. The same is true of the experiences, struggles and opinions of women in several troubled states in the north-eastern region of the country, despite the fact that both individual women and women's groups have played significant roles in efforts to build and maintain peace. As a result,

citizens in other parts of the country are deprived of a real understanding of the nightmare of life in Jammu & Kashmir, as well as
some parts of the north-east, where the ordinary, innocent people
who constitute the majority of the population are caught between
the rock of militancy and the hard place of the military.

By seeking out women and talking to them about their experiences of and opinions on violent conflicts of various kinds,
journalists would not only be fulfilling their professional duty
but also ensuring that their stories are out of the ordinary. For
example, when a group of us went to Ahmedabad in 1985 specifically to inquire into the role of women in and the impact on women
of the caste and communal clashes in the city during the first
half of the year, we came across many important aspects of the
disturbances that the media had till then completely missed. This
was mainly because we made it a point to speak to women in the
affected areas as well as a women's organization working among
them.[24]

One of our most significant discoveries, for instance, was the
devastating impact of prolonged curfew on the lives of ordinary
citizens, particularly the poor. Women spoke about the difficulties
of feeding hungry families for days on end with the meagre provisions available at home when curfew was imposed and of rush-
ing out to get food in the brief periods when it was occasionally
relaxed. They also revealed the debilitating economic hardships
suffered by the poor, especially those working in the informal
sector—a large percentage of them women—because home-based
workers were unable to go out to get raw materials or deliver
finished products and vendors found it impossible to operate in
most parts of the city for months on end. These are not the kinds
of issues normally highlighted by the 'authorities' or 'community
leaders' who usually form the primary sources of information
tapped by the media in such situations. Yet they are important
concerns for those struggling to survive the multi-faceted ordeal
of conflicts they have not created.

As I wrote a few years ago in the context of the war in Afghanistan
(though it is equally applicable in other situations of internal
and external conflict):

The gender angle to war coverage cannot be seen exclusively in terms of reports on violations of women's right to physical security, including rape, sexual

harassment and sexual exploitation—widespread and serious as these tend to be. It needs to also take into account women's heightened experience of violence and trauma during periods of conflict—both physical and psychological, both within the home and outside it. It needs to spotlight the ways in which 'culture' and 'tradition' are often used during times of political tension and strife to curtail women's human rights. It needs to take note of the additional social and economic burdens placed on women's shoulders at such times, when they often find themselves solely responsible for their families (including the very old, the very young and the sick) under circumstances where even food and shelter are not always available. And it certainly needs to focus attention on women's political rights, including their right to participate in decision-making and governance.[25]

With regard to politics—another media staple—the quantum of coverage given to women in the 'public' political arena (particularly party and electoral politics) has improved marginally in recent times, if only because of the news-making qualities (for better or worse) of some prominent female politicians. However, the gender angle to political coverage cannot be restricted to reporting the sayings and doings of colourful, quotable women leaders; occasional articles on women in Panchayati Raj institutions; and the customary he said—she retorted style of reportage on the enduring, unseemly tug of war over the proposed reservations for women in Parliament and Legislative Assemblies, especially since such coverage remains largely uninformed by independent inquiry into the position, role, experiences and opinions of rank and file women within political parties, organizations and structures.

Even within the traditional, narrow view of politics generally reflected in the media—which appears to unquestioningly accept the false dichotomy between the public–political sphere and the private, supposedly apolitical, realm—much is still missing. For example, ordinary women are certainly prominent in photographs and footage of elections—e.g., at political rallies, in queues at polling booths—but their views as voters rarely figure anywhere in the coverage. Further, although most parties now routinely list 'women's empowerment' in their election manifestos, they are seldom quizzed about what exactly they mean by it, let alone what they have done or at least plan to do about it. Nor are they asked about their policies or plans regarding current gender-related issues.

What, for example, is their stand on sex selection, which has become a national issue (and the subject of several media sting operations) ever since the trend–highlighted by the women's movement over two decades–finally got some overdue attention, thanks to the alarming figures on the skewed sex ratio of children in the 0–6 age group released by the Census of India, 2001 (and subsequent research studies)? What steps will they take to combat violence against women in its multiple forms (variously described as a global pandemic and the world's most pervasive human rights challenge), and to reduce the scandalously high rate of maternal mortality or to remove the persistent impediments in the path of girls' education (both critical to the achievement of the Millennium Development Goals set by the United Nations)? How do they plan to meet women's need for remunerative work as well as credit? Do they realize that water and sanitation are women's issues, since poor women are especially the ones who suffer the most from inadequate supply of the former and lack of facilities for the latter?

Then there is economics, which also occupies pride of place in the media's scheme of things. When Finance Minister P Chidambaram introduced the concept of 'gender-budgeting' during his presentation of the Union Budget 2005–06, a financial daily admitted that the proposal was 'something quite a few of us in India would have heard [of] for the first time.'[26] I was reminded of an incident a couple of years earlier, when a journalism student I had assigned to interview a senior editor about the gender implications of the newly presented budget was sent away with the dismissive question: 'What does the budget have to do with gender?'

Yet gender budgets–earlier sometimes known as women's budgets–have been around in different parts of the world at least since the mid-1980s.[27] The current term, gender-responsive budgets (GRB), refers to the analysis of the impact of actual government expenditure and revenue on women and girls as compared to men and boys. It is meant to help governments decide how policies need to be adjusted, and where resources need to be reallocated, to address gender inequalities, especially in the context of poverty.[28]

According to advocates of GRB, although national budgets may appear to be gender-neutral policy instruments, government expenditures and revenue collection often do impact women and men differently. Gender-responsive budget analysis provides a way to hold governments accountable to their commitments to gender equality and women's human rights by linking these commitments to the distribution, use and generation of public resources.[29]

GRB is not confined to so-called women-specific schemes. It neither advocates separate budgets for women nor aims to solely increase spending on programmes specially targeted at women. This is because, as Vibhuti Patel points out, most policies and programmes outlined and provided for in official budgets–at the national, state and panchayat levels–impact women in particular ways.[30] These range from the increasing privatization of health care services to the huge outlays for defence expenditure; from the interest rates on small savings to the number of families covered by anti-poverty schemes; and from the prices of agricultural inputs and produce to the incentives and disincentives operating in various industrial sectors.

Clearly, then, covering gender has nothing to do with being 'too gender sensitive' or being burdened with a 'women's ghetto mentality'. The budget has everything to do with gender, as do other aspects of economics, as well as various high profile areas of media coverage such as politics, war, social conflict and disasters. The stories are out there. If few of them make it to the mainstream media, it is because gender awareness is still missing in most newsrooms.

There is today no dearth of sources and resources that can be tapped to figure out whether or not an event or process has any special implications for women, including different categories of women, as well as other vulnerable sections of society whose voices are not commonly heard in the media.[31]

Yet, according to the Global Media Monitoring Project (GMMP) 2005,[32] which surveyed nearly 13,000 news stories in 76 countries across the world, women's points of view are rarely heard in the topics that dominate the news agenda, such as politics and the economy. In stories on politics and government, only 14 per cent of news subjects are women; in economic and business news the corresponding figure is 20 per cent. Women are, of course, rarely central to such stories, featuring centrally only in 8 per cent of political stories and in 3 per cent of stories about the economy. According to the authors of 'Who Makes the

News?'–the comprehensive report of the most extensive international research into gender in news media to date, 'The absence of a gender angle in stories in the "hard" news topics reflects a blinkered approach to the definition of news and newsworthiness.'

Unless gender is acknowledged as one of several factors that affect people's experience of almost everything, and accepted as one of the 'angles' to be explored while covering anything, the media will continue to tell only part of the story–whatever that story may be.

'Gender' clearly involves and should be of concern to both men and women. Indeed, men and masculinities are the new buzzwords in the gender field. The relatively new focus on men is not just about understanding their roles and responsibilities vis-à-vis women. If the construction of gender under patriarchy impacts women and girls in certain ways, it cannot but affect men and boys as well–after all, human society is made up of both sides of the gender divide and their lives are closely intertwined. If males of the species benefit in certain obvious ways from the patriarchal system that privileges men in particular ways, they also lose out in some important, though perhaps not so obvious, ways as a result of rigidly defined gender roles in general and the narrow construction of maleness and masculinity in particular. So, events and issues need to be examined from that angle too. But with so many miles to go even with relatively old concerns about women and news coverage, the other side of gender will have to be the subject of another chapter.

Notes

1. Deepa Kandaswamy, 'Media forgets female face of tsunami', *Women's E-News*, 27 July 2005. Available at: http://www.womensenews.org/article.cfm/dyn/aid/2390.
2. Ammu Joseph, 'Gender, media and tsunamis', February 2005. Available at: http://www.indiatogether.org/2005/feb/ajo-genmedia.htm. Partly based on a presentation on gender-sensitive journalism made at a Creative Media Workshop organized by the Mahanirban Calcutta Research Group, Kolkata, in Bhubaneshwar, Orissa (7–10 January 2005).
3. See, for example: Oxfam, 'The tsunami's impact on women', Oxfam Briefing Note, March 2005. Available at: http://www.oxfam.org.uk/what_we_do/issues/conflict_disasters/bn_tsunami_women.htm.

Disaster Watch Special Issue, 'One year after tsunami', December 2005. Available at: http://www.disasterwatch.net/tsunami_i1.htm. Damyanty Sridharan, 'Double discrimination', Available at: http://www.indiadisasters.org/tsunami/views/2005/12/double-discrimination.html. Accessed on 26 December 2005. South Asia Disasters Special Issue, 'Tsunami, gender, and recovery', 12 October 2005. Available at: http://online.northumbria.ac.uk/geography_research/gdn/resources/tsunami%20-genderandrecovery.pdf. 'UNIFEM responds to the tsunami tragedy'—Articles and information from various sources. Available at: http://www.unifem.org/campaigns/tsunami/information.html. Gender and Disaster Network, 'Why gender matters'. Available at: http://online.north umbria.ac.uk/geography_research/gdn/why_does_gender_matter. htm. Accessed on 10 November 2005.

4. Complete statement available at: http://www.apwld.org/tsunami_statementpostchallenges.htm; for more details see: http://www.apwld.org/.

5. 'Gender bias in disaster recovery process', posted on Tsunami Response Watch, 28 August 2005. Available at: http://www.india disasters.org/tsunami/response/2005/08/gender-bias-in-disaster-recovery.html.

6. Fatima Burnad, 'The tsunami exacerbates Dalit women's sufferings from caste discrimination', 2005. Available at: http://www.apwld.org/tsunami_dalitwomen.htm.

7. See Ammu Joseph, 'Learning from Latur', the *Hindu*, 26 October 2003. Available at: http://www.hinduonnet.com/mag/2003/10/26/stories/2003102600480100.htm; Ammu Joseph, 'Shaken to the core', *Infochange Features*, November 2003. Available at: http://www.infochangeindia.org/features139.jsp; Ammu Joseph, 'Indian women shaken into action by earthquake', *Women's E-News*, February 2004. Available at: http://www.womenenews.org/article.cfm/dyn/aid/1716/context/archive.

8. Oxfam, 'The tsunami's impact on women'.

9. Joni Seager, 'Noticing gender (or not) in disasters', *The Chicago Tribune*, 14 September 2005. Available at: http://online.northumbria.ac.uk/geography_research/gdn/resources/seager-geoforum-katrina.doc.

10. 'Social causes behind high women casualty in earthquake', *Reuters/Gulf News*, 15 October 2005. Available at: http://archive.gulfnews.com/articles/05/10/15/186877.html.

11. Aditi Kapoor, 'Diary from Kashmir', Oxfam, 15 October 2005. Available at: http://www.oxfam.org.au/world/emergencies/asiaquake/docs/kapoor3.html.

12. Church World Service, 'Pakistan/Afghanistan, Situation Update', 14 December 2005. Available at: http://www.cwspa.org/earthquake/update14122005.htm.

13. Prakriiti Gupta, 'Kashmir quake: Chilling tragedy continues', *Women's Feature Service*, December 2005.

14. Laura J Winter, 'Pakistan theatre renovates as women's hospital', *Women's E-News*, 25 November 2005. Available at: http://www.womensenews.org/article.cfm/dyn/aid/2538/context/archive.

15. Ibid.

16. Edward Parsons, 'Pakistan: Female quake survivors losing property', *IRIN News*, 3 January 2006. Available at: http://www.irinnews.org/report.asp?ReportID=50925&SelectRegion=Asia&SelectCountry=PAKISTAN.

17. Suzanna Koster, 'Women in quake-hit Pakistan break old barriers', *Reuters*, 12 January 2006. Available at: http://in.today.reuters.com/news/newsArticle.aspx?type=topNews&storyID=2006-01-12T062118Z_01_NOOTR_RTRJONC_0_India-231386-1.xml.

18. Ritu Sharma, 'Disasters dramatize how women's poverty is lethal', *Women's E-News*, 5 January 2006. Available at: http://www.womensenews.org/article.cfm?aid=2587.

19. Oxfam, 'The tsunami's impact on women'.

20. See Ammu Joseph, 'Gender, sectarian violence and the media', June 2003. Available at: http://www.iwmf.org/features/7579.

21. UNIFEM, UNIFEM Gender Profile–Iraq–Women, War & Peace. Available at: http://www.womenwarpeace.org/iraq/iraq.htm. Accessed on 9 May 2006.

22. Including articles by Muzamil Jaleel, Sudha Ramachandran and Sonia Jabbar.

23. Urvashi Butalia (ed.), *Speaking Peace: Women's Voices from Kashmir* (New Delhi, Kali for Women, 2002).

24. Women and Media Group, 'Report on the impact on women of the caste and communal disturbances in Ahmedabad' (Bombay, 1985). Also excerpted in Ammu Joseph and Kalpana Sharma (eds), *Whose News? The Media and Women's Issues* (New Delhi, Sage Publications, 1994 and 2006).

25. Ammu Joseph, 'Women, War and the Media', *The Hoot*, 10 November 2001. Available at: http://www.thehoot.org/mediagender/afghan.asp; updated for IWMF website, available at: http://www.iwmf.org/ewirc/7731/7732/ch-7737.

26. 'Budget: No fair deal for fair sex', *Financial Express*, 3 March 2005. Available at: http://www.financialexpress.com/fe_full_story.php?content_id=84236.

27. Debbie Budlender, 'Review of gender budget initiatives,' Community Agency for Social Enquiry. Available at: http://www.international budget.org/resources/library/GenderBudget.pdf.

28. See Gender Responsive Budget Initiatives (GRBI) Website (http://www.idrc.ca/en/ev-80429-201-1-DO_TOPIC.html).

29. Ibid.

30. Geeta Seshu, 'Budget, women and the yawning gap', *India Together*, July 2003. Available at: http://www.indiatogether.org/2003/jul/wom-gendbudg.htm.

31. See, for example, the 'Women & Tsunami' section of the Disaster Watch Website, at: http://www.disasterwatch.net/women_tsunami.htm.

32. For more information on the findings of the GMMP 05, see www.whomakesthenews.org.

2

The Problem with Media Reportage of Queer Lives

Siddharth Narrain

On 4 January 2006, national and regional newspapers reported an incident in which four homosexual men were allegedly caught having sex in public in Lucknow. The Lucknow police lodged a First Information Report (FIR) in Gudumba police station, charging them with an offence under Section 377 of the Indian Penal Code (IPC), the law that criminalizes homosexual activity in India.[1] The police, in their FIR, said the men were 'part of an association' of more than 1,600 persons, who, amongst themselves, talked about homosexual sex and related issues. The FIR specifically mentioned the names and phone numbers of 13 persons other than the four accused persons, with whom the men were in touch. The police released photographs of the four men to the media, along with their names and occupations. The men were paraded before the media and forced to reveal details regarding their private life.

Local media reports dutifully reproduced the police version of the incident. The headlines of some of the newspapers reports tell the story of the media coverage around the issue. 'Four members of International Homosexual Club Held' screamed the *Dainik Jagran* (5 January 2006), 'Gay Club Running on Net Unearthed–4 Arrested' read the *Times of India* (5 January 2006). Not to be left behind, 'Cops Bust Gay Racket' went the *Hindustan Times* headline (5 January 2006).

Media reportage around the incident was widely condemned by queer-rights[2] activists. A fact-finding team of the National

Campaign for Sexual Rights (NCSR), which investigated the incident, found that the cases against the accused were fabricated by the police and that the police had no witnesses to corroborate their version of events. In their report, the fact-finding team found that as per the information they had gathered, none of the men were having sex in public. The police, under the supervision of the Senior Superintendent of Police, had arrested one of the men in his home. They forcibly obtained the names and mobile numbers of the other men mentioned in the FIR. On the following day, they forced him to call the other men and ask them to meet him at a restaurant. The police arrested three men as they arrived in the restaurant. The report came down heavily on the media reportage of the incident and said that the sensational media coverage had contributed to the men being denied a free and fair trial.

This is not an isolated example of prejudiced reporting around queer people's lives. On 14 August 2004, two persons were found murdered in Anand Lok, a posh residential area in South Delhi. One of them was found naked, his hand and legs tied, and his throat slit. The other man was found in the bedroom wearing a pair of shorts, similarly bound and with his throat slit. There was a stash of pornographic material in the room that included photographs of naked men and VCDs. Residents of Delhi woke up the next day to find their newspapers full of reports describing the lives of gay men in Delhi. Every stereotype of the homosexual was suddenly being reproduced in the media—how they cruised the streets of Delhi in search of young boys, how obsessed with porn they were, and how they 'came out of the shadows' in the evenings to lead their sleazy lives in secret. Newspaper reporters used the murders to speculate on the numbers, lifestyle and 'proclivities' of homosexuals in Delhi.

The People's Union for Civil Liberties (Karnataka) (PUCL [K]), in its report on 'Human Rights Violations Against the Transgendered Community', describes how media reporting around queer issues in Karnataka follows the heterosexist logic of seeing queer communities as lurid, sleazy and evil. The report goes on to describe cases of news stories that reveal underlying attitudes of the mainstream media towards queer people. One such case is that of the arrest of four male sex workers by the police of Upparpet station in Bangalore on 5 July 2002. The police alleged that they had recovered stolen property worth Rs 3 lakhs from the accused. They accused them of waylaying people in the Majestic and Cubbon Park areas of Bangalore and taking them to hotels, where they alleged that the accused coerced people into sex and then blackmailed them. The police booked 20 cases of theft and robbery against the four sex workers and illegally detained them in the Upparpet Police Station for more than 25 days. They did not file charge sheets against them for six months after the incident. This case was widely reported in the English and Kannada press. The reports were sketchy and depended exclusively on the police files. Most of the reports linked the criminal offences to the sexual orientation of the accused. The PUCL (K) report said that the media reports seemed to suggest that homosexuals are naturally, and more likely than others, drawn towards criminality. The PUCL (K) report said that the reportage was becoming a 'step towards constructing homosexuality itself as a crime'. The report notes that the Bangalore police had gone to the extent of officially resorting to criminal profiling of *hijras* (eunuchs), alleging that all of them were doing sex work in order to solicit customers and rob them later.

Another case documented in the PUCL (K) report is that of the death of Chandini, a *hijra* who died of severe burns in her home in Bangalore on 1 December 2002. She was married to a painter, Jnanaprakash, who claimed that he was unaware of Chandini's gender identity until the day before her death. According to him, outraged by his discovery, he had threatened to expose her to her parents, which had driven her to commit suicide. But many of Chandini's *hijra* friends alleged that Jnanaprakash had always known about her identity and had in fact murdered Chandini for her money and jewellery. On 4 December 2002, local English and Kannada newspapers reported the news of Chandini's death in a sensational manner. A news report in *Lankesh Patrike* on 18 December 2002 supported the police version of Chandini's suicide. In this article the author uses terms in Kannada to describe the *hijras* that translate as 'freaks of the underworld', 'ghosts condemned to eternal wandering' and 'a race apart'. The news report used derogatory words like *'khoja'*, *'chhakka'*, *'gandu'* and *'napumsaka'* to describe those who did not identify as heterosexual. The PUCL (K) report says that the journalist had failed to comprehend the complex reality of relationships in queer communities that did not conform to the regime of heterosexist and patriarchal morality.

The Problem of 'Objective Reportage'

While the mainstream media, especially the English language media, has been increasingly progressive in its editorial stance on homosexuality in India (most leading English dailies have argued for the abolition of Section 377 of the IPC, which criminalizes homosexuality in the country), the reportage of the issue has most often been homophobic. While queer rights groups have been arguing that they need to engage with the media more proactively, the reportage around the Lucknow incident has shown that though mainstream newspapers have begun taking progressive stands around queer issues, not much has changed since when it comes to the reporter on the daily beat covering local issues. One reason for this is the continued faith in the criteria of 'objective reporting' among journalists in India. Any attempt to contest contemporary forms of news coverage of queer issues will not be successful unless journalists realize the limitations of 'objective reportage'.

Media theorist Stuart Allen describes objectivity in journalism as denoting a set of rhetorical devices and procedures used in composing a news story, and in this sense having no bearing on the truthfulness or validity of the story. Objective reporting, Allen argues, means avoiding as much as possible the overt intrusion of the reporter's personal values into a news story and minimizing explicit interpretation in writing up the story. Reporters do this by eschewing a value-laden vocabulary and by writing in the third person impersonal, not the first person personal. Reporters try to attribute the story, and especially any interpretation of what it means, to 'sources'.[3]

Allen traces the history of 'objective journalism' to the rise of the 'pauper press' in Britain and the 'penny press' in the United States. These newspapers, which aimed at covering news for the masses ignored by the more traditional newspapers, began using content that focused on facts rather then opinion, and encouraged journalists to present facts in the most literal way possible. The emergence of 'journalistic objectivity' is entwined with the invention of the telegraph and its consequent use in the 1840s. In 1848 the Associated Press (AP) was formed by a group of newspapers. This was a major move towards standardized news.

Popular disillusionment with state propaganda after World War II led to newspapers placing a premium on 'neutral reporting'. In 1923, the American Society of Newspaper Editors announced their 'canons' of journalism that included impartiality or distinguishing clearly between news reports and opinion. Thus, objectivity meant that news was considered legitimate when it satisfied the rules that were established by a professional community of journalists. The canon of objectivity along with the structured format of news that emerged may in fact lead to reporting on issues devoid of historical or societal context and perspective, thus lending itself to supporting existing moralistic positions and discriminatory attitudes. In the mid-1970s the Glasgow University Media Group analysed hundreds of hours of recorded news broadcasts focused on industrial items such as strikes. They found that the news consistently favoured the interpretation of the already powerful, because journalists share assumptions with them about the real world, which are rarely seriously questioned, such as strikes being harmful and disruptive.[4]

News sources that are needed to fulfil the requirements of 'objective reportage' are usually drawn from existing power structures and therefore tend to support the status quo. News judgement requires journalists to share assumptions about what is normal in society, and, by focusing negatively on the deviant, journalists implicitly supports the norms and values of society. Michael Schudson, in his book, *Discovering the News: A Social History of American Newspapers*,[5] emphasizes that the belief in objectivity in journalism is not just a claim about what kind of knowledge is reliable but clearly points to a direction of thinking that journalists are expected to engage in—a direction that often is that of maintaining the status quo. In this case the status quo is the prejudice against queer persons in India, which is reflected in institutions of the state, the medical establishment and the media.

Both the ruling United Progressive Alliance (UPA) government and the previous National Democratic Alliance (NDA) government have opposed a petition before the Delhi High Court that has challenged Section 377 of the Indian Penal Code[6] on the grounds that it violates the right to privacy of homosexuals as well as their right to life by affecting adversely HIV/AIDS prevention work. They have defended Section 377 as reflecting societal norms in the country.

There is plenty of documented material that shows that, in India, the law, along with the medical establishment and institutions of state like the police, have marginalized queer persons in India. If a reporter who is covering a story that involves queer persons does not take into account the context of queer lives in the country, then there is a high chance of a prejudiced and inaccurate report. In order to avoid this, it is not enough for the reports to be 'objective' by quoting both the police and the queer persons involved. In the case of the Lucknow arrests, the reports mainly quoted the police as saying that they had exposed a 'gay club'. The media relayed details put out by the only 'official' source available to them. The police claimed they conducted their entire operation because homosexuals were a threat to society. However, there were examples of comprehensive media reports like the CNN-IBN story on the arrests in January 2006–the first in the mainstream English and Hindi media to cover the story in an unprejudiced manner. The story began by contrasting the incident and the criminalization of homosexual acts in the country to the recent legalization of civil unions in Britain. It also quoted the accused, the police and gay-rights activists protesting the police action throughout the country.

In recent years, there has been extensive debate and rethinking around the canon of journalism within the journalistic community. In 1996, The Society of Professional Journalists in the United States, a body dedicated to protecting and improving journalistic standards, dropped the word 'objectivity' from its code of ethics. It replaced objectivity with terms like 'truth', 'accuracy' and 'comprehensiveness'. Media reporting around queer issues cannot be divorced from the reality of queer people's lives. If the Indian media has to address the issue of homophobic reportage, it has to stop clinging to the canon of objectivity. What the media needs are standards that will ensure that journalists recognize and take into account the ways in which queer persons and communities negotiate existing discrimination against them, in place of the 'objective' standards that reinforce such prejudices.

Notes

1. The Section reads:

   Unnatural Offences:

   Whoever voluntarily has carnal intercourse against the order of nature, with any man, woman, or animal, shall be punished with imprisonment for life, or for imprisonment of either description for a term that may extend to ten years and shall also be liable to fine.

   Explanation: Penetration is sufficient to constitute the carnal intercourse necessary to the offence described in this section.
2. In India though the word 'queer' is not commonly used, it is being increasingly employed as a term that could capture a diversity of lives and ways of living which the embedded nature of heterosexism in law, culture and society. It includes *hijras, kothis*, lesbian, gay, transgendered and bisexual persons. See Arvind Narrain, *Queer: Despised Sexuality, Law and Social Change* (Bangalore, Books for Change, 2004).
3. S Allen, *News Culture* (Buckingham, Open University Press, 1999), pp. 8–15.
4. G Branston and R Stafford, *The Media Student's Handbook*, 3rd ed. (London, Routledge, 2003), pp. 145–46.
5. Michael Schudson, *Discovering the News: A Social History of American Newspapers* (New York, Basic Books, 1978).
6. *Naz Foundation v. Union of India and others*, filed in August 2001. It asks for the 'reading down' of the law to decriminalize private consensual sex between adults.

3

At Least Some Children Get *'Mosambi'* Some of the Time

Sandhya Rao

When I was little, my grandmother told me lots of stories. I only had to say, *'Ajji, kathe helu'* ('Grandma, tell me a story').' Lakshmi Ajji was never too busy to put everything aside and begin: *'Seri baa, koothuko. Onde ondu ooralli ...'* (Okay, come, sit down. Once upon a time ...). We always conversed in Kannada.

One of her favourite stories was about Draupadi, the most important character in the Mahabharata. When she described how Yudhishthira, Bheema, Arjuna, Nakula and Sahadeva went to the court of King Drupada to attend the *swayamvara* or 'spouse-choosing ceremony' of his daughter, Draupadi, I knew that Lakshmi Ajji had been there too. And when Arjuna shot an arrow through the fish's eye, Lakshmi Ajji and I both cried out in wonder.

By the time the Pancha Pandavas, the five Pandava brothers, returned home after the *swayamvara*, it was twilight. Their mother, Kunti, was busy lighting lamps for her evening prayer.

'Look, Amma,' said Yudhishthira, 'look what we have brought for you. *Ondu hennu'* (a girl).

Once, when I was telling a friend about my grandmother, he said, 'Not *hennu* (girl). Yudhishthira said *hannu'* (fruit).

'Hennu,' I insisted angrily. 'Lakshmi Ajji always said *hennu.'*

Anyway, Kunti was busy. Besides, she wasn't paying too much attention. So she said, *'Hannu?* Share it,' and went back to her prayers.

That is how Draupadi ended up with five husbands.

At the end of the story, Lakshmi Ajji always gave me, and whoever else was with me, fruit to eat. Mangos in the mango season, jackfruit in the jackfruit season, and *mosambi* (sweet lime) all year round.

Well, that was my grandmother. She was special.

'They don't listen to us!' children have been complaining over the last six years at the writing workshop I facilitate at the Goodbooks Bookstore in Chennai. After the first couple of sessions when they have begun to feel comfortable with me and with each other, the children open up. Inevitably they talk about their troubles at school, and sometimes at home. Why don't you talk to them? I ask. 'They don't listen to us!' is the reply every time from every child. Not teachers and, often, not even parents.

Typically, this is how we treat children in India—almost as if they didn't exist. Apparently, this is how children were treated in Europe too, back in the Middle Ages. And a century or two ago, the US even had a Stubborn Child Law. In fact, legislation on the prevention of cruelty to animals was passed before legislation on prevention of cruelty to children, and the 'first cases of child abuse were brought before the courts on the basis that the child victim was an animal.'[1]

Although India is one among several countries to have ratified the UN Convention on the Rights of the Child, 1989, the ground reality is that children continue to be non-status items and are subjected to extreme forms of oppression: from the rape of babies to being made victims of vote-bank politics, and from being exploited as labour to thousands of children not being in school at all. Having said this, we also have to concede that varying and wide-ranging socio-economic-cultural-linguistic considerations influence the degree to which these generalizations apply.

However, what does all this have to do with magazines for children? It seems about as relevant as asking: 'Why did the banana go to the doctor's?'[2]

According to the UN, four children are born in the world every second, making for a staggering 129,384,000 new persons being added to the population every year. It seems that the current generation of young people is the largest in the history of the world. That is a huge number requiring good quality reading material, assuming we are in agreement that a good education is the basic right of every child.

Although the Convention on the Rights of the Child specifically emphasizes the need to 'recognize the right of the child to rest and leisure, to engage in play and recreational activities appropriate to the age of the child and to participate freely in cultural life and the arts,'[3] children continue to be trapped in the insecurities of war, conflict, disease, malnutrition, forced labour and illiteracy. As the well-known Sri Lankan children's writer and illustrator Sybil Wettasinghe has said, they experience 'a loss of childhood'.[4] Childhood is certainly becoming increasingly stressful, as this poem[5] tries to suggest:

Bus-Stop
The bus was very crowded–
They almost always are, you know.
Not this one please, I pleaded–
We almost always do, you know.
Hurry, quick, no time to waste–
They're almost always late, you know.
Boom! Rattle! Zoom! Zip!–
They almost always will not wait.
Nobody was left behind–
They almost never are, you know.
All except for me, of course–
We almost always are, you know.

Afraid that children will get completely left behind in the frenetic tumble, Zimbabwean writer Chiedza Musengezi refuses to sugar-coat her comments. 'People don't mind buying beautiful clothes, but will not spare a thought to buy books. On the other hand, they complain about the price of books,' she says. Of course, she is talking about Zimbabwe, but what she says is equally true of India: 'It's true, not many here have disposable incomes, but I am shocked by the attitude of those who do. It's time they worried about their children's intellect, because reading puts words at the command of children. It makes for better citizens, more difficult to manipulate.'[6]

Since magazines are cheaper and therefore more accessible to children, at least in principle, what goes into them assumes greater significance. The fact that most children are starved of reading material and will read anything they can lay their hands on poses the stiffest challenge to producers of such materials.

This raises questions I have been grappling with for some time now. How much of the material available by way of magazines for children in India empowers them? How many children get empowered? How many children do magazines reach? How many children read? How many children *can* read? How many children are equipped with the skills to read?

The printed word came to India in the early 19th century, thanks to the printing press, better communication and the efforts of early Christian missionaries who translated the scriptures into local languages, and also produced grammars and dictionaries. Some of the earliest children's magazines in India were *Balak Bandhu* in Bengali, *Bal Prabhakar* and *Bal Vivad* in Hindi, *Bacchon ka Akhbaar* and *Phool* in Urdu, *Bal Jivan* in Gujarati and *Bala Deepihai* in Tamil. They carried stories, poems, riddles, jokes, cartoons and pictures. The thrust was mainly instructional, motivational and value-based. Sometimes, some of the magazines carried writings by children.

Of the approximately 4,000 newspapers and periodicals published in India today, the share of publications for children is about 120 to 150. All of them follow more or less the same philosophy: to educate and to entertain. There are folk tales, fairy stories, original writings, riddles, jokes, poems, pictures, competitions, bits of history, geography, science, sometimes fun with mathematics, information, hobby corners, agony aunts, health corners, cooking tips, stories, puzzles, crosswords, comic strips, how-to-dos and how-to-makes, letters, tips for exams and trips, environment corners and concerns, pen-pals, news items, and quizzes. To take examples of the last:

1. Which is the hormone that the pancreas secretes and that regulates concentration of sugar in human blood? a. adrenalin; b. thyroxine; c. insulin; d. progesterone.[7]
2. Which commonly used office stationery was invented by Johan Waaler?[8]

There are broadly two kinds of magazines: those written for children and those written mostly by children or at least based on ideas from children, with the latter gradually gaining currency. 'Do children like to read what other children write?' a journalist friend once asked. One 15-year-old boy expostulated quite unequivocally, '*Ayyo*, children's writings are *semma* bore. The worst children's magazine I've ever read is *Champak*. It makes *Tinkle* seem like Shakespeare.'[9] Of course, this is one child's opinion;

other children have other opinions. A creative, well-read 11 year-old declared, 'I am very fond of craft, writing, humorous stories, etc. I would like to read about all these things, but I honestly feel that a magazine cannot be complete without general knowledge facts or a quiz in it.'

'I like articles written by children because it is at our own level,' said another even more well-read 11-year-old. 'I mean, no grown-up would normally write a joke using Harry Potter and pottering around, or at least not in the same way that a kid would. Children also have similar tastes. So 99 per cent of the articles written by kids are great. I also like adult articles but most of them aren't as good as the ones by children.'[10]

An immensely popular comic-magazine almost entirely assembled with ideas contributed by children regularly features an immensely popular character called Suppandi. In one story, Suppandi is walking along when an old man stops him and asks the way to the temple. 'Hmmm,' says Suppandi. 'Way to the temple, did you say? Well ... straight down this road is a crossing. If you turn right and walk for a while you will see eight shops. Behind the eighth shop there are three houses. The third house has two rooms. The room on the left has a Bhagavad Gita in it. I place my hand on it and swear, sir, I do not know the way to the temple.'[11]

Everybody knows *Chandamama*. Originally published in Telugu in 1947, and mirrored since in many other languages, it is currently available in 12 languages. This includes Santali, for which the Olchiki script is used (the software is available!) making it the first time ever that a children's magazine is being published in a tribal language. Santals constitute a million-strong population, of whom some 50,000 are literate and live in Bihar, Jharkhand, Bengal and Assam.[12]

Several high-quality English children's magazines have folded up over the years owing to lack of sponsorship, the non-viability of having to depend upon subscriptions, and the unreliability of the English-speaking, urban market base. Experience has shown that it is usually magazines riding on corporate or financial or business patronage that manage to survive. The exception is *Chandamama* which generates its own income through subscriptions, retail sales, and advertisements. Labour and financial problems forced a 20-month suspension of its publication in the late

1990s, but it was reborn in a new *avatar* and has not looked back. It now has a sister publication, *Junior Chandamama*, as well as a special bilingual Singapore edition, which is supported by the Singapore Tamil Teacher's Union.

In fact, a dynamic and creative team that was producing an attractive, intelligent product for the English market called *Chatterbox* through sheer idealism and willpower has now turned to creating content for a Singapore-based company. Of all the magazines produced in English, *Chatterbox* is one example that gave equal importance to content and form, writing that resonated, and interactions that challenged its young readers. In an in-between avatar as *Wizkids*, they also tried to introduce a newspaper for kids. While that adventure ended quietly, *Gobar Times* is hanging on firmly to the sari '*pallu*' of *Down to Earth*, a greatly respected environment magazine. My gut feeling is that some of the best magazines for children in India are those related to nature and wildlife. Some also have various jokes on related subjects:

> Charan: Miss, may I keep this rabbit with me during maths class?
> Teacher: What on earth for?
> Charan: My dad says they multiply very fast![13]

Computers have 'maxiplied' the efficiency quotient of most things, including the collection and collation of material. Errant contributors can be chased to death by e-mail, and elusive illustrators can be tracked down and hunted far more easily, although not quite as effectively, as writers. The visual element is as important as the textual element, and hence calls for tremendous staying power on the part of the editorial team. While the production process has become as smooth as a happy dream, the technology wave has also succeeded in dissolving the unique into sameness and similarity. Many of the products look bright and slick but there does seem to be less by way of intellectual or creative stimulation.

The easy way is of course so much easier and quicker. When someone once suggested to Chiedza that materials simply be photocopied so that they could be available to more children, she retaliated, 'Children hate ugly books.' As one child so wisely put it, 'I think it is very important to give a nice name to the magazine and to put an attractive cover page as that's what all of us coax our parents to buy.' Offering tips on writing mysteries,[14] Ranjit Lal cautions,

> If you are writing about the supernatural—i.e., about ghosts, goblins, witches, wizards, spirits, ectoplasm, etc.—you have a lot of power because your characters can do just about anything. The trick is to use this power only to the extent that the reader believes, 'Hell, this is possible!' If you use this power or magic as an easy way out of a sticky situation then you'll be cheating your reader and he or she will lose interest in your story. If all problems can be solved by waving a wand, well, where's the story? ('Writing Mysteries' in *Chatterbox*, February 2003, Vol. 2, Issue 4)

Sometimes it seems that the children who receive a third kind of magazine (as distinct from the first two kinds mentioned earlier), almost always generated by NGOs mostly engaged in health and literacy and science issues while at the same time working towards giving children a sense of self-worth, are luckier. Their materials are so much more carefully thought-out, attractive and challenging. Much of the time they are published in Indian languages and cater to non-city readers.[15]

For the greater part, however, the world of children's magazines is a mish-mash driven by pressures of the school system, by the need to make children literate and to make them super-achieve, and by the forces of commerce that determine whether a product is viable or not and what will make it so, never mind the profile. Again, the kind of choices exercised by editors depends upon whether they have the freedom to do so, or whether the business house's policy dictates content.

Still, who can completely grudge the desire to make profit? But at the cost of maintaining the status quo of children as non-persons? At the cost of providing enriching experiences? That is the point. 'Reading materials affirm a child's identity,' says Chiedza. Whatever my quarrels with the kinds of identities various magazines affirm, I must admit that children experience ownership of the magazines they have access to, especially those who are allowed to buy or, better still, subscribe to their own magazines. They are not necessarily always the best, but they are available, and they keep their 'customers satisfied'. But is that all we want? Is that at all what we want?

As if this were not enough, South African writer Doris Lessing[16] says that we patronize children. 'No one ever said to me, Don't try and read that book—let's say *Oliver Twist*—it is too old for you. It was taken for granted that I would skip what I didn't understand and slowly learn to read difficult words and grasp difficult ideas ... I think children are patronized now. They are capable of much more.'

Editors of children's supplements and magazines will corroborate the fact that hundreds of letters pour in from children, some of them expressing their deepest dreams and fears. As the first editor of a young people's supplement, 'Youthink' in the *Indian Express*, Chennai, several years ago, I can vouch for the incredibly large numbers of contributions and letters the weekly page sparked off. Children exist as flesh-and-blood persons; they have thoughts and ideas; and they wish to express themselves. The only spaces they seem to have are a page or two once a week or once a month, or, if the magazine has folded up, no space at all.

Below are excerpts from two letters, one published in a magazine that is now defunct, and the other in a magazine that is doing well. At least some *'mosambis'* are available to some children some of the time.

'Every month I eagerly wait for *Chandamama*,' writes Ajita Mohanty. 'I read it fully and like every article in it ... I hope you will continue to entertain millions of children like me around the world ....'[17]

'I can't believe how you folks put together such nice issues every month,' says Samyuktha Kartik. '*Chatterbox* has made me 99 per cent extra creative. It makes me think of ways to help animals, be kind to people, keep the country clean and stop violence ....'[18]

Children have the last word.

Notes

1. Savitri Goonesekere, *Children, Law and Justice: A South Asian Perspective* (New Delhi, UNICEF–Sage Publications, 1998).
2. Vaishnavi Nagaraj and Vivek C Vijayan, 'He wasn't peeling well', *Gokulam* (Chennai, Bharathan Publications Private Limited, August 2005).
3. Article 31 of the Convention of Rights of Child says that we must 'recognize the right of the child to rest and leisure, to engage in play and recreational activities appropriate to the age of the child and to participate freely in cultural life and the arts.' It goes on to add that

we must also 'respect and promote the right of the child to participate fully in cultural and artistic life and shall encourage the provision of appropriate and equal opportunities for cultural, artistic, recreational and leisure activity.'

Article 17 states that we shall 'recognize the important function performed by the mass media and shall ensure that the child has access to information and material from a diversity of national and international sources, especially those aimed at the promotion of his or her social, spiritual and moral well-being and physical and mental health.'

4. Seminar on 'Growing up with books: Children's literature in developing countries', held at the 14th New Delhi World Book Fair, 7–8 February 2000.

5. Unpublished poem by author.

6. Chiedza is quoted from 'Meeting Chiedza Musengezi', in an interview to the author in Harare, Zimbabwe, November 1999, published in *Feminist Bookstore News*, Fall 1999, Vol. 22, 3&4, pp. 74–75.

7. In *Chandamama* (Chennai, Chandamama India Limited), August 2005.

8. *Children's Digest*, Vol. 9, No. 8 (Kottayam, Rashtra Deepika Limited, August 2005). The answer is the paper clip.

9. 'Semma bore' would loosely translate as 'big bore'; *'semma'* is a Tamil word.

10. Personal interviews of children conducted during the course of writing workshop, Imagine Words, at Goodbooks Bookstore, Chennai, July–December 2005. The date of the interviews is 19 August 2005.

11. The *Bhagavad Gita* is a treatise regarded as sacred by Hindus. Story idea by Y V K Sridhar, *Tinkle*, No. 516 (Mumbai, India Book House Private Limited, August 2005).

12. Information courtesy K Ramakrishnan, consulting editor, *Chandamama*.

13. Contributed by M Shivani, in *Gokulam*, August 2005.

14. *Chatterbox*, February 2003.

15. Examples of these are *Chakmak*, *Tulir* and *Tamasha*.

16. Quoted in essay, 'Glass Glass Beads', Philip Davis (ed.), *Real Voices on Reading* (London, Macmillan Press Ltd, 1997).

17. Letter to the editor in *Chandamama*, August 2005.

18. Letter to the editor in *Chatterbox* (Chennai, Wheitstone Productions Private Limited, December 2002).

4

The Unwritten Writing: Dalits and the Media[1]

D Ravikumar

Sometimes, however, journeys into the past give you glimpses of what things might look like in the future, as if you were seeing them reflected in the rear-view mirror of a car.

—*Robert Darnton*[2]

I

The print media in India has a history of 225 years. The *Bengal Gazette*, founded by James Augustus Hicky in 1780, was the first magazine in India.[3] Though the first book printed in an Indian language, *Thambiraan Vanakkam* (1578), was in Tamil, the first Tamil magazine appeared only in 1785. Richard Johnstone founded *The Madras Courier* on 12 December 1785. Started as a weekly selling for Re 1, the four-page tabloid carried government orders and advertisements. From a contemporary perspective, it cannot be regarded as a magazine. Four more magazines were started in 1795. One of them was *Indian Herald* edited by S A Humphrey. After the publication of its very first issue, Humphrey was arrested for printing 'gossip' about the marriage of the Prince of Wales, and *Indian Herald* ceased publication.

Lord Wellesley's 'Regulations of the Press', implemented in 1799, demanded that anyone who ventured into publishing should get prior permission from the chief secretary. As a result, individuals in India could not own any press. This condition prevailed till Metcalf did away with the regulations in 1835. However, these regulations did not cover the activities of the missionaries. The Madras Christian Educational League published the *Tamil Magazine* in 1831. Of the 11 monthly magazines published in 1865, nine were published by missionaries. The Hindus published several magazines in protest against missionary activities. The monthlies *Thatthuvapodini* and *Viveka Vilakkam* tried to propagate the ideas of Veda Samaj, an organization aimed at reforming Hinduism.

Magazines like *Viruthandhi, Dravida Deepikai, Janasinegan, Rajavarthinipothini* and *Varthamana Tharangini* were published with a social mission. However, we do not have any other information about these magazines and their founders. Neither do we have the complete list of magazines published during this period. It is against this background that we must see the achievements of the national daily, the *Hindu*. It was founded in September 1878 with an investment of just Rs 1 and 12 annas–that too as a loan. Started as a weekly with eight pages, priced at 4 annas, it initially had a print-run of only 80 copies.[4]

Six angry youths–G Subramania Iyer of Tiruvaiyyar near Thanjavur, his friend M Veeraraghavachariar of Chengalpattu (a professor at Pachaiyappa's College), and four law college students, T T Rangachariar, P V Rangachariar, D Kesava Rao Pant and N Subba Rau Pantulu (members of the Triplicane Literary Society)–who rose against the British newspapers for criticizing the appointment of T Muthuswamy Aiyar to the bench of the Madras High Court, founded the magazine in 1878. By then, the Indian newspaper industry was more than a hundred years old. Subramania Iyer wanted to start a Tamil magazine and founded *Swadesamitran* in association with Veeraraghavachariar on 20 December 1881. Following the third conference of the Indian National Congress held in Madras in 1887, *Swadesamitran* gained popularity by supporting nationalist politics. In 1898, Subramania Iyer quit the *Hindu* and became the editor of *Swadesamitran*. He turned it into a daily on 2 August 1899.

Though the mainstream history of the press does document such information, it is silent about other significant events. The 19th century Dalit intellectual Panditar Iyothee Thass, whose work has witnessed a revival in the post-Ambedkar centenary phase, has recorded the fact that the Parayars were the first to publish Tamil magazines in the Madras Presidency.[5] According to Thass, Pandit Tiruvenkidasamy of Pudupettai published the magazine *Suryodayam*, and Swami Arangaya Thass published *Sukirdavasani*. 'Besides, people of this community published numerous magazines and books,' writes Thass.[6] Magazines like *Adi-Dravidar, Mahaavikada Toothan, Booloka Viyasan* and *Adi-Dravida Mitran*,[7] which were published by Dalits, validate Thass' claim. This data renders our attempt to identify the first magazine in Tamil difficult.

Iyer, who started the *Hindu* and *Swadesamitran*, founded the Madras Mahajana Sabha in association with Anandacharyulu, Rangaiah Naidu and Ramasamy Mudaliar in May 1884. However, eight years earlier, Panditar Iyothee Thass had founded the Advaitananda Sabha at Nilgiris in 1876; he founded the Dravida Mahajana Sabha in 1891. There is hence reason to believe that the untouchables, who were active in philosophical and political spheres, would have been pioneers in the press too. People of this community, Iyothee Thass argued, would have produced a lot of books:

The original Brahmins–the Buddhists–who were destabilised by the false-Brahmins [sometime after the 10th century CE], suffered innumerable hardships. Buddhist scholars were vanquished, many Buddhist scriptures were destroyed and lost. The few Buddhist texts like *Kumarasamiyam*, *Sothidalangaaram* and *Varushadi Nool* that have survived were preserved and published by Valluva Markkalinga Pandaram. Kuzhandaivelu Paradesiyar published *Manikanda Keralam*. Kandappan, the butler of George Arlington, had handed over the palm-leaf manuscripts of *Nayanar Thirikkural, Naaladi Naanooru* and *Araneri Deepam* to Lord Ellis,[8] who established the Tamil Sangam. Ellis published them with the help of his manager, Muthusamy Pillai....

Kuzhandaivelu Pandaram of Mylapore published the songs of the Siddhars (mystic poets). Punditar Tiruvenkidasamy of Pudupettai published the *Vaidya Kaviyam, Sivavaakkiyam* and *Rathina Karandakam*. Vee. Iyothee Thassa Kaviraja pandithar brought out medical texts such as *Bogar 700, Agasthiyar 200, Simittu Rathina Surukkam* and *Balavagadam*.[9]

Besides the palm-leaf manuscripts of *Arichuvadi, Varikkuvaai Paadam, Peyarchuvadi, Aatthichuvadi, Konraivendan, Vetriverkkai, Moodurai, Tivakaram, Nihandu, Ensuvadi, Nellilalakkam, Ponnilakkam* and other important Tamil texts were preserved by families which had knowledge of the Tamil

Buddhist tradition. These statements of Iyothee Thass demand the attention of present-day historians. According to Anbu Ponnoviyam, an upholder of the Tamil Buddhist tradition and a chronicler of the life and times of Iyothee Thass, 'Since other forms of literature like poetry, essays and plays produced between 1860 and 1910 by Adi-Dravidars have not survived, it is difficult for us to know the history of untouchables.'[10] Thanks to Ponnoviyam, all the issues of the magazine *Tamilan* (founded by Iyothee Thass in 1907) were preserved and published. Otherwise, the history of the untouchables in Tamil Nadu would have been further distorted.

It is not surprising to note that the magazines run by the untouchables are not to be found now. If the publishers of the *Hindu* could not admittedly locate a single issue of the first three years of their magazine, who can be blamed for the loss of the magazines run by Dalits?

II

The *Hindu* celebrated its 125th anniversary on 13 September 2003; whereas not a single issue of *Parayan*, which was started about the same time as the *Hindu*, has survived. The *Hindu* has grown into a Rs 400-crore empire, though founded with just Rs 1 and 12 annas.[11] In such a context, a critical assessment of the newspaper is necessary, not only from a general perspective but from a Dalit perspective as well.

We have already seen that the *Hindu* was started in response to the criticisms levelled by the English editors of the British-run press against the appointment of Muthuswamy Aiyar as a high court judge. However, the founders of the *Hindu* did not register their protest in a direct manner. Describing the circumstances that surrounded the founding of the newspaper, they said: 'It will always be our aim to promote harmony and union among our fellow countrymen and to interpret correctly the feelings of the natives and to create mutual confidence between the governed and the governors....'[12] Though they claim to have represented the feelings of the natives, this can be contested. The term 'natives' does not refer to a monolithic bloc; it does not consist only of the Brahmins. The opinions of the untouchables, who too were 'natives', were not similar to those of the founders of the *Hindu*. They felt that people like Muthuswamy Aiyar should not be given the position of a judge. Raobahadur Rettamalai Srinivasan, who later in his life represented the untouchables along with B R Ambedkar at the Round Table Conference in London in 1931, describes an incident–similar to Iyer's appointment as high court judge–that took place in 1893. This pertained to the conduct of simultaneous exams for civil services in Britain and India:

> Only British citizens who cleared the Civil Service Examination conducted in London became collectors and judges and occupied other administrative positions of national significance. The Congressmen submitted a petition to the British parliament urging them to conduct the examination in India. Realising that it would help the caste Hindus occupy powerful positions and harass the poor untouchables, the members of 'Parayar Maha Jana Sabha' gathered in large number at Chennai's Wesleyan Mission College hall in December 1893 and condemned the move. They submitted a 112-feet-long memorandum with 3,412 signatures to General Sir George Chesney protesting the Congress demand. Later, the Congressmen withdrew their petition.[13]

Even after this incident, the untouchables stuck to similar stands on such issues. This is conveyed by Iyothee Thass through a news item that appeared in one of the issues of *Tamilan* in 1908.[14] Titled 'Power of District Magistrate for Indians', the news item observes that such positions should not be given to Brahmins, and adds: 'The self-styled Brahmins migrated to this country from alien lands.' Treating Brahmins on a par with Englishmen and Muslims, he said:

> If we give the power of District Magistrate to these people, they will employ the people of their caste and cheat common Hindus. There will be endless troubles if high positions are given to those who call themselves 'higher caste' .... They regard even the British as inferior to them. They don't have intellectual, physical, economic or even numerical strength. They have only the strength that comes from calling themselves people of high caste.

This statement of Thass, and the consistent stance taken by *Parayan* on such issues, leads us to infer that the untouchables would certainly not have supported Iyer's appointment as a judge. More pertinently, this demonstrates that the *Hindu* surely did not represent *all* the natives.

We can appreciate the stand taken by the untouchables only if we can set it against the background of the state of justice in

19th century India. Pointing out that those regarded as lower castes were put into stocks and the so-called 'higher' castes were given simple imprisonment in 1816, Iyothee Thass says that this trend changed only during the regime of Queen Victoria. She made it clear that anyone who committed a grave offence can be put into stocks regardless of whether he belongs to a higher or lower caste. She was aware of the atrocities committed by the *tahsildars* and divested them of their position as magistrates (who act as judges) and declared that magistracy is distinct from that of a *tahsildar's* position. Ambedkar's assessment that Hinduism has lawlessness as its law and has been offering injustice as justice, owes his distress to similar situations.

Taking such a state of affairs into account, we can say that apart from representing the feelings of the natives, the founders of the *Hindu* had a different intention. This found subtle expression in the first issue of their magazine: 'The Press does not only give expression to public opinion, but also modifies and moulds it according to circumstances,' they wrote.[15] Hence it would not be wrong to say that they actually operated with a caste bias and represented the 'interests of the higher caste' and projected these as the feelings of all the natives. It showed that the founders were motivated not by patriotism but by an affinity for their caste.

Fifteen years later, in October 1893, Rettamalai Srinivasan founded the magazine *Parayan*. It was started as a monthly with four pages for 2 annas. The total cost of production including the advertisement was Rs 10. Srinivasan did not make claims like the founders of the *Hindu* did. Explaining the reasons for starting the magazine, he said:

> One who pronounces his 'I' as a *mantra* would become a saint and would know himself as well as have a vision of the all-knowing Almighty. One who does not ignore his community and speaks the truth without fear or shame would be honoured and would live in peace and prosperity. So, those belonging to the Parayar community should come forward openly to say, 'I am pariah.' Otherwise, he cannot enjoy freedom. He will lead the life of the suppressed and remain poor. That is why I have started a magazine, crowning it with the name 'Pariah'.[16]

Four hundred copies of the first issue of *Parayan* were sold out in just two days, bearing testimony to the literacy rate among the untouchables in Madras city. The first edition's sale was five times higher than that of the *Hindu*'s–which printed only 80 copies with 10 times *Parayan*'s investment.

In a letter to S Srinivasa Raghava Aiyangar, Inspector General of Registration in Madras Presidency, written in 1893, Iyothee Thass pointed out that among the untouchables within the municipal limits of Madras, there were 112 candidates qualified for the post of *Dubashies* with proficiency in many languages.[17] The same letter lists the fact that there were 148 qualified butlers from among Parayars at that time. This helps us surmise that efforts like Thass' *Tamilan* and the Srinivasan's *Parayan* survived with the support of the untouchables. The same was true in the case of the literary texts as well.

In the history of Tamil, the production of literary texts has been possible only with the support of patrons. During the second half of the 19th century, *palayakars*, *maths* and *zamindars* were serving as patrons.[18] When A Sheshayya Sastry served as *diwan*, the prince of Pudukkottai conducted a 'Navarathri festival' in which he honoured poets and scholars with sums up to Rs 100. Sheshayya Sastry supported scholars like C Vai. Damodharan Pillai and U Ve Swaminatha Iyer.

Ponnusamy Thevar (1837–70), brother of the prince of Ramnad, was a lover of literature. He always had a scholar around him to read and discuss poetry and encouraged the publishing efforts of Arumuga Naavalar. He supported scholars like Thillaiyambur Chandrasekara Kavirayar, Mahamahapathiyaya Raji Sastrigal and Vidhwan Thiyagaraja Chettiyar. Pandithurai Thevar (1867–1911) continued the services of his father Ponnusamy Thevar. It was he who funded U Ve Swaminatha Iyer's publication of the Sangam poetical text *Purananooru* and the epic *Manimekalai*. Besides these, Marudhappa Thevar of Ootrumalai *zamin*; Ramalinga Thevar of Siruvayal *zamin*; Duraisamy Reddiyar, the *zamindar* of Namakkal; Pethachi Chettiyar, the *zamindar* of Chokkampatty; and the *zamindar* of Aandipatty also served as patrons and played a crucial role in the publication of several texts. Saiva maths in Tiruvaaduthruai, Dharmapuram, Tirupanandal, Kumbakonam, Chidambaram, Tiruvannamalai, Thoraiyur and Mayilam also played a significant role in the production of literary texts and supported many poets. What is more, landlords and heads of castes also served as patrons.

It is quite certain that the untouchables would not have had the support of such patrons. This becomes even clearer if we look into the kind of texts edited and published by these poets and scholars. Apart from the lack of support, the 'wealth' of knowledge of the untouchables was destroyed by the caste Hindus who envied and hated them. Talking about this, Iyothee Thass said in the 2 March 1913 issue of *Tamilan*:

> Besides encouraging casteism, these people earn money by spreading lies through the business of religion. When the Jain saints and Buddhists condemned their [Hindus'] ritual of sacrificing the goats, horses and cows and drove them out, the enraged and envious Brahmins won the support of the local chieftains and a majority of the people, killed the Jain/Buddhist saints, destroyed their places and burnt the palm-leaf manuscripts preserved by them.[19]

In the 25 February 1914 issue of *Tamilan*, he pointed out that the untouchables managed to publish those palm-leaf manuscripts that had survived these atrocities:

> Even though the Buddhists were regarded as lower caste and were put to a lot of trouble and were expelled from their inhabitations, they managed to publish their ethical, philosophical writings and almanacs, which they had preserved. A quarter of the native medicinal texts were published only through the so-called 'lower castes', who also published their original, ancient sources.[20]

Before the publication of *Dinavarthamani*, a Tamil weekly published in 1855 by Reverend Pater Percival 'Iyer',[21] Pandit Tiruvenkidasamy published *Suryodaya* from Pudupettai. He also published the *Cittar Songs, Gnana Kumbikal, Theraiyar Vaithiyam 500, Dhanvandhriyar Nihandu*. From these details provided by Iyothee Thass, we can infer that the untouchables preserved their wealth of knowledge and spread it without the help of patrons.

Apart from literate Brahmins and the caste Hindus, the British administrators and native kings too supported the *Hindu*. It is important to look at Muthiah's reference to the following editorial to understand that the founders of the *Hindu* remained 'Anglophiles': 'How enormously the Indian people are indebted to British rule for everything that makes human life worth living. For everything that imparts to them happiness, dignity and the quality of progress.'[22]

Muthiah further adds that the *Hindu* was deeply involved in disclosing the misuse of power, criticizing power-mongering officials and in opposing Anglo-Indian magazines. These activities of the *Hindu* need to be understood also through its support for '*swadeshi*' politics. If from a secular point of view we compare its support for Hindus during the communal clash in Salem in 1884, and its condemnation of the arrest of B G Tilak in 1887, we can understand how truly 'progressive' it was.

Muthiah says that Iyer, one of the founders of the *Hindu*, was actively involved in the uplift of women. Besides supporting widow remarriage, which was strongly opposed during his time, Iyer got his daughter, Sivapiriyammal (who became a widow at the age of 13), remarried during the Congress conference in Bombay in 1889. Muthiah also says Iyer was concerned about Dalits and quotes him as saying that 'the degraded condition' of the Dalits was 'notorious and the peculiarities of the Hindu social system was such that from this system no hope whatever of their amelioration can be entertained.' Also: 'No amount of admiration for our religion will bring social salvation to these poor people.'[23] All the same, Iyer did not take any measures for the uplift of Dalits as he did for women (by way of getting his widowed daughter remarried and by sending his family priest to perform the ritual for the death of a widow's child). There is little doubt that the *Hindu*, which has not bothered to employ a single Dalit on its editorial staff in 125 years, had the same 'progressive' attitude even during the time of Subramania Iyer.

While the *Hindu* got advertisements and received financial support from the Vijayanagara emperor, Aananda Gajapathi, *Parayan* did not receive any support except from the Parayars. 'It talked in support of the Parayars, demanded help for them from the government and promoted goodness.'[24] It was therefore quite natural that the Parayars supported the magazine. Srinivasan further said: 'Wherever they gathered, they talked about the magazine with great enthusiasm.' It grew very fast with the support of Parayars. It was turned into a weekly in a short span of three months. Within two years, it established even a separate press. If we compare it with the five years that the *Hindu* took to start its own press, we will understand how far the untouchables had been involved in issues of social growth, self-respect and political awareness.

The *Hindu* had differences with the magazines like the *Mail* and the *Madras Times* and often wrote against them. Such contradictions and competition could be seen even among the Parayars. Besides, the Congressmen, caste Hindus and missionaries too attacked the *Parayan*. In fact, there was an occasion when even an arrest warrant was issued against Rettamalai Srinivasan on the ground that he was fleeing the nation. However, the arrest did not take place. In 1896, a case was filed against *Parayan*, citing a letter to the editor, and the editor was taken to the court. A fine of Rs 100 was imposed on him. 'The people of this community came to the court in good number. On their turbans and chests, they sported the name '*Parayan*' and had come with some money.'[25] Someone in the crowd paid the fine to express his love for the community, according to Srinivasan.

The *Hindu* also faced such litigation during much the same period. It had to pay a large fine for three out of the four cases filed against the magazine. It incurred heavy losses due to the fall in advertisement revenue. The ill feeling among its founders in this connection led to their parting. Their animosity went to the extent of Subramania Iyer filing a defamation case against his one-time friend, Veeraraghavachariar, for publishing an article in his Tamil magazine *Hindu Desam*.

The parting of ways of the founders and Veeraraghavachariar's inept leadership led to the decline of the *Hindu*. His efforts to compensate the loss by leasing out a part of its building and by printing school textbooks proved futile. The circulation came down to 800. It was at that time that he decided to sell the *Hindu*. Kasturi Iyengar, their then legal advisor, bought it for Rs 75,000 in 1905. The magazine started with an investment of just Rs 1 and 12 anna was sold for Rs 75,000 after 27 years. Starting with a circulation of just 80 copies, it sold 800 copies in 1905. After Kasturi Iyengar took charge of the magazine, it ran smoothly, according to the present editor N Ram: 'Walking on "two legs"– serious, independent, quality journalism, and business viability and success–along the path worked out by the *Hindu*'s second founder has brought the newspaper to where it is today: the front ranks of the world's major newspapers.'[26]

What happened to the *Parayan*? Started in 1893, it continued publication till 1900 without any disturbance. When Srinivasan went to London 'for the cause of the untouchables', it had to be stopped as there was no one equipped to run the magazine. When Subramania Iyer went to London, there was this Veeraraghavachariar to run the *Hindu*. When it faced a loss, there was a Kasturi Iyengar to buy the magazine. There was good support for the *Parayan*; yet there was no one to run the magazine. Though Iyothee Thass later started the magazine *Tamilan*, the closing of *Parayan* was a major loss in the political life of the untouchables. *Parayan*'s defeat is a mere story, whereas the success of the *Hindu* becomes history.

III

Seven years after *Parayan* ceased publication, on 19 June 1907 Iyothee Thass launched a weekly, *Oru Paisa Tamilan*, from Royapettah. It was printed at the Buddhist Press of Adimoolam, a Buddhist. The first issue of *Tamilan* clearly states its aim: 'Some philosophers, natural scientists, mathematicians and littérateurs joined together and published this *Oru Paisa Tamilan* to teach fairness, the path of truth and honesty to those who cannot otherwise discriminate between the excellent, the mediocre and the bad.'[27] The weekly appeared until his death in 1914. Subsequently, it was produced by the editorial team of G Appadurai and P M Rajarathinam of Kolar. *Tamilan* and *Parayan* were not one-off instances. Dalit interest in the media in the late 19th and early 20th centuries seems to have been a serious affair. M C Rajah, an important Dalit leader of the period, lists the following publications run by Dalit leaders in his book *The Oppressed Hindus* (Tamil edition). Their year of founding is given in parentheses.

Suriyothaiyam [Sunrise] (1869)
Panchama [The Outcaste] (1871)
Dravida Pandian, edited by John Rathinam (1885)
Andror Mitran, edited by Vellore Panditar Munnuswamy (1886)
Magha Vikata Thoothan, edited by T I Swamikannu Pulavar (1888)
Parayan, edited by Rettamalai Srinivasan (1893)
Illara Vozukkam (1898)
Poologa Vyasan, edited by Dasavathanam Poonjolai Muthuveera Pavalar (1900)
Dravida Kokilam, edited by the Association of Dalit Christians of Madras (1907)

Oru Paisa Tamilan, edited by Pandit Iyotheedass (1907)
Tamil Woman, edited by K Swappaneswari Ammal (1916)

We know very little about *Madurai Pirapandam* and *Rangoon Piravesa Tirattu* published in 1896. Besides pioneers in the press, leading intellectuals among the Dalit community contributed to various spheres of knowledge such as medicine, literature and philosophy.

Swami Sagajananda[28] (1890–1959), a contemporary of Iyothee Thass and Rettamalai Srinivasan, who outlived Ambedkar, produced a magazine called *Paranjothi* and had authored several books. They include *Aalayam Enbadu Arisanangalukke* (The temple is only for Harijans), *Theendaamai Ozhippu* (Annihilation of Untouchability), *Vachirasoosikai Upanishad, Chidambara Rakasiyam* and *Nadarajar Thandavam, Theendaamai is not Sastriam* (Untouchability is not Part of Sastras), *Thazhthappattor Arisanangal Thotram* (The Origin of the Downtrodden Harijans), *Theendamai* (Untouchability), *Namathu Thonmai* (Our Antiquity) and *Pannaiyal Paadukappu Cattamum Arasangathin Kadamaiyum* (Landowners' Protection Act and the Duty of the Government).

What is the present state of Dalits, who made a distinct mark by publishing magazines, and writing or editing scholarly books way back in the 19th century? Today how many Dalits work in the Indian dailies, whose combined circulation is nearly six crores? Political scientist Robin Jeffrey says:

> In more than ten years studying Indian-language newspapers, including twenty weeks of travel in which I stayed in twenty towns, visited dozens of newspapers and interviewed more than 250 people, I did not—so far as I know—meet a Dalit journalist working for a mainstream publication, much less a Dalit editor or proprietor. My colleague Oliver Mendelsohn, co-author of an extended study of Scheduled Castes, could offer only one suggestion, a Dalit from Karnataka who had worked for the *Deccan Herald* and *Prajavani* before starting a Kannada weekly in 1985. This was Indudhara Honnapura, whose weekly *Suddhi Sangaati* claimed a circulation of 44,000 in 1987.[29]

Despite the fact that Dalits constitute one-fourth of India's population, we find no Dalit today working as a reporter or sub-editor. Jeffrey continues:

> There were no Dalit editors and no Dalit-run dailies. Dalit periodicals, where they existed, were fringe publications, often with a literary emphasis and with

limited influence beyond the circle that produced them. The most senior journalist I met in more than ten years of studying Indian newspapers had never worked for a commercially run daily.[30]

The only journalist that Jeffrey met was T S Ravindradass in Chennai. He was the president of the Tamil Nadu Union of Journalists. But he never worked in any mainstream magazine. When he was elected from among the 800 members, no one knew that he was a Dalit.

'If you ask an Indian journalist, "Do you know any Dalit journalists?", the answer could be a long pause and then, "Could you give me a couple of days." Sometimes it was a considerate no,' notes Jeffrey.[31] There were some Dalit journalists in *Malayala Manorama*, but they worked in less significant positions.

Magazines in the US showed special attention to news regarding the African Americans as early as in the 1920s. The African Americans in the US form 13 per cent of the American population. Though the percentage of Dalits in India is higher (at 16 per cent), the picture in India is a complete contrast to that in the US. African Americans started a magazine in 1827. It is significant that the untouchables in India started theirs around the same time. By 1891, more than 150 magazines were run by blacks. Most of these were run either by the Christian missionaries or with the help of those involved in business. Jeffrey argues that there were no such religious or educational institutions to support Dalits. However, Iyothee Thass established both religious and educational institutions.

We need to find out how many Dalits work in the leading Tamil dailies—*Dinamalar*, *Dinakaran* and *Dinathanthi*. It is mostly those belonging to the Nadar caste who are appointed as reporters in *Dinathanthi*. The situation is the same with *Dinakaran*.[32] In *Dinamalar*, it is the numerically strong among the shudra castes in a given region who are appointed as reporters.

When asked in 1999 by Jeffrey about Dalit journalists, R Kumaran, the then managing editor of *Dinakaran*, said: 'It is not an issue at all. While appointing reporters, we don't normally ask their caste.... So it is impossible to say how many Dalits work in our institution. A few of them may be Dalits.'[33] R Krishnamoorthy, editor of the *Dinamalar*, echoed the sentiment: 'Yes. There are a good number of Dalits in the printing section ... may be two or three in the editorial department too....

We don't select candidates on the basis of caste. We are not interested in such things. We want only eligible and efficient candidates.'[34] The editor of *Dinamani* said in 1999 that they had one photographer and a sub-editor from among Dalits.

It was a great shock for B N Uniyal, a Delhi-based journalist, that there was not even a single Dalit journalist accredited by the Press Information Bureau. Following his article (published in the *Pioneer* on 16 November 1996), Chandra Bhan Prasad and Sheoraj Singh Bechain submitted a memorandum to the Editors' Guild and the Press Council of India. In their memorandum, they demanded that Dalit journalists must be appointed in the mainstream media, taking the American experience as their model and by fixing 2005 as the target date.[35] After five years, the owners and associations of the press have not paid attention to their demand. The state of the press too remains unchanged.

Of the magazines published in India, a considerable number are from Tamil Nadu. As far the dailies are concerned, Brahmin domination was wiped out a long time ago.[36] The same holds good for the visual media too. All the same, the magazines in Tamil Nadu seem to adopt a much more oppressive policy vis-à-vis Dalits than other states. For them, social justice means caste justice.

In the last 50 years, there has been a decline in landholding and education among Dalits in Tamil Nadu. Their social status also has come down. There are several places—such as Keeripatti and Pappapaptti in Madurai district—where Dalits could not, till the 2006 local elections, contest for the post of panchayat president even in reserved seats.

The power and influence of the press are very high in this state. When the Tamil Nadu government attempted to take action against the *Hindu* in November 2003, the government faced a crisis. If the press uses its undoubted power to achieve democracy and equality, it will hasten social change. But the editors and owners of the press here do not have such a 'graceful' attitude. Running a magazine is not similar to owning an industry. Since the press is regarded as one of the pillars of democracy, it plays a significant role in shaping democracy. Therefore, demanding the inclusion of Dalits in the media should not be merely regarded as a plea for jobs. It is a demand for democracy, like that of the demand for representation in the assembly and parliament. In fact, it is equivalent to seeking due representation in the judiciary. The demand for space in the mainstream media is not to say that the Dalits should not develop their independent media. Given that the Dalits have successfully published weeklies a hundred years ago, they could well produce dailies today. Such initiatives should be undertaken forthwith.

Notes

1. First published in Tamil as 'Ezhudha Ezhuththu' in *Dalit*, February 2004. Translated by R Azhagarasan. 'Ezhudha Ezhuththu' was how Tamil literary circles in the late 18th century described printing technology—writing that did not require the act of writing; hence the unwritten writing.
2. 'The Bookless Future: An Online Exchange Between Robert Darnton and Keiji Kato', available at: http://www.honco.net/100day/03/2001-0607-dk1.html.
3. The magazine founded by J A Hicky on 29 January 1780 was popular among the European non-professionals for the 'gossip' it carried. For details regarding the state of Indian press during colonial rule, I have relied on K Mohan Ram's *Tamil Press and the Colonial Rule* (Chennai, Prism Books, 2003).
4. S Muthiah, 'The Hindu Experience,' the *Hindu* (Special Supplement), 13 September 2003.
5. See Gnana Aloysius (ed.), *Iyotheethasar Sinthanaigal*, Vol. I (Palayamkottai, Folklore Resources and Research Centre, 1999), p. 146.
6. Gnana Aloysius (ed.), *Iyotheethasar Sinthanaigal*, Vol. I, p. 146.
7. See Anbu Ponnoviyam, 'Foreword', in *Iyotheethasar Sinthanaigal*, Vol. I, p. xxv.
8. Lord Francis Whyte Ellis joined the administrative service in the Madras Presidency in 1796 and served as collector in several districts. Expert in judicial and political matters, Ellis collected Tamil palm-leaf manuscripts through his Tamil teacher Panditar Saminatha Pillai. He also wrote notes for the first 13 chapters of *Tirukkural*. For more details about Ellis, see Mayilai Seeni.Venkatasamy, *Chistianity and Tamil* (Chennai, Nam Tamilar Publications, reprint 2004), pp. 70–71.
9. *Iyotheethasar Sinthanaigal*, Vol. I, p. 146.
10. Ponnoviyam, ibid., p. xxv.
11. N Ram, 'Yesterday. Today. Tomorrow', the *Hindu* (Special Supplement), 13 September 2003, p. 1.

12. S Muthiah, 'The Hindu Experience', p. 2.
13. Rettamalai Srinivasan, 'Jeevida Carithira Surukkam' (Autobiographical Sketch), *Dalit*, No. 5, May–July 2002, p. 56. The mainstream nationalist history records this as a struggle between the Indian National Congress (INC) and the British. But the reports that appeared in *Parayan*, edited by Srinivasan, prove that the actual fight was between the INC and the untouchables.
14. Gnana Aloysius (ed.), *Iyotheethasar Sinthanaigal*, Vol. 1, pp. 21–23.
15. Quoted in Muthiah, 'The Hindu Experience', p. 2.
16. Srinivasan, 'Jeevida Carithira Surukkam', p. 47.
17. Gnana Aloysius (ed.), *Iyotheethasar Sinthanaigal*, Vol. 2, 4. For the original English text of this letter, see G Aloysius, *Religion as Emancipatory Identity: A Buddhist Movement among Parayars in Colonial Tamil Nadu* (Hyderabad, New Age International, 1997), p. XXX.
18. A R Venkatachalapathy, 'A Social History of Tamil Publishing, 1850–1938', Ph.D. dissertation submitted to Jawaharlal Nehru University, 1994.
19. Quoted in Anbu Ponnoviyam, 'Foreword,' p. xxxvii.
20. Ibid.
21. Rev. Pater Percival of the Wesleyan Mission Society came to Jaffna in Sri Lanka in 1833. He learned Tamil from Arumuga Navalar. Besides publishing a collection of 1,873 proverbs, he also published a Tamil dictionary. He produced a weekly, *Dinavarthamaani*, in 1855. The surname 'Iyer' was appended to the names of several missionaries, including Percival, and was used as an equivalent of the Brahmin caste. In several cases, the missionaries too assumed the name and used it in formal contexts.
22. Muthiah, 'The Hindu Experience', p. 2.
23. Ibid., p. 3.
24. Srinivasan, 'Jeevida Carithira Surukkam', p. 48.
25. Ibid., p. 56.
26. Ram, 'Yesterday. Today. Tomorrow', p. 1.
27. G Alyosius, *Religion as Emanicipatory Identity*, p. 61.
28. See Dr Pon. Subramaniyam, *Swami Sagajananda* (Madras: Santha Pathipagam, 2000).
29. Robin Jeffrey, *India's Newspaper Revolution: Capitalism, Politics and the Indian Language Press*, 2nd ed (New Delhi, Oxford University Press, 2003), p. 161.
30. Ibid., p. 161.
31. Ibid., p. 162.
32. At the time of writing this article in Tamil in 2003, *Dinakaran* was under the management of the Nadar caste. By 2005, the daily was taken over by Kalanidhi Maran, the chief managing director of the

Sun Network. However, there is no reason to believe that Dalits would have made space for themselves in *Dinakaran* now, given that even Sun TV has not had any policy of affirmative action.

33. Ibid., 163.
34. Ibid.
35. 'End Apartheid from Indian Media, Democratise Nation's Opinion', Memorandum prepared by Chandra Bhan Prasad of Dalit Shiksha Andolan and Dr Sheoraj Singh 'Bechain' of Dalit Writers Forum and submitted to the Press Council of India, 1999.
36. The Brahmins dominated the press during the Congress-led 'nationalist' movement and in the immediate post-Independence period. The Brahmin monopoly was successfully challenged following the Dravidian movement in Tamil Nadu in the realms of literature, cinema, press and in politics.

5

Dalit Murasu: Surviving a Difficult Decade

V Geetha

This is the record of a conversation with Punitha Pandian, *chief editor,* Dalit Murasu, *a radical anti-caste Tamil monthly that is now entering its 10th year of publication.* V Geetha *interviewed Pandian for this volume. She has also written a brief introduction, placing* Dalit Murasu *in the context of Tamil political and cultural life.*

Introduction

Giuseppe Fiori's biography of Antonio Gramsci recounts an incident involving Gramsci's days with the Italian left paper, *L'Ordine Nuovo*. Impatient with the habitually vague rhetoric of his party men, as well as the lack of intellectual rigour in their writing, Gramsci is believed to have remarked that a revolutionary party, expecting to capture state power, cannot afford to treat its paper with such scant respect. For, the running of a newspaper, according to him, was akin to the running of a state.[1]

Nearer home, Dr Ambedkar comes to mind. His Marathi newspaper announced a new politics and ethics and anticipated a just social order. In the Tamil context, the Dalit writer and thinker Iyothee Thass, who founded and published the weekly *Tamizhan* in 1907, and E V Ramasamy Periyar, founder of the radical anti-caste and anti-brahmanical self-respect movement, who founded *Kudiarasu* (*The Republic*) in 1925, were both keenly aware of the power of the newspaper. The former was determined to keep alive and sustain a forum for articulating a dissident 'non-caste' and 'Dravidian' point of view. *Tamizhan* in fact announced itself as just such a forum. Periyar was all too aware of the manner in which newspapers in colonial Madras not only spoke to and with their readers, but also in their name. It was not for nothing that Annie Besant's *New India*, which spoke for Madras Brahmins, nationalists and reformers, loyal citizens of empire and conservatives, considered itself a veritable '*vox populi*' (voice of the people) and ran a column by that name in its pages. Periyar wanted the Tamil self-respecters to write and publish papers that would proclaim their representative worth and radical thought.

Dalit Murasu belongs to this tradition of self-conscious journalism. Its lineage goes back to the mid-19th century, to the early decades of anti-caste and Dalit publishing. And, like its illustrious forebears, especially *Tamizhan* and *Kudiarasu*, it is acutely conscious of its historic responsibilities. As its editor Punitha Pandian indicates (see interview later), it sees itself as performing a hegemonic function of persuading the public at large of the virtues of anti-caste radicalism. Further, it seeks to universalize a point of view that is usually considered subaltern or marginal, and thereby urges its claims to speak on behalf of a decent, civic humanity, and one committed to social and economic justice. The 'Dalit' in *Dalit Murasu* is both an invocation of an oppressed condition that has to be remembered, as well as an invitation to a future, where the oppressed become the measure of all that is to be human and imagine and build a brave new world.

This universalism is unique in the Tamil context, in that the anti-caste movement in the state has never really possessed its own news forums since the heyday of the self-respect movement. That is, it has never really successfully and in a sustained fashion proclaimed its will to a new and radical politics and ethics. *Viduthalai*, which started out as the voice of self-respect, speaking for a range of voices united in the cause of social justice, has long since become the official organ of the Dravidan Kazhagam. Various assorted papers that emerged in the days of Dravidian political success have since disappeared or become official party papers. *Dinamani* (belonging to the Indian Express group) and *Dinamalar*, which endorses the Hindu Right, are not really papers that inherited or laid claims to the Dravidian, self-respect inheritance. In this sense *Dalit Murasu*, which self-consciously situates itself in the context of anti-caste radicalism, is the only existing serious alternative political monthly in Tamil Nadu.

The first issue of *Dalit Murasu* was published a decade ago, in 1997. Those were the years of Dalit militancy in the Tamil country, when the public sphere in Tamil Nadu was held captive to the emergent discourses of Dalit liberation and assertion. The terrain of progressive politics was consequently transformed as new definitions of human rights, gender justice, cultural identity and literary worth were proposed and argued. Since that time, the tide of Dalit dissent has ebbed and retreated in the sphere of politics, though it continues to work its molecular effects in the world of culture. *Dalit Murasu* is perhaps one of the very few experiments to have survived the tumultuous excitement of that time–and it has done so with much grit and grace. It has evolved into an instance of mature journalism, not afraid to speak truth to power or to disturb both the facile calm as well as the disingenuous political correctness of civil society.

There are several reasons for the magazine's survival and growth: first, the unwavering conviction of its editors and founders that its continued existence was necessary, and that the magazine must not be allowed to perish; second, the public perception of this necessity, with the magazine serving as a space for dissident thought and critique that draws inspiration from the great catholic traditions of Tamil anti-caste radicalism and socialism; third, the nature of its content, lively political articles, reporting on public events in the community and Dalit parties combined with its deep ideological commitment to Ambedkar's views on caste and Hinduism; and, finally, its attempts to build a Gramscian historic bloc, comprising a range of dissenting voices, that would resist the logic of the *varna* order and build an alternate political comradeship.

None of this has been easy to accomplish: apart from persistent problems with financial support and distribution, *Dalit Murasu* has had to fight hard to sustain the political integrity and credibility which got attached to the Dalit cause in the mid-1990s. There are two important reasons for the struggle being a hard and difficult one: for one, political developments in the state, especially the wildly changing positions that the leading Dalit parties have come to adopt this past decade, appear to compromise the essential justness of the Dalit cause. Second, the magazine has not found it easy to retain for itself a coherent sense of Dalit interests and needs. Very real material and symbolic contradictions structure relationships between Dalit castes and threaten to divide the oppressed. The sense of an overarching comradeship such as the one proposed in the 1930s by the Tamil self-respect movement appears elusive, as particular castes and groups amongst the Dalits proudly assert their prescriptive identities. Further, comradeship itself, as a social virtue, does not appear desirable, since some amongst the current generation of Dalit intellectuals and activists consider it a conspiracy hatched by Periyar and others to perpetrate caste Hindu hegemony. On the one hand, they assert a unique 'Dalitness', if you will; on the other hand, they inscribe this Dalitness within particular caste memories. It is clear that they feel oddly burdened by the non-Brahmin Dravidian legacy of the past, including the life and thought of Periyar. They appear both unable to render that legacy critical and meaningful, as well as to reject it in strident terms. Much of this criticism remains cynical and unproductive, as *Dalit Murasu* has never failed to point out in its columns.

In the face of this desperate cynicism, both of political leaders and certain Dalit thinkers, *Dalit Murasu* has to work doubly hard to identify and champion Dalit interests and concerns. While it invokes a comradeship of all dissenting anti-caste groups and individuals, irrespective of their caste origin, in its attempts to build a historic bloc, it has also to contend with the political reluctance of even progressive non-Dalit political groups to make Dalit issues their own, except in a tactical sense.

The pressure to retain a clear and principled political point of view and not give into the very real allure of an identity politics, whose imaginative energy is contagious and compelling, has come to define the magazine's tone, which is sober, defiant and zealous. Political acuity has also meant that the magazine does not succumb to celebrations of Dalit culture or cultural achievements, except when these are directly linked to the cause of Dalit liberation. By not allowing too much room for art and literature, especially for imaginative play and fantasy, which, in their own way, possess the power to disturb the caste imagination, *Dalit Murasu* seems excessively weighed down by an unrelenting politics. On the other hand, if one were to consider the plethora of 'little' magazines devoted to art and culture in Tamil, which are not particularly sensitive to Dalit politics or social life, as they might be to Dalit literature, the burden that *Dalit Murasu* carries appears inevitable.

However a sustained engagement with culture cannot be wished away. Cultural criticism in *Dalit Murasu* has to transcend the limits imposed by the traditions of rational thought and criticism, popularized by Periyar and his fellow thinkers. For these latter do not allow a patient, nuanced engagement with the life worlds of caste society–something which is required if one is to understand, for instance, the alarming hold of Hindu practices in Dalit lives; or the manner in which Dalits claim a 'Tamil' cultural identity. *Dalit Murasu* is prone to considering these as instances of an imposed ignorance or false consciousness. They certainly are that, but perhaps it is critically important to also see how such practices are central to selfhood in caste society. Thus, if one is to reclaim caste subjects for an anti-caste politics, it might be equally important to build on cultures of living and relating. In some ways, this is precisely what Dr Ambedkar attempted when he converted to Buddhism.

Yet *Dalit Murasu* does not hold its principles as dogmas. It has always been sensitive to historical changes and attentive to the anxieties of the hour. In the late 1990s and until 2000–2001, it gave into the tide of genuine political and cultural excitement, as Dalits appeared to be at the helm of those changes that would usher in a new social order. When this gave way to the disillusionment and opportunism of the election years that followed and which affected Dalit politicians and parties, the magazine did not give up on its faith in social change. It retained its sense of what Dalits required to do: fight caste violence on the one hand, and build an expansive anti-caste historic bloc on the other. Even when a section of Dalit intellectuals appeared to denigrate and cast aspersions on the possibilities of such a bloc emerging in Tamil Nadu, the magazine's editors stayed calm and reasonable and continued to affirm the importance of both Ambedkar and Periyar. Since its earliest days, *Dalit Murasu* has remained consistent in its fundamental opposition to both Hindutva and Brahminical Hinduism and to a globalization process that only further perpetrates the *varna* order.

These past few years have seen *Dalit Murasu* committed to recording and bearing witness against the everyday violence and humiliation that caste society fosters. It is thus fighting a sustained war against forgetting–for the provisional successes of Dalit magazines and the public visibility enjoyed by some Dalit leaders sometimes make it seem that Dalits are no more the victims they once were. While this is true, it is equally true that the victories they have snatched in this past decade have also induced a social forgetting. It is as if the visibility of the Dalit cause has rendered it routine. *Dalit Murasu* has therefore realized that it is as important to capture the nature of life in caste society as it is to record stories of deliberate violence. It thus fights on, being both a measure of a Dalit will to change society, as well as the conscience that directs this will.

How did you come to edit Dalit Murasu? *Was it in the context of an overall Dalit militancy that burst upon the historical stage in the 1990s?*

Actually it was a combination of interest and circumstance. I must say that I was not really aware of being discriminated against as a Dalit when I was growing up–not in the sense that I understand discrimination today. Nor did I think much about these matters then. I grew up in Ambur in northern Tamil Nadu. There is a sizeable Muslim presence in this region, reflected in place names and so on. For example, our house in Ambur was in an area known as 'B' Kasba ('A' Kasba was where the caste Hindus lived), and it was assumed that if you were from this neighbourhood then you are a Dalit. My father was the headmaster of a local municipal elementary school. He taught in schools in both the Dalit colony and in the non-Dalit neighbourhoods.

Later on, it struck me that the school that I went to in 'B' Kasba was actually in an area where the public toilets were located. So, in a sense, there was no escaping the identity of being a Dalit, being part of a world that was considered unclean and polluting. But, as I said, it did not bother me too much then. I assumed that if you are from 'B' Kasba, you were poor and considered to be of a lower class. I held this identity as if it were entirely natural. I realize now that others of my generation also felt that way then. When we discuss those times now, we marvel at how we did not really comprehend discrimination as we do today.

I remember being given a copy of *Annihilation of Caste* as a birthday present (a friend of my father gifted the book) when I was in my early teens, but I did not read it at that time. I did not know what 'annihilation' meant, and did not think of referring to a dictionary to find out. Nor did I ask anyone.

During this time, the politics that we knew had to do with the Dravidar Kazhagam (DK) or the Dravida Munnetra Kazhagam (DMK). There was a generalized sense of this politics being anti-Brahmin and anti-caste. Many Dalits also subscribed to the idea of being Tamil—felt Tamil pride, so to speak. This is not surprising, since being Tamil was something that was part of being anti-Brahmin ….

It was in college in Vellore (the famous Voorhees College) that I became acquainted with social issues. Here, I must recall Professor Elangovan who preferred to devote his classes to such discussions as he felt were important for us to be part of. Like many others, he too adhered to a generalized anti-caste, Tamil/Dravidian ideology (he had participated in the anti-Hindi agitations of the 1960s); but he had also read a lot of Ambedkar. Later on, when he was active in the university teachers' association, he revealed a socialist side to his thought.

During my college days, he helped me comprehend the subtle slighting that I and others experienced in the world outside, something, which I did not fully understand as yet. When we did the train journey from Ambur (where I lived) to Katpadi (the station nearest to Vellore), we would often witness heated political discussions on board the train. And whenever questions regarding the reservation policy came up, we realized that some of our co-travellers, older men, working or teaching, revealed all sorts of biases. They used to talk of the ill-effects of the reservation policy and of how some people were unfairly benefiting from it. It was not accidental that they subscribed to magazines such as *Tughlak*, edited by Cho Ramasamy, which were in the forefront of defending caste privilege.

Initially, I did not realize how this pertained to me or to anyone I knew—until one day one of my friends pointed out that these men were actually talking about us, Dalits. I remember being bothered by this and wondering if I should tell these people that I had a copy of Ambedkar's book at home, but was not sure what responses this would provoke. Actually many of us did not know what to say.

When I discussed the matter with Professor Elangovan, he would urge me to put such remarks about merit and reservation aside and get on with my studies. 'Of course we need reservation. In any case Dr Ambedkar fought for us to have this right, not them. So why should you bother about what they say? Let us just use this opportunity and get on with our learning.' I was somewhat nonplussed by his seemingly airy dismissal of my concerns. But later on when I was one of the two candidates (the other was a Brahmin boy) who obtained a pass in the BA literature course–introduced for the first time in our college–I remember him being unusually exultant. I had vindicated his faith that we could use these opportunities and actually move forward from where we were.

My interest in social matters took me onwards to study at the school of social work in Tirupathur (for a Master's degree in the discipline), but I must say that I was disheartened with what I found in that Catholic institution. By then, I was familiar with anti-Hindu criticisms, voiced by several people linked to the Dravidar Kazhagam. But I was not prepared for the disenchantment that I experienced in the school of social work. For one, I did not learn anything about social work–for example, there was nothing in my education that explained or helped me critically understand caste and injustice. Whatever I have since learnt about society I owe to the writings of Dr Ambedkar and E V Ramasamy Periyar.

The most important influence on my mind and thought during this period was the Tamil nationalist struggle in Sri Lanka for the establishment of Tamil Eelam. I used to sporadically read such literature that came my way, usually again through Dravidar Kazhagam comrades; even more so when I was in Chennai and looking for a job. I think what impressed and inspired me at that time was the manner in which this literature, especially that published by the Liberation Tigers of Tamil Eelam (LTTE), communicated their concerns, outlined their ideologies of struggle. I particularly liked the manner in which the Tamil Tigers linked their cause to diverse causes for justice–to past events in Cuba and in parts of Africa, where national liberation struggles had been waged.

I think this is what prompted me, when I came to edit *Dalit Murasu*, to remain alert to international contexts and struggles. We serialized the life and thought of Malcolm X, carried articles on the Durban conference and were even part of a movie-making initiative on caste, which resulted in a documentary film titled *The Untouchable Country*, which was screened in Durban.

To come back to what I found impressive about the propaganda texts from Sri Lanka: they were all aesthetically designed and with well-presented and coherent arguments. This is also why, I think, they left a lasting impression on me. It was these texts that helped me develop a sense of graphic design. They were my journalistic study aids, in a sense.

It is curious how political and intellectual trajectories of the most unexpected kind produce a sense of social unease and indignation in us. I would have thought the most important influence in your life was to be associated with the Dalit militancy of the 1990s ....

That came later, but you must realize that one had to be prepared in some way to receive that. And for me, in that sense, my early days in Chennai were crucial. That was the time I got to know a group of individuals that was interested in things I had not heard of before: human rights, environmentalism ... I must recall here Nedunchezhiyan (Chezhiyan)–he used to be part of a group then, 'Poovulagin Nannbargal', which did a lot of publicist work on environmental issues. But at the time that I met him, he was printing and distributing in the hundreds copies of the United Nations Charter of Human Rights. That was the time that I also happened to hear of Amnesty International (AI) through a report that they had done on the Indian Peace Keeping Force's rights violations in Sri Lanka. I recall being astonished that there existed global forums such as this one, and this, along with the notion of rights communicated by Chezhiyan, proved very exciting and inspiring.

Chezhiyan did more–he provoked me to think beyond my obsessive interest in the Eelam struggle. For instance, I would file away stories of human rights violations against the Tamils, and sometimes even sent them to organizations such as AI. Chezhiyan pointed out to me that the Tamil nationalists did not really need me to do this–they had a very sophisticated publicity and propaganda wing in place and could communicate the logic of their struggle without help from individuals such as me! He also pointed out that there were other social issues that I could turn my attention to: the environment or caste injustice.... But I must say that I did not really see myself merely planting trees or writing about the environment. I wanted to do something else. By this time, I was reading widely on caste and visited the Dravidar Kazhagam library regularly. I was slowly getting to know Periyar's and Ambedkar's views and ideas....

Did you have a sense of wanting to be a journalist at this time?

Actually, yes. After my days with the social work school, I had decided that I wanted none of that, and instead wanted to write and be a journalist. But how does one start? What does one write about? I was working at odd jobs then and was not really in a position to set off on my own as a journalist. Christodass Gandhi, an IAS officer who knew my family, realized that I was not getting anywhere with the sort of work that I was forced to accept. He recommended me for a post with World Vision, a Christian organization. I went for my interview and when asked whether I was a believer stoutly said, 'No, I am not'. The man who interviewed me was stunned. He was also embarrassed, because he obviously could not employ a non-believer. Yet he did not want to, in fact, could not, really send me away. After all, Mr Gandhi had recommended my case. So, he asked me what he to tell Mr Gandhi. I replied, 'The truth, of course'. He was quite taken with my response and I think he decided then that he would somehow find me a job. Thus, I found myself with a non-governmental organization that worked on issues of Dalit education and liberation.

Working at the Dalit Liberation Education Trust, at Henry Thiagaraj's office, I found myself not quite wanting to do the routine work that was expected of me, viz., editing a small newsletter for visitors to Chennai. I demanded more fulfilling work. I wanted to be able to read English, read English texts. And Henry, always generous, asked to me read and translate articles on human rights and related issues from the English for a human rights newsletter that his organization published. Called *Manitha Urimai Murasu* (Human Rights Drum), this newsletter provided me with my first serious opportunity to compile, translate and edit articles that I found inspiring and socially relevant. It was in this context that I came to publish articles on Dalit lives, the rights violations Dalits suffered, Dalit political organizing, Dr Ambedkar's ideas.... The year was 1993, just before the Vienna Human Rights conference, and there was plenty of talk about rights and charters and so on, and our focus on Dalit concerns helped link this latter to a larger and more global argument on rights.

Did you focus on Dalit issues from time to time, or was the newsletter devoted to Dalit concerns entirely?

Manitha Urimai Murasu was a prototype of *Dalit Murasu*. Though we did run articles on human rights, women's rights and on the gradual erosion of rights in the face of an impending globalization of economies, we made it clear that we were articulating a 'Dalit' point of view. In fact, you will notice from the letters to the editor that we received that the newsletter was perceived as a Dalit forum. For one, we ran a regular column titled, 'Ambedkar Speaks'. I was inspired by the 'Thus Spake Ambedkar' column in V T Rajsekhar's *Dalit Voice* (published from Bangalore) and decided to run one in the newsletter. This appeared in every issue. Besides this, we also featured essays by Ambedkar on a range of subjects, from his critique of Gandhism to the significance of education for Dalits. We carried articles by Periyar—on women's rights, obscurantism, the importance of the so-called shudras and Dalits uniting in the face of *varnadharma*.... Then there were articles on Dalit literature, history, politics.... The newsletter was quite popular and some regular readers urged me to bring it out as a regular magazine, but that was not possible given the circumstances that I was working in (*Manitha Urimai Murasu* was published well into 1996).

I was a regular reader of *Dalit Voice* around this time. Earlier, I had been particularly impressed by an article on 'Hindu Unity', published in 1991, before the demolition of the Babri Masjid. Even at that time, I translated it and even got it printed as a pamphlet. And I remember thinking, 'Why can't we do something like this on a sustained basis?' I found out that there did exist a Tamil version of *Dalit Voice*–*Dalit Kural*–which was occasionally brought out by Dalit Ezhilmalai, who was then with

Dr Ramdoss' Pattali Makkal Katchi (PMK). I decided that my future would be tied with this magazine, that I wanted to edit *Dalit Kural*. I wrote to Rajsekhar and asked him if I could do this. I did not expect him to reply at once, and was amazed when he wrote back–on a postcard–that I had his support and that I should approach Dalit Ezhilmalai and work out matters with him.

I approached Dalit Ezhilmalai with this request, but he was not convinced this would work. Nor did he think that Rajsekhar's assurance–which I had got–would help. But I did not give up. I got in touch with Rajsekhar again. He invited me to Bangalore to his very modest office, piled with books and with not much else in it. We talked for a long time, at the end of which I was sure I had his support. I felt triumphant. But actually things turned out to be rather difficult. Ezhilmalai, for instance, did not really relish handing over the magazine to me, much less backing it financially. He claimed that he had been in touch with Rajsekhar and that the latter too had not really committed himself to supporting the effort to revive *Dalit Kural*.

I was aghast. Anticipating support and encouragement, I had planned out the first issue. For instance, I had got in touch with Ravikumar, the Dalit activist from Pondicherry. (This was a heady and exciting time in Tamil Nadu, when there was plenty happening in the areas of politics and culture, dominated chiefly by debates and arguments advanced by Dalit and anti-caste writers, intellectuals and performers. I used to attend these meetings and workshops enthusiastically.) He had planned a conference on double electorates–Dr Ambedkar's original demand–at Neyveli and so we thought we could release the first issue of the magazine at that time.

And now I was being told that there might be no magazine at all. I was most upset and quite dejected. I did not think I could really face up to doing things as I had earlier. And I did not feel like meeting people or doing anything. However, I found myself at this all-party conference convened by Dalit leaders–there was an election in the offing–and met P Chandragesan, convenor of Ram Vilas Paswan's Dalit Sena in Tamil Nadu. He wanted to know what I was doing–he appeared to know that I wanted to start a magazine and that I was unhappy at not finding support.

I did not know of this then. After that meeting, he telephoned me and requested me to visit him.

When I did, he brought up the magazine question and said he would like to support such a venture. I was astounded, and could not quite believe what he said. In fact I remember telling him that I was not interested in half-hearted attempts, that I did not want to edit a Dalit magazine that folded up after three issues, that I wanted to edit a magazine that would survive for at least five years....

Were there other Dalit magazines at this time?

Yes, of course, *Kodangi, Aravurai* (run by Anbu Ponnoviyum) and many others were published later. Unjai Rajan's *Manusanga*, for instance, and Ravikumar's *Dalit* (which is still published occasionally). *Kodangi* has been re-issued as *Pudiya Kodangi* and Sivagami remains the editor.

But to resume my story of how I came to edit *Dalit Murasu*: Chandragesan appeared quite serious about his offer. I made it clear though that the magazine would function independently, and while it would feature the Dalit Sena (as it would other Dalit political organizations), it would not identify with its politics or point of view. Instead it would strive to retain its critical independence Chandragesan appeared agreeable to all of this–he only requested that the first issue be got ready as soon as possible. There was to be a Dalit Sena meeting in the city, Paswan was to attend–he was the Minister for Railways then–and Chandragesan wanted the magazine released on the occasion. I had already missed the Neyveli conference, but here was someone offering me another context for bringing the magazine out.

I had my own plans for the magazine. I had wanted to have articles ready for at least three issues, I wanted to work through design and layout carefully–as I had seen in the magazines published by the Eelam Tamils–but now I could not afford any of this. I had to act immediately, and I decided I would.

The very first issue would of course carry a picture of Dr Ambedkar–that was not in dispute. But what else? I decided then that I would carry quotes from Babasaheb and Periyar. I owed my intellectual development to both these thinkers and the traditions they represented. And I wanted to express a point of view that combined a critique of Hinduism and caste with arguments for Dalit rights and dignity. As I see it, Ambedkar's critique of Hinduism had been anticipated by and found expression in Periyar's famous acts of iconoclasm: breaking of Hindu idols, public denunciations of *Manusmriti*, his sustained arguments against Hinduism and the *varna* order.... So, as far as I am concerned, these two thinkers cannot be seen in isolation.

And since then, your Periyar and Ambedkar columns have become permanent features of Dalit Murasu—*Ambedkar on the inside front cover and Periyar on the inside back cover....*

That's right. As you know, many readers find it hard to believe that I still repose faith in the Dravidian movement, still seek to remember its ideologues. I am also told that I ought not to compare Periyar and Ambedkar, that the former does not really deserve this comparison.

But they don't understand: Periyar cannot be seen only in the context of the Dravidian movement. He understood Brahminism and Brahmin hegemony as very few did, and he also resisted the caste system and Hinduism throughout his life. I also find it wrong that those who criticize Periyar do so simply because he was not a Dalit. I sometimes think that those who criticize Periyar would probably have said the same things about Dr Ambedkar if he had been a non-Dalit!

In any case, to return to the first issue of *Dalit Murasu*: When it was released, it seemed to many that it was a magazine of resolutions framed at various Dalit conferences. It did appear so, since we had covered the Dalit Sena's conference for this issue. But this is still a policy with us—to grant space and visibility to Dalit movements, to people's movements, and to Dalit leaders. It is in that sense that you'll find a few references to Paswan .... And you will also see that we have always striven to capture the many voices within Dalit movements and parties. We have carried interviews with diverse Dalit leaders: not only Thirumavalavan (of the Dalit Panthers of India) and Dr Krishnaswamy (Puthiya Tamizhagam); but also Adiyaman of the Adi Tamizhar Peravai; and Kalyanasundaram, the left-leaning Chandra Bose. We have carried articles by Aranga Gunasekharan....

Yes, sometimes you don't remember that this is a magazine supported by the Dalit Sena....

Well, not any longer, as you know. It is more than three years now since Chandragesan withdrew support to us (this happened in 2003), and now we are on our own. We have re-constituted our editorial committee and while our financial prospects appear bleak, we have enough writers and issues to want to go on....

But let us look at what happened next, at how you went about organizing content, your constituency....

Well, we decided that we would print around 10,000 copies. And we have, until the last two years done so. Of this, over 5,000 would be subscriptions, and the others were given away. Our readership is a mixed one–both Dalits and non-Dalits read *Dalit Murasu*. Some Dalit readers, especially those in government service or holding high posts elsewhere, are uneasy at being seen with the magazine. So we get these requests: 'Please mail the magazine to my office, and not to my house.' The reason is that the reader in question has not let on that she or he is a Dalit and so would not like her or his neighbours to find out. *Dalit Murasu* is delivered in a cover that bears the magazine's name, so it is a highly visible magazine, and cannot be easily hidden away.

But there are others, hundreds of Dalits and non-Dalits who look forward to receiving their monthly issue. And while we sell mostly through agents, we also have a few select outlets where the magazine does well. There is a small store in the Chennai Central Station, for example, which sells more than 75 copies.

But let me get back to the magazine. As you must have noticed, the magazine that I came to edit was, of course, not *Dalit Kural*. So we set about finding a name for it. Several were suggested: *Nyaya Chakram* (*The Wheel of Justice*), *Samooga Needhi* (*Social Justice*) and so on, but finally *Dalit Murasu* appeared the best and most representative of what we wished to be known for. I wanted the name 'Dalit' in the title. There was resistance, though– some said this was not a Tamil name. But this is a name that has become synonymous with struggle, suffering and defiance, and I wanted to proclaim it....

Once we had this in place, I had to think of the content. From the beginning I was clear that the magazine would reflect a range of concerns: politics, gender, the environment, human rights ...

and not restrict itself to so-called Dalit issues alone. In any case, what is not a Dalit issue?

I remember an exchange in 2002, I think, between you, A Marx and S V Rajadurai, on why the environment and its problems should matter to Dalits....

Yes. And other things should matter to Dalits: e.g., the struggle in Sri Lanka. Or the experiments that have gone on in Fidel Castro's Cuba. Or intellectual work that supports the Dalit cause. I also think it is important to link class and caste concerns, so you will find *Dalit Murasu* looking at economic issues, especially those thrown up by globalization. S V Rajadurai's *Dalits and Globalisation*, which we serialized, was a very important step in this direction. And we continue to carry articles on this subject.

As I had noted earlier, we wish to link up with other struggles. Following the UN conference at Durban on race and other forms of discrimination, Ravikumar began a series of articles on Malcolm X, which proved very successful. And you, I remember, interviewed a visiting German political scientist and he spoke against the dangers of political fascism, especially the denial of religious and cultural pluralism. We have consistently denounced Hindutva, and remained alert to chauvinism and discrimination in the church.

Much of course depends on the writers. Gender, for example. I often have to solicit articles. Earlier, we had Jeyarani working for us full-time—a young, brilliant Dalit woman photojournalist who also grasped conceptual issues very fast and whose contributions were always exceptional. She did several lead stories, using a variety of pseudonyms, and whether she wrote on the plight of tribal people who bore the brunt of police violence during the Special Task Force's operations against Veerappan or on Dalit washerpeople caste, who are considered untouchable even by Dalits; or on Arunthatiyars, who are looked down upon by other Dalit castes, she focused on women's lives, on how events affected women. Her point of view was fearless and feminist....

I recall that she did a sharply worded pieced against derogatory remarks about Muslim women in sections of the Tamil Muslim press....

Yes, I remember that. While we have all along emphasized Dalit–Muslim unity, we are also sensitive to unease over gender matters in the community, and, in this instance, we were convinced that Jeyarani's argument was entirely valid. I must mention here all the others who have written consistently for *Dalit Murasu*. Azhagiya Periyavan, who is as eloquent a prose writer as he is a writer of fiction, has written many important articles, including his essays on the educational system and how it is inimical to the educational needs of Dalit students; his analysis of natural disasters such as floods or drought, from the point of view of the poorest of the poor, who are invariably Dalits; his thoughts on Dalit literature, etc. A P Vallinayagam's biographical essays on early Dalit intellectuals, publicists and community leaders have been received very well. He has returned to Dalits a history that many of us do not even know we possess. Earlier, Sangamitrai regularly wrote on Buddhism, and Gautama Sannah was, until recently, writing on Dalits, political life and the historical tasks expected of the Dalit community. Then there is Yaakkan, the artist, who writes eloquently on the problems plaguing Dalit politics, and who has not hesitated to criticize the inadequacies of Dalit political parties and their leaders. All these are Dalit writers, but we have also had non-Dalits writing regularly: Subaveerapandian and Viduthalai Rajendran, both of whom are associated with the non-Brahmin, anti-caste Periyar traditions, S V Rajadurai who writes on a range of subjects from a socialist–Dalit point of view....

I write the editorials myself, often focusing on matters of imme-diate interest. But over the years, I find that there has been both an evolution of arguments as well as a constant reiteration of certain ideas. We have thus all along maintained the importance of widening the basis of the struggle against caste, bringing to-gether Dalit leaders and ideologues and anti-caste and secular intellectuals. We have also insisted on defining and re-defining the Dalit struggle as one that represents the struggle of the most oppressed against all forms of social and economic discrimination. In this sense, we are not seeking to articulate a restricted Dalit point of view, centred only around demands for reservation in education and political life; nor are we interested in defining our goals chiefly in terms of an increased and more democratic access to political power. I, for one, hold with Ambedkar and Periyar, that unless we push forward our agenda for a social revolution, political transformations will prove futile and cosmetic. This is why *Dalit Murasu* continues to pursue the argument that 'Dalits are not Hindus' and that 'Hinduism has to be resisted and countered'. This is also why we have featured articles on religious conversions and their implications for Dalits.

In a more specific and empirical sense: we acknowledge the importance of the Dravidian movement and its role in enabling some of us to resist caste, but we have never feared to criticize the DMK, the AIADMK and the other so-called Dravidian parties. Likewise with Tamil nationalism. You will notice that we have mercilessly interrogated nationalists such as Nedumaran—we have asked them if they have consistently considered the question of caste and untouchability in relationship to the nation, to being Tamil. We have asked if Tamil nationalism has a position on Hinduism, on the caste order....

Do you see Dalit Murasu *as having done things other magazines have not?*

I will speak for myself, for what we have been able to do. Here, I would like to recall two things that have made *Dalit Murasu* distinctive: our transcripts of interviews with a range of social and political thinkers and activists, and our book pages. It appears to me that we have developed the interview as a communicative form to a fine art. We have carried some really wonderful ones, interviewing both Dalits and non-Dalits, encompassing a range of progressive voices: from Dr Balagopal, the civil rights activist from Andhra Pradesh and the labour and rights lawyer Chandru to cultural activists like Gaddar, Parattai and Dalit Subbaiah. We have also carried interviews with former prime minister V P Singh, the journalist P Sainath, and anti-Hindutva writer and human-rights activist Teesta Setalvad. Sometimes, we translate interviews that have appeared elsewhere, such as the one with the Marathi poet Limbale, which is featured in our 10th anniversary issue. We have done over a 100 interviews to date.

Our book pages are very important. We carry a page of book announcements in each issue, giving details of the title, publisher, author and also a short blurb. Besides, we carry extracts from books that we consider germane to the Dalit cause and for the cause of social revolution, reviews of titles that have appeared in not only Tamil, but also in English. Our book pages are much appreciated and at the last count, I found that we had carried around 489 book-related news stories this past decade.

*Let me ask a specific question: What is the 'Dalit' content of
Dalit Murasu? And how do you balance specifically Dalit interests and concerns with those that animate radical movements
in general?*

This is a difficult balance and one we fight to maintain. Let me
explain: our point of view, as I have noted earlier, is Dalit; we
look at issues from the point of view of those who suffer most in
this social order; and from a perspective that is based on comradeship, mutual respect, dignity, equality, justice. That is, we are
aware of specific injustices Dalits face within the caste system,
but also see the caste system as being linked to other forms of
injustice—towards the so-called most backward castes, women,
the *adivasis*, minority nationalities, and, in today's context, the
victims of globalization and imperialism.

But there is also the pressure on us, and one we feel ourselves,
to address the needs of our immediate constituency: and this we
do, in our rights violation reports, in records of Dalit meetings
and conferences, by carrying articles on Dalit leaders and so on.
We have also carried stories on the Bhopal document (urging
Dalit participation in the market economy and asking for positive
discrimination in this context—*editor*), and on reservation in the
private sector. But we do not see ourselves doing this exclusively.

More generally, we want to look beyond the historical present, the contingent moment, and focus on larger ideological
issues, such as Brahminism, the caste system, the problems with
Hinduism and so on. Some Dalit intellectuals think that much of
this is a waste of space and time, that we should really devote
time to the here and now, to practical politics and lobbying ...
but we do not think so. We want to suggest there exists another
consistent point of view, which we must work to make universal.

*I was wondering in this context why your culture pages are few
and far between....*

Yes, that is indeed so. We do not publish much poetry or fiction. But we do have the occasional culture article. We carried
two major sets of articles: one on the music of Ilayaraja by K A
Gunasekharan, and one on the poet Bharathi by Madimaran.
We have also commented upon the relationship between caste
and culture in films, whenever we have felt the need to. But yes,
we do not really address culture, as such. We see ourselves more

as a magazine whose focus is political argument, and thought and culture is invariably brought in as a part of this.

But I must also say here that my own understanding of culture is more expansive than is usually allowed. For me, culture does not merely mean art, song, dance and performance. It is what makes a person; it is therefore a point of view, a set of ideas, a way of living one's life ... so, in a sense, we are working hard on cultural matters, since we are chipping away at all that is wrong with our social contexts and all that goes to make a person the sort of social being he or she is in caste society.

However, we are not averse to publishing essays or notes on culture, even if some of the content is not immediately relevant. R R Srinivasan, for example whom we got to know as the man who filmed the infamous Tamarabarani massacre—of protesting Dalits by the police—wrote an engaging column for some time on cultural oddities. He also taught us to use visuals more creatively. And we do have an unusual sense of the visual. Jeyarani pioneered the photo page—a striking image, accompanied by a poem, often on a social theme. This was done in such a marvellous fashion, not using predictable slogans or being boring. But ultimately Dalit cultural expressions ought to bear the mark of Ambedkar's legacy, his insistence on social revolution, for us to take them seriously.

I would like to return to you interest in publishing on a range of issues. But it appears sometimes—and this is not particular to Dalit Murasu—*that caste issues, in a conceptual sense, are seldom linked to other concerns. For example, violence against Dalits is only seen in terms of vicitmization and rights violations, seldom as part of an overall developmental process that affects all castes, though with varying implications....*

It is my belief that we are trying to do this, attempting to link up Dalit lives and concerns with larger realities; trying to analyse reality in a more nuanced fashion. But this is not easy, since the larger public and intellectual culture in Tamil Nadu is not open to critical and reasonable debates. But if you look at our reporting on caste violence, you will notice that we do attempt to go beyond the simple 'backward classes versus Dalits' argument. We argue that caste cannot be countered by violence, or by pointing to the fact that those who earlier benefited from social change are now themselves the perpetrators of caste violence.

As I see it, caste prejudice or hatred is not merely physical or contingent, it is also in one's head, in one's consciousness. One cannot challenge or counter this using only economic or cultural arguments–one has to suggest an entirely different way of living, working and thinking, and this is what Ambedkar's legacy is all about. Being a different kind of person, and as Periyar made it clear, one who subscribes not to *manudharma* but *samadharma*. This requires sustained argument and reasoning and there are no easy ways of doing this.

Unfortunately some Dalit political leaders and parties, both here and in North India, imagine that by merely seeking a share in power they could achieve the social changes they claim they want. Their political imagination is very limited–it is drawn to party politics, poll alliances and power, but remains impervious to radical Ambedkarite thought that is committed to social revolution. On the other hand, they easily play into an obvious identity politics, and sometimes end up supporting the interests of one Dalit caste alone. *Dalit Murasu* has taken a principled stand against this animosity that exists amongst Dalits as well–several articles have been published denouncing this tendency to play off one Dalit community against another.

Dalit Murasu *is interested in engaging with the Tamil national question, in supporting the cause of nationalities within the Indian union. How do you view this aspect of your agenda in the context of Ambedkarism. Dr Ambedkar after all wanted a strong centre....*

Dalit Murasu is interested in the Tamil struggle in Sri Lanka because it is a just struggle, and one being waged against a very brutal government. Some Sri Lankan Tamils have pointed out that much is wrong with Tamil society itself, that it is also a caste society and that untouchability is present there as well. I see that, but I think that this is a matter that cannot be resolved outside of the national liberation struggle. It has to be thought of within its terms.

In a more general sense, though, I am not interested in nationality issues because I believe in a given cultural or historical identity. For me, as I learnt from Periyar, being Dravidian is being sensitive to the wrongs that are part of my world here. I am interested in tending this earth, and I firmly believe that unless I do this, unless I work this earth carefully, nurture and cultivate it, I cannot really hope to do the same elsewhere. Besides, I do think that there are problems with centre–state relations in India, and there are all sorts of justice issues that must be sorted out–in Kashmir, for example. For me these are nationality issues in as far as they refer to lived realities for those who live in them, and who cannot think of rights or justice outside of this context.

I also don't believe that Ambedkar's plea for a strong centre takes away from his essentially universal plea for a good, just and humane society. He was being strategic when he argued for a strong centre. You know that when he met Periyar in 1940, and the latter defined his plea for a separate Dravidian nation as one animated by a desire to live in a caste-free society, Dr Ambedkar said that in that case he too would support the cause of a Dravidasthan!

Dr Ambedkar possessed a sense of citizenship that was truly universal. His final conversion to Buddhism shows that he wanted to be part of a community that was ethically and politically committed to and could realize universal values of justice and equality.

How do see your magazine's future?

We will go on–we want to expand our readership, make sure that in every district we have a core group of readers who support us and extend our reach. We can rely on donations or other kinds of support only temporarily. For, in the final analysis, we can only count on our readers and on our eagerness and commitment to communicate a different worldview and politics for those who are uneasy and angry with the social order.

It has not been easy. Though we had sustained support in the past, we still had to engage with discrimination and rejection in ways that were both indirect and relentless. For example, we have had to shift three offices this past decade. Initially, we functioned from an office space near Chandragesan's residence. Later on, when we had to move from there and look about for another office, we found the going difficult. And when, finally, we did manage to rent a space–this belonged, not surprisingly, to a Dalit doctor who was at that time not living in India–we had to face up to local pressure. The apartment owners' association accused us of all sorts of things, though we were actually model tenants. We had to give up that place, when it seemed that if we stayed on we would only be creating trouble for the doctor. We found a second place, but at the last minute we were told that while the son had promised us the house, the father had already contracted it out to someone else!

All who refused to rent us an office space were very inventive in their reasoning. In one instance, we were told that if our magazine did not carry the word 'Dalit' it would be easier for us to find a place! Some others told us that they knew that Dalits were all trouble-makers, and so wanted nothing to do with us. One time, we had moved all our things, including shelves and tables, when the house-owner refused permission for us to take possession of the office.

What I mean to stay is that to remain a magazine that is not afraid to call itself Dalit is itself a struggle. Our very visibility as a forum for Dalit thought is threatening to some, 'polluting' to others....

But we will remain what we are—Dalits fighting to change the way caste society lives and thinks. We will continue to urge the case for a social revolution, keep faith with democracy and aspire to being the sort of universal citizens Dr Ambedkar wanted us to be. In the coming years too, *Dalit Murasu* will take its inspiration and cues from that very important book, *Annihilation of Caste*.

Note

1. Giuseppe Fiori, *Antonio Gramsci: Life of a Revolutionary* (New York, Schocken Books, 1973), p. 151.

6

'What is the Spanish Word for Appeasement?'

Subarno Chattarji

The bombings of commuter trains in Madrid in March 2004 marked the first time that Al Qaeda (or terror groups inspired by Al Qaeda) struck in Europe. As with all such moments of crisis there was blanket media coverage and expressions of a general sense of horror at the outrage perpetrated on innocent civilians. Post 9/11, Madrid took its place in an ever growing roster of places round the world struck by Islamic terror. The representation and conjoining of Islam with terrorism, as well as the ways in which dominant political and media rhetoric have seen this phenomenon as an assault on a way of life, are both crucial and commonplace. Of course, the picture is complicated when such events take place in non-Western nations such as Indonesia and Morocco, but the complexity is undercut by creating a larger narrative of a rampaging, atavistic Islam.

I propose to examine four articles in the *New York Times* that were not reports of the Madrid bombings but reflections on what they meant for democracy, relations between the US and Europe, and the best ways to counter the Al Qaeda threat. The *New York Times* articles create what Michael Wolff calls 'the *Zeitgeist* story':

> It's the larger package which holds the smaller packages. A great editor (who's going places in the business) is a creator of *Zeitgeists*, able to summarize or synthesize where we are now. Who we are. What we want. This is a judgement that is intrinsically commercial—what's selling now. And political—where are the winds blowing? [...] You're trying to anticipate both the story you think

your audience wants you to be telling and the story that will be told—and then
shining a hot light on it.[1]

Wolff's essay is primarily about the 'storifying' of news and
how the US media totally failed to call the bluff on the Weapons
of Mass Destruction (WMD) claims made by the Bush administration in the run-up to Gulf War II. However, the desire to create
a *Zeitgeist*, to reflect on 'Who we are' and 'What we want' are
important aspects of the articles I focus on, since the writers
(and by extension the paper) pontificate on the shortcomings of
Spanish democracy and its implications.

It is significant that even within a span of four articles there
was no homogeneity. An editorial was much more reasonable
than pieces by op-ed columnists and one article dealt with complex issues thrown up by the bombings and its electoral aftermath.
This plurality of views might bolster the idea of a free play of
meanings that seems to be the essence of a free media, and at
one level it is. At another level, however, the dominant tenor
was one of condescension and arrogance, and the 'reasonable'
articles were framed, as it were, by the more vociferous ones.
Because the latter group voiced the temper and opinions of a
larger political constituency, they are indicative of symbiotic
relations between political and media discourse.

Following from the shameful record of the US media in its ac-
quiescence to the justification of war in Iraq, the meditations
on Madrid are one of a piece. It is possible to argue within this
media trajectory that the dissenting or 'balanced' articles are an
attempt by the *New York Times* to distinguish itself from the so-
called illiberal press, the likes of Fox News Television and Rupert
Murdoch's *New York Post*. The very fact, however, that some
fairly egregious views are given prominent op-ed space in the
New York Times is indicative of a consensus about what constitutes a good story and what will sell. To quote Wolff once more:
'No matter how hoity-toity a news organization you are, you
can't not participate in what has been storified, whether it is
Jessica Lynch, or Swift boats, or, say, Monica.'[2] The Madrid
bombing reflections need to be placed within the 'storification'
of the war on terror and its continuing reverberations in Iraq.

David Brooks' 'Al Qaeda's Wish List' begins with first person
condescension: 'I am trying not to think harshly of the Spanish.'[3]

This is an opening gambit that leads to a summary of the Spanish election results:

> The Spanish government was conducting policies in Afghanistan and Iraq that Al Qaeda found objectionable. A group linked to Al Qaeda murdered 200 Spaniards, claiming that the bombing was punishment for those policies. Some significant percentage of the Spanish electorate was mobilized to shift the course of the campaign, throw out the old government and replace it with one whose policies are more to Al Qaeda's liking.
> What is the Spanish word for appeasement?
> There are millions of Americans, in and out of government, who believe the swing Spanish voters are shamefully trying to seek a separate peace in the war on terror.

Brooks omits the fact that a majority of the Spanish people also found the policies of the Aznar government 'objectionable' and that may have motivated their vote against the incumbent. He also avers that not supporting the US in Iraq and Afghanistan is a vote for Al Qaeda. Right through this opinion piece Brooks adheres to the rigid 'You're either with us or with the terrorists' syndrome articulated after 9/11. Not only does this us-versus-them matrix obliterate complexity, it is extended here to question the judgement of the Spanish electorate and the legitimacy of the government about to be installed. One obvious irony in this criticism of Spanish democracy is that it is precisely the sort of free and fair election held in Spain (no commentator questioned the electoral process itself) that the US would like to replicate in Iraq and the rest of the Middle Eastern region. Or perhaps not, because democracy might subvert the wishes of the democratizing force—a fear that surfaced later during the Iraqi exercise.[4]

Brooks' use of terms from the Second World War such as 'appeasement' and 'separate peace' create a contextual and moral frame within which the Spanish people are seen as 21st century successors to Neville Chamberlain. Within this framework, Al Qaeda is equivalent to Hitler, just as Saddam Hussein was once seen as the Hitler of a new century. In American historical memory, the Second World War is the 'good war', where the just cause of the Allies, powered by US military might, defeated the unmitigated evil of Nazism. This trajectory of justice is sought to be imposed on the current 'war on terror' so that contemporary complexities can be subsumed within a master narrative of good triumphing over evil. While this is problematic in itself, Brooks also ignores more tangled contexts within Spain, particularly the Spanish Republican fight against dictatorship during the Spanish Civil War and Spain's tryst with totalitarianism under General Franco. That Spanish democracy emerged from the shadow of fascism and that the 2004 result could also be seen as a triumph of its democratic credentials is not considered by Brooks, because of the moral lens through which he views the bombings and their aftermath.

Brooks hammers away at the culpability of Spain's electorate. 'Al Qaeda has now induced one nation to abandon the Iraqi people. Yesterday the incoming Spanish prime minister indicated he would pull his troops out of Iraq unless the UN takes control. The terrorists sought this because they understand, even if many in Europe do not, that Iraq is a crucial battleground in the war on terror.' This is a repetition of Bush administration rhetoric, ignoring the fact that terror strikes have actually increased since the invasion and that Iraq serves as an impetus for new recruits.[5]

Brooks also conflates US rhetoric of saving Iraq with contempt for the UN. It is interesting that in Spain and Iraq there are amorphous 'people' who have either appeased Al Qaeda or who must be saved from it. When these 'people' express an opinion–as the Spanish did–they are portrayed as traitors. When they remain largely silent sufferers–as do the Iraqis–they become iconic objects of salvation. While the US agenda is to bring democracy to Iraq, US political managers and media commentators such as Brooks are wary of a democratic process that cannot be micromanaged, in much the same way as the evangelicals were managed in the 2004 Bush re-election campaign. As Jean Baudrillard writes: 'Democracy itself (a proliferating form, the lowest common denominator of all our liberal societies), this planetary democracy of the Rights of Man, is to real freedom what Disneyland is to the imaginary.'[6] It is the spectacle of democracy rather than its substance that matters and in Spain the spectacle collapsed in the face of some determined and thoughtful voting.

Brooks goes on to analyse the 'aftershocks from the Spanish election': 'The rift between the US and Europe will grow wider. Now all European politicians will know that if they side with America on controversial security threats, and terrorists strike their nation, they might be blamed by their own voters.' Once again Brooks obliterates inconvenient contexts such as Europe's solid and heartfelt support for the US in the immediate aftermath of 9/11, as well as many European nations' own histories of grappling with terrorism–from the Red Brigades in Italy to Germany's Beider Meinhof to Spain's Basque separatist movement, Euskadi Ta Askatasuna (ETA). There seems to be an assumption that there is no history of terrorism anterior to 9/11, until America became a victim and then an avenger. Brooks also makes no mention of anti-war protests in Spain and the rest of Europe, that Aznar committed his nation to war despite the will of his 'people'. Within a particular discourse propagated by George W Bush, Tony Blair, and media pundits such as Brooks, the Spanish electoral result is an aberration because the 'people' actually exercised democratic power in jettisoning an unpopular government. While the war in Iraq is equally unpopular in the UK, Blair managed to survive, which is the norm of democratic disjunction between leaders and voters.[7]

Brooks concludes with a dose of self-flagellation:

> Nor is America itself without blame. Where was our State Department? Why hasn't Colin Powell spent the past few years criss-crossing Europe so that voters there would at least know the arguments for the liberation of Iraq, would at least have some accurate picture of Americans, rather than the crude cowboy stereotype propagated by the European media?

America is blamed not for the mess in Iraq but for not getting the message across that its mission has been and continues to be noble. That Colin Powell lied to the UN and the world about Iraq's Weapons of Mass Destruction arsenal is not enough for Brooks. (That the nobility of purpose would get even murkier with the Abu Ghraib revelations is something Brooks could not anticipate at this point. It is interesting, however, to look at Brooks' jingoism in the context of the prisoner abuse scandal, for nothing could highlight the disjunction between the 'people' and the mission more effectively than the antics of Lyndie England and her ilk.)

Brooks latches onto a favourite whipping boy, the European media, which–rather than the actualities of US policy–is blamed for the 'crude cowboy stereotype' of the American in Europe. One can only wonder if Bush's 'Wanted Dead or Alive' statement, among other memorable words and deeds, were the creation of the European media. Throughout the article, Brooks stereotypes the Spanish and Europeans and that, of course, is neither crude nor uncalled for.

Edward N Luttwak in 'Rewarding Terror in Spain' continues Brooks' theme: 'It must be said: Spanish voters have allowed a small band of terrorists to dictate the outcome of their national elections. This is not how democracies are supposed to react when they are attacked by fanatics.'[8] That Spanish voters were unhappy with Aznar's support of the US war in Iraq, that they had demonstrated their opposition to that war, and that the vote could be perceived as an expression of anger at being steam-rollered by an unresponsive government, does not figure in the analysis. A free and fair election is thus seen as a failure of democracy.

In Luttwak's vision, the Socialists and the media are to blame for the electoral reversal suffered by the government. 'It was an act of colossal irresponsibility for the Socialists and the Spanish news media to excoriate the Aznar government for asserting that ETA, the Basque separatist movement, was probably behind the attacks.' Luttwak would rather that the opposition had gone along with the lie perpetrated by the government.

Luttwak then reverts to some pop-history combined with stereotypes: 'Under Muslim law, no land conquered by Islam may legitimately come under non-Muslim rule. For the fanatics, Spain is still Al Andalus of the Middle Ages, which must be reclaimed for Islam by immigration and intimidation.' Luttwak remembers an Islamic history in Spain and associates it with fanaticism and an undefined 'Muslim law'. One wonders if such a connection with the Spanish Inquisition, for instance, would be offered if the terrorists had espoused Christianity. The bombings are seen as a replay of the Crusades, with the spineless Socialists refusing to play the role of the valiant Christian soldiers. This sub-text of the clash of civilizations is par for the course for advocates of the war on terror.

The most insidious aspect of the argument is the collation of immigration and intimidation, implying that impoverished Moroccans–a significant group of illegal migrants–risk death and deportation to come to reclaim 'Al Andalus'. Economic inequit-ies–the main reason for migration–are obliterated in favour of religious fundamentalism. The implication is that Islamic terrorism and Muslim immigration are a finely coordinated, two-pronged strategy to swamp Europe and change its 'Christian' character. Perhaps Al Qaeda is behind the hordes of illegal immigrants who wish to enter Europe. The xenophobia that has characterized some of the debates surrounding immigration and the concept of fortress Europe are reiterated here.

For Luttwak, there is only one solution to the problems created by the Socialist victory: 'Paradoxically, Mr Zapatero can redeem Spanish democracy only if he repudiates the popular mandate he received and announces that there will be no withdrawal from Iraq because of any act of terrorism, Muslim or Basque.' Luttwak is forced, finally, to admit that Mr Zapatero did receive the popular mandate and he advocates that like his predecessor he should ignore the will of the majority that voted him to power. After all, Blair and Berlusconi have done that with panache.

Although both Brooks and Luttwak construct a rhetoric of redeeming Spain and Spanish democracy, what they are most concerned about is the (il)legitimacy of the coalition of the willing in Iraq. In their desperation to maintain the façade of the quest for democracy in Iraq, they are willing to repudiate its results in Spain. That the *New York Times* carried these opinions is proof of their mainstream legitimacy. Luttwak's position as a senior fellow at the Center for Strategic and International Studies adds to that process of legitimization at the same time that it reveals the easy symbiosis between think tanks, academia and government in the US.

On the same day that Brooks and Luttwak were berating the Spanish, the *New York Times* editorial, 'Change in Spain', made observations that disagreed totally with their opinions. 'Sunday's vote became an expression of national pride and mourning. Spaniards who might not otherwise have voted turned out in large numbers and voted against a government that they opposed before the bombs went off. Others may have turned against the government over its early emphatic insistence that the bombings had been the work of Basque, rather than Islamic, terrorists. Either way, it was an exercise in healthy democracy, in which a change of government is simply that, and not a change of national character. It is possible to support the battle against terrorism wholeheartedly and still oppose a political party that embraces the same cause. [...] Here in the United States, as much as the White

House would like the elections to be about fear and national in-security, they are a choice between two men and two political philosophies—not a referendum on terrorism.'[9] The editorial is a model of balanced reasonableness and its appearance in tandem with Brooks and Luttwak emphasizes the plurality of views that the *New York Times* publishes.

This editorial, along with an article on 17 March, are the seem-ing epitome of press freedom. Yet these two pieces were in a minority and did not express a majority view in the US media and polity. Edward Herman and Noam Chomsky's articulation of a media propaganda model for elections in Guatemala, El Salvador, and Nicaragua in the 1980s is apposite for attitudes expressed here: 'A propaganda model would anticipate mass media support of the state perspective and agenda. That is, the favored elections will be found to legitimize, no matter what the facts; the disfavored elections will be found deficient, farcical, and failing to legitimise—again, irrespective of facts.'[10]

'Mass media support of the state perspective and agenda' was on display, amongst others, in articles by the *New York Times*' Judith Miller, who steadfastly proclaimed that Iraq did have WMDs. That her source was Karl Rove and that Rove had an inter-est in keeping these stories in circulation mattered little within contexts of media and political consensus. Similarly, Brooks and Luttwak delegitimize the Spanish elections because they do not fit into the model of the war against terror; and Luttwak, in rhet-orical desperation, asks Zapatero to ignore the election verdict. The editorial redresses the balance and is followed by a more complex analysis of the bombings and the election verdict.

Lizette Alvarez and Elaine Sciolino begin with a question: 'Who really won on Sunday, the Socialists or the terrorists?'[11] This question creates a false dichotomy and indicates the media frame within which the debate occurred. Alvarez and Sciolono admit that 'Spain, with Britain, had embraced the American war effort in Iraq, despite widespread popular opposition.' This 'widespread popular opposition' is the problem in representations of demo-cratic models in the West and their clones elsewhere. The anxiety is quite clear—whether the Spanish election would have a domino effect and others in the coalition would be affected. Fortunately,

Britain, Italy and Australia did not follow Spain's example, but obviously the writers were not to know that: 'Now the Madrid bombings raised the possibility that Europe was a fresh target for violence and that terrorists could undermine democracy and manipulate elections.' The insinuation that Spain's elections were somehow manipulated is absurd and its persistence is indicative of the dominant discourse.

To their credit, Alvarez and Sciolino attempt to provide some contexts that may explain Zapatero's victory:

> Voters flooded the polls on Sunday in record numbers, especially young people who had not planned to vote. In interviews, they said they did so not so much out of fear of terror as anger against a government they saw as increasingly authoritarian, arrogant and stubborn. [...] Voters say they were enraged not only by the government's insistence that the Basque separatist group ETA was responsible, despite mounting evidence to the contrary, but they also resented its clumsy attempts to quell antigovernment sentiment.
>
> For example, the main television channel TVE, which is state-owned, showed scant and selective antigovernment demonstrations on Saturday night, just as it ran very little coverage of the large demonstrations against the war in Iraq last year. It also suddenly changed its regular programming to air a documentary on the horrors of ETA.
>
> That was the last straw for some Spaniards, who said it evoked the nightmare of censorship during the Franco dictatorship little more than a quarter of a century ago.

Alvarez and Sciolino highlight the arrogance of the government and the parallels with the Franco era in terms of media censorship. They also pointedly refer to Aznar calling 'top editors of Spain's major dailies twice on the day of the attacks', saying 'he was convinced that ETA was responsible'. None of the *New York Times* analysts wonder why Aznar was so keen to pin the Madrid bombings on ETA. Aznar's zeal *not* to blame Al Qaeda is atypical in the post-9/11 world, and perhaps reflected his anxiety that democracy was finally catching up with him.[12] Alvarez and Sciolino do highlight the ways in which media is manipulated to suit governments in power, a point ignored by Brooks and Luttwak.

The Franco context is crucial because Spanish democracy is relatively new and Aznar's censorship and arrogance would have great resonance. Contrary to Brooks and Luttwak, the Spanish election was actually a victory for democracy, a model worth emulating. The article ends with this idea:

> 'The election,' Mr Alberto Martin, a 31-year-old nuclear physicist added, 'is a victory for the people, not for terrorism. You see, I am now going to take the train.' Mr Martin also says, 'Look at the war in Iraq. Aznar thought he was God! There was no dialogue.'

While democracy is projected by the US administration and the media as a panacea for Iraq, it is seen as an inconvenient irritant, a sign of appeasement and capitulation, when it actually functions in the West. The arrogance of democratically elected leaders co-exists with the idea that a disconnect between the ruler and the ruled is good for the people and for democracy, not in an abstract sense, but in terms of US geopolitical interests, particularly vis-à-vis Iraq. The re-election of Blair is an ideal case in point.[13]

For all its contextualization and attempt to present multiple aspects of the story, Alvarez and Sciolino do not entirely debunk the idea that terrorism won. They quote Ana Palacio, foreign minister in the Aznar government: 'We are giving birth to a new world, and it is sad and dangerous and sick. We are giving a signal to terrorists that they can have their way because we have given in.' After delineating Aznar's attempts to fix the media, the authors write: 'Meanwhile, within 24 hours of the terrorist attacks, the Socialists, through their own intelligence and diplomatic contacts in the Muslim world, were already leaning toward the theory that Al Qaeda and not ETA was responsible, two senior Socialist Party officials said.' The reference to 'diplomatic contacts in the Muslim world' is a sly one, insinuating that only Socialists and others of their ilk have such shady contacts. Did Aznar's intelligence agencies have no such contacts and if not, why not? Inadvertently it highlights a major intelligence failure on the part of the government—a point ignored by all analysts. Of course, within the ideological logic of absolute and blind support for the war in Iraq, it is better to have failures of intelligence than 'diplomatic contacts in the Muslim world'.

Perhaps the best way to indicate Brooks' and Luttwak's closed analysis and insensitivity to any point of view that is not American is to contrast their pieces with one written on the London bombings more than a year later.[14] Gary Younge's 'Fallujah and London–In Deepest Denial' emphasizes the need to make connections:

> As the identities of the missing emerge, we move from a statistical body count to the tragedy of human loss–brothers, mothers, lovers and daughters cruelly blown away as they headed to work. The space to mourn these losses must be respected. The demand that we abandon rational thought, contextual analysis and critical appraisal of why this happened and what we can do to limit the chances that it will happen again, should not. To explain is not to excuse; to criticise is not to capitulate.[15]

Younge makes a distinction between explication and justification that many in the US media have refused to consider since 9/11. He also makes connections that are often unavailable in mainstream media:

> We know what took place. Certain people, with no regard for law, order or our way of life, came to London and trashed it. With scant regard for human life or political consequences, employing violence as their sole instrument of persuasion, they slaughtered innocent people indiscriminately. The trouble is there is nothing in the last paragraph that could not just as easily be said from Fallujah as it could from London. The two should not be equated–with over 1,000 people killed or injured, half its housing wrecked and almost every school and mosque damaged or flattened, what Fallujah went through at the hands of the US military, with British support, was more deadly.
>
> But they can and should be compared. We do not have a monopoly on pain, suffering, rage or resilience.

Younge concludes:

> 'Collateral damage' always has a human face: its relatives grieve; its communities have memory and demand action. These basic humanistic precepts are the principal casualties of fundamentalism. They were clearly absent from the minds of those who bombed London last week. They are no less absent from the minds of those who have pursued the war on terror for the past four years.

That these imaginative and analytical links were not made by Brooks and Luttwak are indicative of the ways in which media (and political) discourses remain cocooned within nationalist and limiting frameworks. To connect the Madrid bombings and its electoral result with events in Iraq is not to justify the bombings in any sense. It is to point to the ways in which competing fundamentalisms merely perpetuate the cycles of violence.

One significant aspect of Younge's article is its lack of equi-
vocation and, in this sense, Brooks' and Luttwak's pieces are
obverse images, particularly in their refusal to articulate connections and contexts for an earlier outrage. Alvarez and Sciolino
appear to be balanced but biases are embedded in their piece.
Their article can be compared to one written by Thomas Friedman
on the London bombings.

In 'If it's a Muslim problem, it needs a Muslim solution',
Friedman offers a clear analysis and even a solution to the problem of Islamic terror. He begins by expressing solidarity with the
victims: 'Thursdays bombings in central London are profoundly
disturbing. In part, that is because a bombing in our mother country and closest ally, England, is almost like a bombing in our own
country.'[16] It is interesting that none of the analysts I have cited
express any sympathy for the victims of the Madrid bombings.
While England is a steadfast ally, Spain was shifty and the elections proved the Spaniards' unreliability. The London bombings
fortuitously occurred after Blair had won, albeit with a reduced
majority. The UK elections become a model for how to manage
a democracy in spite of majority outrage at Britain's role in Iraq.

Friedman then goes on state that *jihadi* attacks are an assault on 'open societies' which 'depend on trust', and that trust is
diminished by such assaults. Friedman is entirely right about the
demolition of trust, as was evident from the hate mail and attacks
on minorities within Britain, and he articulates this without
ambiguity:

> When *jihadist*-style bombings happen in Riyadh, that is a Muslim–Muslim
> problem. That is a police problem for Saudi Arabia. But when al-Qaeda-like
> bombings come to the London Underground, that becomes a civilizational
> problem. Every Muslim living in a Western society suddenly becomes a suspect,
> becomes a potential walking bomb. When that happens, it means that the
> West is going to be tempted to crack down even harder on their own Muslim
> populations.

Friedman gets to the nub of what Abdel-Bari Atwan calls
the perpetuation of circles of suspicion, hatred, and violence.[17]
Friedman also admits that since the West has no obvious target
to retaliate against, it will do so in a crude and blanket manner
'by simply shutting them out, denying them visas and making
every Muslim in its midst guilty until proven innocent'. His

solution to this downward spiral in Muslim–Western relations is to advocate that Muslims do their own policing. 'The greatest restraint on human behavior is what a culture and a religion deem shameful.' He gives two examples of such change: the Palestinian ceasefire with Israel and King Abdullah's conference in Amman calling on moderate Muslims to retrieve their faith from the hands of extremists.

Without a doubt there are Arab societies where moderate voices have been sidelined. There is a sense, however, in which Friedman places prime responsibility on Muslim societies to reform themselves or face the wrath of an intolerant and paranoid West. The truism of cultural and religious shaming hides an essentialist bias: that Islamic culture does not deem acts of terror as shameful. One wonders if the same argument would apply to Abu Ghraib or Guantanamo Bay, in terms of what the dominant culture or religion values. In conclusion Friedman avers, 'The double-decker buses of London and the subways of Paris, or the markets of Riyadh, Bali and Cairo, will never be secure as long as the Muslim villages and elders do not take on, delegitimize, condemn and isolate the extremists in their midst.'

While one could hardly disagree with this argument, one is also astonished that Friedman absolves the West of any responsibility and agency in this terrible cycle of violence and counter violence. His arguments are reasonable up to a point, but they are underpinned by a white Anglo-Saxon bias, evident in the phrase 'our mother country'. Considering that the US is not any longer exclusively the land of white immigrants, many citizens of the US would disagree with that appellation, even if they were entirely sympathetic to the victims in London. There seems to be a subliminal desire to return to the mythical whiteness of the US or Britain, but that hardly helps the present situation.

The point of the comparison is to emphasize the continuity in media language and representations of the acts of terror that have blighted Europe's landscape since the Madrid bombings. The articles on the Madrid bombings that I have focused on are circumscribed by and reiterate media frames within which acts of terror and democracy are represented. They relate specifically to the *Zeitgeist* of 'Who we are' and 'What we want'. In that specificity, they tell us more about US policies, desires and anxieties than they do about the victims of those policies in Madrid,

London, and Iraq. Younge's piece is exceptional in its attempt to redefine that *Zeitgeist*, to provide an alternative set of contexts. It stands out because it is rare in a media field awash with the certainties of Brooks and Luttwak or the not so subtle biases of Friedman. As readers we remain 'overexposed to the media, underexposed to memory'.[18] The events themselves fade into the haze of history, the war on terror continues to unfold, and mainstream media rush headlong into the next catastrophe.

Notes

1. Michael Wolff, 'The Plot to Sell the News', *Vanity Fair*, November 2004, pp. 184–90.
2. Wolff, 'The Plot to Sell the News', p. 188.
3. David Brooks, 'Al Qaeda's Wish List', *The New York Times*, op-ed, 16 March 2004.
4. See Seymour M Hersh, 'Get out the vote: Did Washington try to manipulate Iraq's election?', *The New Yorker*, 25 July 2005.
5. A US National Intelligence Estimate report, *Trends in Global Terrorism: Implications for the United States*, concluded in April 2006 that the US campaign in Iraq has increased the threat of terrorism.
6. Jean Baudrillard, *The Illusion of the End*, trans. Chris Turner (Stanford, CA, Stanford University Press, 1994), p. 27.
7. For a detailed analysis of this disjunction, see Suman Gupta, *The Theory and Reality of Democracy: A Case Study in Iraq* (London and New York, Continuum, 2006).
8. Edward N Luttwak, 'Rewarding Terror in Spain', *The New York Times*, op-ed, 16 March 2004.
9. 'Change in Spain', *The New York Times*, Editorial, 16 March 2004.
10. Edward S Herman and Noam Chomsky, *Manufacturing Consent: The Political Economy of the Mass Media* (London, Vintage, 1988), p. 88.
11. Lizette Alvarez and Elaine Sciolino, 'Spain Grapples with Notion That Terrorism Trumped Democracy', *The New York Times*, 17 March 2004.
12. Even in a pre-9/11 scenario Islamic terrorists were the immediate suspects, as in the Oklahoma bombings.
13. For an excellent analysis of this disjunction, see Noam Chomsky, 'Preventive War: The Supreme Crime', ZNet, 11 August 2003. Available at: http://www.zmag.org/content/showarticle.cfm?ItemID=4030. Accessed on 15 October 2005.

14. US media contempt for British media, particularly the BBC and *Guardian*, after the London bombings was emphatically stated by *Fox News's* Bill O'Reilly, who said, 'What good does it do al-Qaeda to alienate the BBC and all of these major organizations that have basically not dealt with the threat in a realistic way?'
    This prompted a guest to add: 'In certain respects, the BBC almost operates as a foreign registered agent of Hizbullah and some of the other jihadist groups.' O'Reilly has also laid into the *Guardian* since Thursday's bombings, asking one guest: 'Have you read the *Guardian* lately? I mean, it might be edited by Osama bin Laden. I mean, that's how bad the paper is.' See Jason Deans, 'Fox News presenter's comments "beneath contempt" ,' 13 July 2005. Available at: http://media.guardian.co.uk/bbc/story/0,1527895,00.html. Downloaded 17 October 2005.

15. Gary Younge, 'Fallujah and London–In Deepest Denial', 12 July 2005. Available at: http://www.hindu.com/2005/07/12/stories/2005071206981100.htm. Downloaded 20 July 2005.

16. Thomas L Friedman, 'If it's a Muslim problem, it needs a Muslim solution', *The New York Times*, 9 July 2005.

17. See AP, 'After bombings, Arabs debate whom to blame: Islamic leaders condemn London attack; some say US, Britain fuel violence', 8 July 2005, AP. Available at: www.msnbc.com. Downloaded 9 July 2005.

18. Baudrillard, *The Illusion of the End*, p. 63. 'Events now have no more significance than their anticipated meaning, their programming and their broadcasting' (p. 21).

7

Prophetic Misreading

Anjali Kamat

The row over the cartoons of the Prophet Muhammad, far from quietly subsiding, has grown more impassioned with every passing day. The controversy reveals a dangerous and virulent anti-Muslim racism that will almost certainly return to haunt us in the near future. While the United States has recently distanced itself from the 'free speech at all costs' position, this is only a pragmatic move aimed at sustaining its military ambitions and must not obfuscate the decisive role that US media and policy have played in demonizing both Muslims and their faith.

The 12 cartoons, originally published in September 2005 in Denmark's largest-selling daily, the conservative *Jyllands Posten*, drew the ire of Muslim diplomats and of a section of Scandinavian Muslims, but the controversy seemed to have died a largely un-noticed death until they were republished in the Norwegian Christian publication, *Magazinet*, in January 2006. Protests erupted across the so-called 'Muslim world'. In response to the official condemnations, the closing of Saudi Arabian, Libyan, and Syrian embassies in Denmark, threats against the editors, protests from Gaza to Yemen, and an incredibly well-orchestrated boycott of Danish goods in the Gulf States, newspapers across Western Europe republished the cartoons 'in defence of the freedom of expression.' Also at stake, according to these editors and the defenders of the cartoons, are the core values of a democratic, modern society—the most crucial of which, judging by the current furore, is a keen sense of humour. 'Yes, we have the right to caricature God!' screamed the front-page headline of the French newspaper *France Soir* on 1 February 2006.

To frame the issue as a battle between free secular democracies and an Islamic world defined by narrow religious orthodoxies and a criss-cross of indelible 'red lines' limiting the freedom of expression is to be trapped within a claustrophobic vision of humanity. Such a vision infuses Samuel Huntington's 'clash of civilizations' theory with the renewed vigour of a self-fulfilling prophecy. The debate raging across Europe, blinded by its discourse of a humourless Islam versus a playful Freedom, is unwilling and unable to see the cartoons for what they are: hateful and racist.

Depicting the Prophet as a wily blind sheikh with a sword and flanked by two wide-eyed veiled women, or with a bomb growing out of his elaborate turban, is not offensive simply because it 'hurts the religious sentiments of Muslims' or because it is an affront to the Prophet. The images are violent, and they incite and rationalize further violence against Muslims. They are inseparable from overused platitudes about Islam as a ticking bomb, which in turn cannot be understood apart from policy and national security decisions based on a tacit understanding of all Muslims as potential terrorists who have no rights under the law.

Jyllands Posten commissioned the 12 cartoons in defiance of 'the self-censorship which rules large parts of the Western world'[1] after a Danish author completing a book on the Prophet could not find a single artist willing to illustrate his work—apparently for fear of reprisals along the lines of the infamous murder of Dutch film-maker, Theo van Gogh. When Muslim diplomats demanded an official apology in October 2005, Danish Prime Minister Anders Fogh Rasmussen was quick to draw a line separating European from Muslim governments: 'The Danish government cannot apologize on behalf of a Danish newspaper. That is not how our democracy works ... and we have explained that to the Arab countries.'[2]

In early 2006, as protests grew within and beyond Europe—from Nigeria to the Philippines—and the boycott proved remarkably successful (causing Danish firm Arla Foods to lose over $1 million each day), theories of a civilizational schism between 'European' culture and the 'Muslim' culture of a quarter of the world's population, including some 20 million first- and second-generation Middle Eastern, North African and South Asian immigrants in Western Europe, grew apace. *Jyllands Posten*'s culture editor offered the following explanation: 'This is about the question of integration and how compatible is the religion of Islam with a modern secular society—how much does an immigrant have to give up and how much does the receiving culture have to compromise.'[3]

Neither the trope of Islam as intolerant nor the intolerance with which Islam has been portrayed is by any means unique to the specifics of today's debate. These are old tropes. The picture of Europe and the Islamic world as two fundamentally distinct entities pitted against each other stems from a medieval Christian worldview that was honed to secular perfection during the British and French colonization of the Middle East, North Africa and South Asia. The attacks of 11 September 2001 and the subsequent global 'war(s) on terror' have emboldened an anti-Muslim racist politics, but the specific stereotypes of Muslims as terrorists or intolerant fundamentalists have been fairly consistently deployed since at least the 1970s.

What is relatively new about the current impasse is the defiantly resentful tone of those supporting the publication of the cartoons, who present themselves as a besieged and dwindling community of free speech advocates defending freedom against a violent horde of Muslim fundamentalists gathering at the gates of European capitals. The debate on the cartoons tells us less about fanatic Muslims than about how Europe is choosing to deal with its 'Muslim question' and its growing anxieties about Muslim demographics.

The 2005 riots in the poorest slums of France and the violent anti-immigrant policies of right-wing political parties across Western Europe speak volumes about the sordid reality of repression, racism and poverty that most European Muslims have to contend with. The hysterical tone of some free speech defenders, comparing official apologies for the cartoons to a dangerous form of appeasement, thus betrays a fantastic sense of delusion. Wake up, Europe! This is not Munich in 1938. The real siege is in Iraq, Afghanistan and other sites of the US-led war on terror, not in the editorial offices of European capitals. Indeed, if a comparison must be made to that era of impending fascism, then recalling the anti-Semitic cartoons of the 1930s and 1940s would be more appropriate.

It should not bear repeating, but to depict the most revered figure in Islam as essentially and fundamentally violent, to reduce the Prophet to the level of media-spewed images of terrorists and Islamic radicals, is deeply offensive and about much more than distorting the life and teachings of the 7th century figure. Leaving aside the fact that many devout Muslims through history have seen no contradiction between their faith and visually depicting the Prophet, fixating on the rigidity of Islam and oversimplifying its impact on the lives of Muslims avoids a crucial point. It is, after all, Muslims who are overwhelmingly at the receiving end of Western violence.

When protestors burn down embassies and hard-line clerics call for 'a day of rage', one need not to turn to crude explanations of 'Muslim rage' that echo the influential Orientalist Bernard Lewis–notorious for his impact on the neoconservatives. A cursory glance at the recent history of European and American violent interventions and overt support for repressive dictatorships across the largely Muslim populations of the Middle East, North Africa, and South and South East Asia would be a far better place to start.

Notes

1. *Jyllands Posten*, 30 September 2005 (as reported on news.bbc.co.uk on 20 October 2005).
2. Per Bech Thomson, 'Danish paper apologizes over Prophet cartoons', Reuters, 30 January 2006.
3. Alan Cowell, 'More European papers print cartoons of Muhammad, fueling dispute with Muslims', *The New York Times*, 2 February 2006.

Part II

THE PLURALITY OF PRACTICE

8

Economics through Journalism[1]

V K Natraj

Economic journalism is apparently regarded as a somewhat specialized affair. That, at any rate, seems to be the perception of editors and newspaper persons in general. This needs to be explained.

It would seem that the analysis of economic events is perceived as being meant for a rather specialized reader. This does not seem to be quite the case for journalism dealing with social and political issues. There are a number of papers and journals which focus on social and political issues, but their style and even the treatment of the subjects does not leave the reader with the impression that she has to have a rather specialized aptitude or skill for reading the material. To put it in gross terms, almost anyone is presumed to have the ability to be her own political advisor.

The situation is different for journals devoted more or less exclusively to economic and financial affairs. A journalist friend recently remarked to me that what we have is not economic journalism so much as journalism dealing with economic matters. He added that in his view economic journalism as it is practised is not aimed at understanding economics in all its dimensions. What he meant to convey is, I suspect, that most of the writing we read on economic matters is not intended to sensitize the reader to economic issues, certainly not on those which are of real consequence to our society, such as poverty, inequality and the like.

It is superfluous to make the point that journalistic writing on economic issues has altered according to changes taking place in the macro sphere. In the past two decades at least, much of the writing on economics has been and continues to be highly influenced by the phenomenon of globalization or more accurately the LPG package–*liberalization, privatization and globalization.* A number of newspapers devote quite an impressive amount of space to a discussion of the implications of globalization. Naturally enough, there is also a discussion of the accompaniments of this process, such as issues relating to international trade, WTO rules and the like. A more noticeable feature of the immediate past and the present is the increased space made available by newspapers, especially in English, to business and commerce. Many aim to acquaint their readers with the world of investment and finance. The reference here is to daily newspapers not specializing in the realm of economics and economic affairs.

The very emergence of newspapers specializing in economics and finance is a reflection of the increasing importance of these fields in everyday lives. At the same time, it also reflects the manner in which developments at the international level have exercised a visible influence and impact on national economic policies. It is not at all uncommon to read feature articles in leading dailies syndicated from prestigious papers published overseas, and most often the subjects written up about are what may be described as economic affairs, in particular those aspects pertaining to the international dimension.

Another dimension which has come to dominate economic news is the stock market. The Sensex and its variations are regularly in the media, print as well as TV. I am reminded of my graduate student days in the UK in the 1960s of the past century, where it was a matter of some amusement for us–a large proportion of us were students of economics–to watch the TV commentator matching his expression to the state of the British economy, which, needless to say, gladdened no hearts. Even so the preoccupation that we now see with the Sensex was unimaginable a few decades ago. We are accustomed to seeing the effects of major economic measures being assessed with respect to the Sensex. Along with the Sensex and its sensitivity to economic policy, there is also the phenomenon of the leaders of the corporate sector being asked to offer their opinions not merely on economic policy but on governance in general. A few months ago several dailies were headlining the controversy between former Prime Minister Deve Gowda and Narayan Murthy, Chief Mentor at Infosys. While it is not argued here that the issues referred to above are not of consequence, it is arguable that other matters of equal importance are often sidelined.

In general the genre of economic writing is divisible into some broad categories. One concerns the world of high finance, the stock market (and, of course, the sensitivity of the Sensex!), and economic developments at the global level. In the same category we may include economic policy statements of the government of the day. Incidentally, ministerial pronouncements routinely secure prominent and often unjustifiably large amounts of space in our newspapers, but since this cuts across most news reporting it cannot be singled out for particular treatment here. In passing it is tempting to state that if a great scientist or social scientist delivers a major speech and this is presided over by a minister, most papers would (with honourable exceptions) feature the latter more prominently. I would like to recall an instance to which I was witness. Decades ago, Raj Krishna, a well-known economist and member of the Planning Commission, visited Karnataka. During his visit he made only one speech, at the Institute of Development Studies in the University of Mysore. Despite a prior briefing, few papers carried a report of the speech, in all likelihood because the occasion lacked a 'ministerial' flavour.

The second category comprises natural calamities and disasters, which invariably cause the heaviest damage to the poor. In this group the reporting is followed by critical analysis of how well or more generally how badly the government of the day has coped with the problem. Another category consists of what, for want of a better expression, can be called reporting of economic issues of everyday concern. Of the three it is this that appears to get the least coverage.

Among natural disasters one has to again distinguish between disasters which could not have been predicted and those which could (and are quite frequently caused by human failure). In the latter group we may include famines, which, as Amartya Sen has demonstrated, are largely the result of governmental policy and not, as was for long believed, due to food shortages. The reaction of the public to natural disasters requires to be seen in the appropriate perspective. With respect to unpredictable events such as the tsunami of December 2005, people generally react with sympathy and show willingness to contribute what they can to mitigate suffering. The response of the public to the tsunami was so generous that NGOs and all those concerned with management of relief began to feel the problem of plenty. What causes this is not merely the unanticipated nature of the disaster but the fact that such events, subject to certain important exceptions, can affect rich and poor alike.

This is not to deny that the poor were more affected by tsunami in terms of loss of livelihood but it is equally true that among those swept away by the tidal waves were several non-poor persons. The public's response is also a measure of this partially non-discriminatory effect of the disaster. Any one of us could be affected by such events; the same cannot be said of a famine, for instance, since those of us who are relatively well placed are quite aware that such an event is not likely to affect us as desperately as it would a poor person and her family. These differing perceptions of disasters, or the different ways in which various strata perceive disasters, exercise an influence over the manner in which journalists treat them in their reports and analyses. Very likely this explains, to a significant extent, why papers give this kind of disaster more continuous treatment compared to other types of disaster.

In dealing with problems like drought and famine, newspapers serve one essential purpose, which is to highlight the existence of the problem. Along with democratic institutions such as the Parliament and the legislatures and now Panchayati Raj institutions, it is the media that plays a vital role in ensuring governmental attention. But for the role of the media, cases of drought might well have gone without requisite attention from the state. To return to Amartya Sen, he has once again argued that it is the functioning of democratic institutions (including the press) that has ensured that independent India has not suffered a famine, although it continues to have droughts as well as malnutrition and chronic hunger.

It is necessary at this juncture to speculate upon the reasons for the last two issues mentioned here not having received continuous attention from the press. The explanation lies in the chronic nature of the problem. Expressed cynically, newspapers, like most of us, are not moved by persistent problems. Hunger, poverty, malnutrition–these are chronic, if one may put it that way; they are 'daily occurrences'; they are not dramatic. To be fair to ourselves as well as to the media, without a certain degree of 'built-in insensitivity' to persistent problems, living itself would become a morally difficult proposition. If I may become personal, I recall being asked years ago by a Britisher whether the appalling poverty around me did not prevent me from eating. My candid reply that I had, in a certain sense, ceased to notice it provoked him into accusing me of crass insensitivity. Yet I think I had spoken the truth. The point is that the print media in many ways takes the cue from us, the readers. Newspapers know how much 'poverty' we can take.

In spite of what has just been said we would do well to examine to what extent newspapers attempt to sensitize their readers to issues of great relevance to our society, many of which have been adumbrated above. It is most probably true that newspapers follow the readers' willingness in terms of how much they can digest on a daily basis, but is there also not a role for papers to mould public opinion? And in doing so, no one can reasonably expect any paper not to entertain its own ideological predilections. Given this, what is the record of our newspapers on matters economic, if we exclude, for the moment, their treatment of the stock market and related questions? Let us consider one example. How much information has been made available to us about the Employment Guarantee Act? More relevant, how aware are we of the implications of this legislation? How often have we read about it and its implementation since it became law? In particular the question is: how aware are non-specialist readers?

This brings into focus another aspect of economic journalism. In issues like employment guarantees, information supplied to the members of the public is of critical importance. This is in order that potential beneficiaries have knowledge of what they can avail themselves of from the state. Additionally, elected representatives in local government also ought to be in the know of state policy, the varieties of programmes it has launched, and the application and ambit of at least the more directly welfare-oriented ones. Can newspapers be expected to fulfil this task? Clearly the answer is somewhat complex.

In the first place, newspapers in English obviously do not have the reach to perform this function, and it is a certainty that the preferred language for most elected local government representatives would be the state languages. Second, it is likely to be the case that for most people at this level of governance–possibly at any level for that matter–the principal source of information is not the print medium but information supplied by the government through its own publicity devices as also official circulars and, perhaps most vitally, what is given to them in meetings, formal and informal, by officials working in local government. Moreover, it would be unrealistic to think that newspapers can devote the space necessary for the dissemination of detailed information on individual programmes.

This still does not answer the question whether the print medium, particularly in the state languages, can take up the challenge of making people aware of state policy and programmes. Here the answer has to be in the affirmative, although it is a moot point whether the function is being adequately discharged at present. On this the best that can be said is that the jury is still out. One of the problems in coming to a definite conclusion is that most of us obtain information from a vast number of sources, with the result that it would be difficult to state with any degree of precision which is the real source in any one case.

In addition to what has been urged above, we have moved from times or eras of information deficiency to a surplus or surfeit of it. Typically it has been a move from too little to too much. It would be interesting for us to inquire even at an individual level into how much of the information we read in the newspapers or come across through other media is actually distilled and retained in our mental archives. The answer, one is entitled to suspect, is that retention is contingent upon how much value we place on the particular piece of information under examination.

When it comes to economic/financial policy issues there is a need to divide the information into two categories. The first of these relates to that which is almost wholly in the public domain. Although we individuals are prone to be affected by the policy on taxation, it is one good example of this genre. The second refers to those policies and programmes which can be availed of by us for our personal benefit. An excellent illustration of this type is the myriad opportunities now advertised for investments, some of which carry the promise of virtually putting a ladder to the moon! It stands to reason that retention would be much more certain in the second case. A strong commitment to a public cause (of which development work is one important instance) would induce people interested to seek, obtain and retain information relating to the first category, which is more public than the second. Reference was made above to the expected preference for the print medium in the regional languages, especially in the rural areas. A point that needs to be added is that newspapers in these languages may not always have the expertise to analyse and disseminate information relating to the economic and financial worlds.

In countries like ours, development is a primordial issue of concern. In the past few decades, the concept of development has become much wider than it was when development studies first became a recognized field of study. One of the major ingredients of development is the participation of the people. This, in addition to human development as measured by the Human Development Index, is perceived today to be the essence of development. Participation is closely linked to decentralization of power and devolution of authority, and these, in turn, share an intimate nexus with information. Without information, people cannot make choices, and much of development actually involves choice between competing alternatives. In the final analysis, the real difference between the rich and the poor is not merely in respect of wealth and possession of resources, important as that is, but, as a great authority and one of the pioneers of the study of growth and development, Arthur Lewis, pointed out over half a century ago, one of the critical differences is in terms of choice. Poverty restricts choice. Similarly lack of access to information (in fact, information in a digestible form) also restricts choice and adversely affects participation. This is the motivating force behind what has come to be called development communication.

One of the other major facets of this dimension of development and journalism is that it has a nexus with accountability and transparency. In relation to both these factors, newspapers have a big contribution to make. Here again the accent is often on the sensational, as witness reports of corruption and bribery and those of officials getting caught or trapped, and rather less on educating people in the nuances of transparent and accountable governance. A newspaper person would possibly argue that it is no part of her brief to educate but to stay confined to reporting of news and views. While there may be some justification for this perspective, it is necessary to remember that values like account-ability, transparency and participation are principal components of development and the print medium has contributed effectively to our understanding of these issues.

One instance I would like to recall is the following. A leading English daily carried a critique of women's participation as elected representatives in panchayats. It was a one-sided presentation but was fortunately most ably countered by another author in the columns of the same paper. And I draw attention to this for the simple reason that, despite the constitutional amendment making reservation for women in local government mandatory, there is a tendency to regard this as futile. In this context, it is particularly necessary that newspapers do not let 'fundamentalist' views go unchallenged.

Given the expanding scope of development, the print medium along with the other media serve the cause by focusing on the constituents of development. Among them may be mentioned sensitivity to poverty, concern for equity, ecological balance and gender justice. While the campaign for all these has been aided by newspapers, perhaps their contribution is especially significant in the case of the environment. It is not improbable that the response which the public at large exudes with respect to the environment is not found to the same degree of intensity in the case of gender or equity in general. The reason is that in the environmental dimension there is the confluence of a number of interest groups, ranging from those who are mainly motivated by aesthetic considerations to those who have an ideological preference for a Gandhian mode of development, whereas in relation to gender, and more broadly equity, such a confluence may have proved elusive. These are spheres in which the newspapers could do more. However, as has been emphasized several times in the text, we need to keep in mind two limiting factors. One is that newspapers are also businesses and have to plan their space allocation with an eye to what will sell. The second is precisely how much of a particular variety of news will be tolerated by the readers. The second of the two considerations will depend upon the manner in which society's value systems keep altering. And of course, that is true of newspapers too.

Note

1. I would like to thank Mr E Raghavan, Resident Editor, *Economic Times*, Bangalore, for several critical insights. I thank the editor, Dr Nalini Rajan, for an initial and helpful discussion and for her infinite patience. Neither is implicated in the views presented in this paper.

9

Media Freedom and the Right to Privacy

Geeta Ramaseshan

The media in India theoretically enjoys the same freedom that is guaranteed to every citizen. As an institution it has no constitutional or legal privilege.[1] The right flows from the right to freedom of expression that is guaranteed under Article 19 of the Constitution. Such a right is not absolute and is subject to reasonable restrictions, and these include the interests of the sovereignty and integrity of India; the security of the state; friendly relations with foreign states; public order, decency or morality; or in relation to contempt of court, defamation or incitement to an offence.[2] The state can therefore make laws under any of these subjects and indeed there are many kinds of legislation in India that restrict or impinge on the right to freedom of expression. Some of these would include the Contempt of Court Act, the criminal law of defamation under the penal code and the Official Secrets Act.

Under the guise of public order, the Indian state has stifled dissent. And when the state has chosen to look the other way, moral brigades have often used these laws to silence artistic expression. Added to this is the fact that the right to information is still to fructify as a valuable right, despite lukewarm legislation that does not offer much in terms of privileges.

Within this context, it is with caution that one approaches the issue of privacy, for any such discussion would actually involve further restricting the media's freedom. But as a collective, the media in India is an extremely powerful institution that often tramples upon individual rights, especially of those who are not in a position to assert them. In such situations 'privacy' or 'the right to be left alone' is a necessary requirement to insulate these individuals from public attention.

The focus in this chapter is not on public figures who would want to keep their private lives out of the public eye. This is not to belittle their concerns. The release and circulation of sexually explicit tapes of a political leader does raise some grave questions on ethics and privacy, even if one were to accept the fact that public figures—in view of their position—will be scrutinized severely by the media. Media releases of photographs of actor Kareena Kapoor found kissing her boyfriend prompted the Supreme Court to ask whether such pictures served any 'public interest'. But such persons, by virtue of their positions, enjoy privilege and power in the Indian context and have the wherewithal to take recourse to remedies available under the law. Such privileges are however not available to the vast majority of persons who are then exposed to great risks by such media exposure.

Let me give you a few examples here. In a public hearing on children's rights in Chennai, child survivors of rape were photographed by some media persons, despite repeated requests by the organizers not to do so. One of them responded that if the organizers did not want journalists to take photographs, they should not have invited the media in the first place. The hearing was public, inasmuch as the survivors narrated their experiences with the judicial system to a select group working on children's rights as well as to members of the jury. The focus of the hearing was to raise awareness about the problems faced by survivors in child sexual abuse trials; it was not to expose children to media attention. The concerned media persons, however, were clearly not willing to distinguish between the public interest that was involved in discussing sexual abuse of children and the latter's right to privacy.

In another example, the Chennai police conducted a series of raids on some residences. The police claimed that brothels were being run in the premises. Photographs of women alleged to have been found during the raid were released to the media. Sections of the media published the pictures of women along with the phone numbers and addresses of the premises. No questions were raised about the modus operandi of the raid or about the lives of the women. As far as the media was concerned, the women alleged to be sex workers had to be exposed with a crusading zeal. Needless to say, not a single male was photographed by the media.

A third example relates to the media coverage of two children who were found to be HIV-positive in Kerala. The children were removed from school by the authorities after their status was revealed, and the media did serve valuable public interest by raising a furore over the matter. But in the process the children's pictures were once again published in some newspapers and television channels, thereby making their identities known to everyone.

Any discussion on privacy would necessarily involve addressing the public–private divide. Issues relating to violence against women and children have for too long been considered as matters to be kept within the private sphere and hence hidden from the public gaze. Arguments concerning honour and family values are often used to prevent survivors from seeking justice in the face of violation. Bringing such issues out of the private sphere has therefore been a great challenge. However, at the same time, issues involve individuals, and such individuals need to be protected from the prying eyes of the public. To such individuals privacy is of utmost importance, since public exposure can have serious repercussions, some of which may be fatal.

In the first and third examples given above, public interest was definitely involved. The media has a powerful role to play in focusing on such issues. However, at the same time, it has a responsibility to perform a balancing act by not revealing the identity of the persons concerned. As far as the second example is concerned, it is my view that no public interest was served. On the contrary, release of such news and pictures harmed the women concerned, apart from reinforcing patriarchal norms.

'Privacy' is a recent development in the area of law, but it has been recognized as a human right. The first judgement of the Supreme Court on the subject related to the intrusion of the police by surveillance. The court held that domiciliary visits by the police without the authority of law were a violation of privacy that flowed from Article 19(1)(d) of the Constitution relating to freedom of movement and Article 21 relating to the right to life.[3]

However it was only in *R Rajagopal v. State of Tamil Nadu*[4] that the court addressed the right to privacy of the individual referred to in a publication. The Tamil weekly *Nakeeran* serialized an autobiography of a death row convict, 'Auto' Shanker (so called because he ran an auto service and then moved on to big-time crime). In his autobiography, Shanker narrated his rise and how it would not have been possible without the connivance of many persons 'in high places', and these were mentioned by name. Shanker was in prison and the dispatches, according to the editor, were sent from prison. The prison authorities stopped the dispatches, prompting the editor, Rajagopal, to challenge their order in court. Shanker, in the meanwhile, refused to acknowledge the serial as his own, presumably under pressure from the prison authorities.

While the case before the apex court was on the right to free expression, the court examined the right of privacy in detail and laid down the following directions:

(*a*) The right to privacy is implicit in the right to life and liberty guaranteed under Article 21 and is a 'right to be left alone'. A citizen has a right to safeguard the privacy of his own, his family, marriage, procreation (*sic*), motherhood, child-bearing and education, among other matters. None can publish anything concerning the above matters without his consent—whether truthful or otherwise and whether laudatory or critical. If one does so, one would be violating the right to privacy of the person concerned and would be liable in an action for damages. The position may, however, be different if a person voluntarily thrusts himself into controversy or voluntarily invites or raises a controversy.

(*b*) The rule becomes an exception if the publication is based upon public records including court records. This is because once a matter becomes a matter of public record, the right of privacy no longer subsists and it becomes a legitimate subject for comment by the media. However in the interests of decency (Article 19[2]), an exception is carved out of this rule, viz., a female who is a victim of sexual assault, kidnap, abduction or a like offence should not further be subjected to the indignity of her name for the incident being publicized in the media.

(*c*) In the case of public officials, right of privacy is not available with respect to their acts and conduct relevant to the discharge of their public duties even when the publication is based on facts and statements that are not true, unless the official establishes that the publication was made with reckless disregard of truth. In such a case it would be enough for the media to establish that they acted after a reasonable verification of facts and it is not necessary for the media to prove that what was published was true unless the publication is proved to be false and actuated by malice or personal animosity.

(d) Government, local authority and other organs and institutions exercising governmental power cannot maintain a suit for damages for defamation.

(e) The Officials Secrets Act or other enactments having the force of law binds the media.

(f) No law empowers the state or its officials to prohibit or impose a prior restraint upon the media.

The court observed that the principles are only broad, neither exhaustive nor all comprehending—'indeed no such enunciation is possible or advisable. This right has to go from case to case development since the concept is still in the process of evolution.'

In the context of privacy and the media, the principles gain significance. While the privacy of a survivor of sexual assault would still fall within the purview of 'decency', the development of the doctrine is a welcome addition to the law. The court has distinguished the private and public role of persons and has recognized the dynamics of power that operate in cases relating to the latter.

In *People's Union for Civil liberties v. Union of India*,[5] the Supreme Court was concerned with phone tapping. The court held that the right to hold a telephone conversation in the privacy of one's home or office without interference could certainly be claimed as 'right to privacy', and that telephone tapping infringed the right to life under Article 21 of the Constitution of India, unless it is permitted under procedure established by law. However the court, while holding it as technological eavesdropping, observed that an individual talking over the phone is exercising his right to freedom of expression under Article 19, and tapping is a violation of that freedom, unless it comes within the restriction of Article 19(2). This would imply that the state can make laws that can permit tapping of phones, but such legislation will have to fall within the purview of reasonable restriction.

In *'X' v. Hospital 'z'*,[6] a hospital breached confidentiality by giving information about the HIV status of one of its patients. In a suit of damages filed by the patient that was defeated all the way to the Supreme Court, the court held that the doctor–patient relationship, though commercial, is professionally a matter of confidence, and that public disclosures of even true private facts may amount to an invasion of the right to privacy, which may sometimes lead to the clash of one person's 'right to be left alone' with another person's right to be informed. The court observed that the right is not absolute and can be lawfully restricted for the prevention of crime, disorder, protection of health or morals, or protection of rights and freedoms of others. In this case the court held that the disclosure of the patient's HIV status to the family of his fiancé did not violate privacy since 'she was saved by such disclosure, or else, she too would have been infected with the dreadful disease if marriage had taken place and consummated.'

The development of case law indicates that the court has tried to balance the interests of the individual with public interest in the context of the media. However it still remains in its nascent stage. In the meantime, new issues are yet to arise before the court. One such example is the intrusion of television. TV channels often flash gory scenes of bodies in accidents or crimes, with scant respect for the dead and the impact of such visuals on the family. During the tsunami, Sun TV in particular kept repeating such visuals, thereby benumbing the viewer. Disasters are big news, but the question arises whether the privacy of families who have lost their near and dear ones should not be respected.

News broadcasts often seem to be highlighting the 'us and them' divide in presentation. One example related to the very private moment of a father who was praying for a last-minute reprieve of the death sentence on his son, Dhananjay Chatterjee. Star News focused the camera on his prayer at his family temple and his breakdown at the exact time when Chatterjee was hanged. No one can forget the late Gudiya in the talk show on Zee TV that attacked her for marrying another man presuming that her soldier husband was dead. The anchor was extremely judgemental, and the audience moralistic, with everyone commenting about her life, thereby leaving Gudiya speechless throughout the programme.

An ideal situation would be for the media to evolve its own code of ethics. But one does not live in ideal times. Privacy exists in many forms in special forms of legislation[7] but these are often violated. There is as of now no move to introduce legislation in this regard. Indeed our experiences with forms of legislation often indicate they are breached as a rule. However, the concerns of privacy, as indicated earlier, are very real. When there is a conflict between the rights of the media and the rights of the individual in the context of privacy, it is my opinion that privacy must reign supreme, if only because we, as a society, give very little importance to the protection of individual rights.

Notes

1. *Sharma v. Srikrishana*, All India Reporter 1959 SC, p. 395.
2. Article 19(1)(a).
3. *Kharak Singh v. State of UP*, All India Reporter 1963 SC, p. 1295. For a detailed reading on role of media and public trials see *Naresh Shridhar Mirajkar v. State of Maharashtra*, AIR 1967 SC, p. 1.
4. AIR 1995 SC, p. 264.
5. AIR 1997 SC, p. 568.
6. AIR 1999 SC, p. 495.
7. Some of the legislation include the marriage laws, the Juvenile Justice Act, and rape under the Indian Penal Code. These prescribe in-camera trials and prohibit publication of proceedings.

10

Exposing the Media Spiel on Rural Women

K Kalpana

To cast aspersions on the authenticity of media-peddled images of grassroots collectives of rural women, using their group-generated corpus of savings and credit to bootstrap their way out of poverty and to launch a multitude of successful enterprises, is surely akin to sacrilege, considering that the year 2005 was earmarked as 'The International Year of Micro-Credit'. The Governor-General of the United Nations has reminded the world community of the responsibility that the international media has—as do national governments and the global development industry—to do its bit in ensuring the proper celebration of the Year of Micro-Credit.[1]

It would seem that the mainstream media in India at least has decided to pay heed to the injunction of the UN Governor-General, judging from the unfailing regularity of heart-warming stories of rural poor women striving towards upward economic mobility, through the resources provided by state patronage of self-help groups—the Indian variant of the global micro-credit phenomenon. If the female victim genre of journalism in Tamil popular dailies marks, as V Geetha points out,[2] a recognition of wrongs suffered by women in an unequal society, the recent mush-rooming of stories recounting the small successes of grassroots women's savings and credit-based collectives marks the media's attempt to come to terms with the near-meteoric explosion of such groupings, sponsored by an assortment of agencies (both state and non-state) and concentrated particularly in rural parts of the southern states of India.

As an activist with the Tamil Nadu Science Forum, which has over the last 10 years organized women through self-help groups (SHGs) in the southern districts of Tamil Nadu, and as a doctoral student grappling with claims of 'empowerment of women' and 'alleviation of poverty' attributed to micro-credit in the development literature, I have followed 'human interest' stories of SHGs in the media (in both Tamil- and English-language dailies) with some dismay. This dismay is on account of finding repetitive, adulatory statements of 'women's empowerment' by powerful actors in the state and in the media. These include narratives of how credit-financed micro-enterprises sustain rural livelihoods, liberate households from dependence on moneylenders, or even enable women to eliminate the practice of female infanticide. Were one to believe the media, it would appear that women organized through SHGs have mounted a dramatic challenge to entrenched structures of power–economic and political–where other more powerful actors, the state and judiciary included, have failed.

One tendency that runs through the media reporting of rural women's credit-based *sangams* or groups that I wish to quarrel with has to do, in particular, with the glossing over of differences among women–of the remarkable heterogeneity that characterizes the lives of women from near-poverty households in Tamil Nadu–so much so that the category of 'rural women' is flattened out, homogenized and rendered without any kind of meaningful social identity. As a young activist attempting to sell women the spiel on solidarity and the potential for collective action that inheres in all-women collectives, my work experience offered me an invaluable insight into the importance and meaning of difference in women's lives, of the fault lines that undercut the ideal of a cohesive sisterhood.

A woman in a hamlet in Kanyakumari district, who quit membership of her group after the suicide of her husband, informed me blandly that she felt shame and feared loss of face at her inability to make the mandated minimum savings following the loss of her family's sole earning member. A SHG, composed entirely of women from the dominant caste in another village, sought with vehemence to stymie the attempts of the local NGO to create self-help groups in the poorer, Dalit hamlets of the village. 'These people never repay their loans. Why should we suffer if banks refuse us credit on account of their repayment record?' went the argument. Caste-based notions of who would honour a commitment (repaying a loan being a case in point) and who would not did, in that instance, permit women of the dominant caste to monopolize access to a development intervention with significant material consequences for poor women.

I also found that stories of SHGs collectively challenging the brewing and sales of illicit alcohol in their villages were sometimes complicated by protest and dissent from within the groups by individual SHG members (usually the poorest in the group), whose livelihood derived from the sale of alcohol. Differentiated by household circumstances, intensity of poverty, levels of education and caste, would not the story of 20-odd women meeting every week to decide how to distribute their meagre resources make for fascinating telling? Why then do we not hear enough of these in the media?

As a research scholar who spends quite some time on the 'field' chronicling the battles of SHG women with local banks and officials of the block development office as they struggle to access bank loans and subsidies of anti-poverty schemes purportedly designed for them, I wonder sometimes how well-meaning journalists doing the 'rural beat' can possibly overlook the numerous instances of SHG women clamouring for a better deal from local development agencies. Surely there are exceedingly interesting stories of both conflict and collaboration waiting to be told? Manoeuvring the maze of paperwork and project reports required to be submitted to banks, negotiating with the block office for a reduction in the 'commission' that is invariably demanded, SHG women have often had to endure the indignity of waiting ('like beggars') for long hours in the sun without a meal, for bankers to grade their loan papers, sometimes of having their account notebooks thrown in their faces in the event of 'unsatisfactory' bookkeeping, of being sent home without an audience with the bank manager who was either out of the office or just too busy.

Bankers' efforts to retrieve defaults on older bank loans (such as the Integrated Rural Development Programme) made to male kin (husbands, sons, even fathers-in-law) of women SHG members have been manifested as threats, such as suspending loan access until the SHG induces its members to make good the unpaid balance to the bank. Forced by bankers' unyielding positions on tying up access to SHG-related bank loans to older, individual-targeted loan schemes of the pre-SHG era, women in self-help groups are turning against their unfortunate co-members whose families have defaulted on earlier government loans, blaming them for queering the pitch for all of them. A classic case of pitting the poor against the poor! Why do these nuances never get reported in the media?

It is indeed unfortunate that this emerging bone of contention between rural women's credit groups and the bureaucracies they interact with on an ongoing basis is not the stuff of front-page news. It surely has all the ingredients of front-page news—oppression (by bankers and block officials), resistance (by SHG coordinators and SHG members who often mince no words when informing officials of exactly what they think of them) and outright valour (when the poor in sheer disgust reject bank loans and declare that their group-generated funds will do)!

Cases abound of repayment pressure-induced dropouts and push-outs of poorer women—women who suddenly find themselves in situations of acute economic stress, women whose credit-worthiness consequently plummets in the eyes of the rest of the group, and women whose male kin's unpaid balances on bank loans have led to eviction from group membership. These are human interest stories as well—stories of solidarity gone sour, of what happens when group empathy frays in a context of competition, acute scarcity of resources and fragile livelihoods, whereby women and poor families turn against each other.

Stories that speak of the harsh realities of sharing resources are an important window into the lives of rural women, perhaps of even greater significance than stories of collective striving and upward mobility. Borrowing from village moneylenders, pledging jewellery, reducing consumption of vegetable and meat, and postponing much-needed medical treatment—these are strategies that SHG women frequently deploy to avoid the ignominy and shame of delaying repayment of a loan and testing the patience and goodwill of one's peer group. These strategies are an integral component of the much vaunted repayment performance of SHGs that the official establishment and the media alike celebrate. However the considerable costs that women incur in order to beat the high-pressure repayment deadlines remain so many untold stories.

Another issue of great concern for SHGs and the NGOs that organize SHGs is the government's facile equation of access to institutional credit with the economic viability of enterprises. The state's refusal to assume responsibility for organizing systematic production-related training, technology upgradation and linkages with markets may rightfully be perceived as the state's disavowal of its obligation to guarantee the means of livelihood to people. SHGs across Tamil Nadu, which attempt to repay enterprise loans by raising cattle, complain of the tendency of the milk co-operative society to transfer its own working capital crises on to the shoulders of poor women by inordinate delays in making payment for the milk. As SHG women in Virudhunagar district ask: 'If payment for the milk is delayed by 45 days each time, how do we repay our bank loans, keep up with our monthly savings, buy fodder for the cows and feed ourselves and our families?'[3]

SHG women also complain of imposition of pre-selected enterprise activities by block administration officials, eager to demonstrate 'variety' and 'diversity' in the choice of enterprises. Examples include toy-making, embroidery, candle-making, handicrafts, small decorative items, etc., in which the women have no prior experience. This is however accompanied by little training and no guarantee of markets. In this context, a question that begs to be asked (frequently and forcefully by the media) relates to the intent of the state, which forces women into unsustainable enterprises at the same time as it withdraws support for village and cottage industries as part of its macro-economic policy. This contradiction is far from theoretical for the women who face both hostile markets and bankers eager to recover loans. How individual women and SHGs, as collective entities, resolve this dilemma, even as they struggle to keep the group together and placate irate bank officials, testifies to crisis management skills that could give any management *guru* a run for his money! However, these struggles remain invisible.

Dealing as I constantly do with the failure of enterprise-related loan schemes targeting SHG women, which are frequently subverted (and with good reason, too) by women to meet pressing consumption-related needs, I admit that I am quite sceptical about the propensity of the media to celebrate the arrival of 'women entrepreneurs' financed by bank loans sourced through their

SHGs. The 'entrepreneurs' that I have frequently encountered in
the course of my work experience with SHGs are women from
below-poverty-line households working long hours at abysmal
wages in unprotected jobs in the informal, unorganized sector.
The word 'entrepreneur' has a glamorous ring to it and belies the
reality of the conditions of labour for the majority of SHG women.

Women who borrow from SHGs in Kanyakumari district to
buy raw materials in bulk (for palm-leaf and coconut-leaf thatch-
ing) often work till midnight, scrimping on sleep and rest in order
to increase their daily earnings by a couple of rupees. Women
beedi workers in Virudhunagar, who use SHG loans to buy *tendu*
leaves from middlemen, complain routinely of 'chest pain, white
discharge and back pain'. An important critique of SHGs is that
they may end up increasing women's work burden, without con-
comitantly enhancing the monetary returns to women's labour.
Much of women's labour in the household, in agriculture and
the informal sector remains invisible, devalued, under-accounted
and grossly under-paid. The visibility accorded to the 'disciplined'
SHG member who attends meetings regularly and makes timely
loan repayments is accompanied by the continuing invisibility of
other dimensions of her life, especially as an unacknowledged
and under-appreciated worker.

Journalism that celebrates the SHG and its small successes
therefore invariably ends up obfuscating as much as it reveals,
and conveys partial truths. In recent years, journalists' reports of
distress-induced migration, starvation deaths and debt-related
suicides in the rural countryside have come to exemplify points
of crises and breakdown in local support systems, state protective
mechanisms and livelihood arrangements. Likewise, tracing fluc-
tuations caused in SHG membership in an area due to dropping
out owing to members' cash-flow crises, and mapping the disinte-
gration or paralysis of the normal functioning of SHGs within
the regional agrarian landscape, can offer a micro-cosmic view
of how households and communities respond to economy-wide
developments. However, we have yet to witness the emergence
of serious journalism that rises above the 'feel-good' nature of
much of writing about rural women's credit groups.

What I am saying therefore is not that the attention that SHGs
have merited in the recent past in the mainstream press is unwar-
ranted. This is far from the truth. The point that I am making is

that SHGs and the windows they offer into understanding rural lives and livelihoods need to be taken far more seriously, far more rigorously, than they have been hitherto.

Notes

1. UN Resolution, 'International Year of Microcredit: 2005', Resolution 1998/28, 45th Plenary Meeting. Available at www.gdrc.org/icm/iym2005/un-resolution.html.
2. V Geetha, 'Gender, Identity and the Tamil Popular Press', in Nalini Rajan (ed.), *Practising Journalism: Values, Constraints, Implications* (New Delhi, Sage Publications, 2005).
3. Personal interviews conducted by author with coordinators of the Thuligal federation of SHGs organized by the Tamil Nadu Science Forum in Virudunagar district.

11

Writing Science: Breaking the Language Barrier

Vijaya Swaminath

It was cold and bright and there was no night. Winds that stop your breath within and a chill that freezes it without made you question your sanity. Four layers of clothes to venture out to use the facilities—all in the name of science. The same snowy desert that makes life as human beings difficult makes it a haven for scientists—neutrino astrophysicists, specifically! Welcome to the South Pole—one of earth's icy caps.

I am a scientist by training. I wanted to start my thesis this way and I can still hear my professor's laughter. 'You are a scientist writing for other scientists,' he said, 'not a storyteller.'

This then is how the battle lines are drawn.

A scientist writing for her peers is walking them through the intricacies of her experiment, calculation or invention. She has their undivided attention and talks to them in a language they are familiar with. She does not focus on the researcher but explains how the data leads to specific conclusions. In fact, 'I' or 'we' are to be avoided according to the holy grail of journal writing because it should not matter what you think or do as an individual.

A science writer, however, will have to be a storyteller even as she unravels the 'science'. She does not have the luxury of a rapt readership familiar with the language of her story—science. In fact, it is quite the opposite.

A sure way to lose your reader is to announce, through style, form and language that you are making him read science. Instead, a little sleight-of-hand, a plot and a story that tickles the innate curiosity of your reader will hook him in.

This is not that hard to do.

Science is done by scientists—people like you and me. It happens in windowless rooms and in the frozen tundra, in labs with beakers and test tubes and in distant space. Find the lure—the science, the scientist, the lab—and take the reader there.

As a science writer, violate a tenet of scientific writing. Tell a story. Build a plot around characters (scientists, animal rights activists, engineers, technicians) and let their voices talk about the science.

The Beginning

In most science stories, the beginning of your story decides if the reader stays on till the end.

Here is a dramatic opening by Jennifer Kahn in her story 'Stripped For Parts', a story about organ transplants, in *Wired* magazine.[1]

> The television in the dead man's room stays on all night. Right now the program is *Shipmates*, a reality-dating drama that's barely audible over the hiss of the ventilator. It's 4 AM, and I've been here for six hours, sitting in the corner while three nurses fuss intermittently over a set of intravenous drips. They're worried about the dead man's health.

The author does not let on that this is a story about organ transplants till the third paragraph. But the reader's curiosity is up by then, what with the patient being a corpse.

Another example of a fast-paced opening is the lead in the story, 'Desperate Measures' in the *New Yorker* by Atul Gawande.[2]

> On 28 November 1942, an errant match set alight the paper fronds of a fake electric-lit palm tree in a corner of the Cocoanut Grove night club near Boston's theater district and started one of the worst fires in American History. The flames caught on to the fabric decorating the ceiling, and then swept everywhere, engulfing the place within minutes. The club was jammed with almost a thousand revelers that night. Its few exit doors were either locked or blocked, and hundreds of people were trapped inside. Rescue workers had to break through walls to get to them. Those with any signs of life were sent primarily to two hospitals—Massachusetts General Hospital and Boston City Hospital. At Boston City Hospital, doctors and nurses gave the patients the standard treatment for their burns. At MGH, however, an iconoclastic surgeon named

> Oliver Cope decided to try an experiment on the victims. Francis Daniels
> Moore, then a fourth-year surgical resident, was one of only two doctors
> working on the emergency ward when the victims came in. The experience,
> and the experiment, changed him. And because they did, modern medicine
> would never be the same.

The drama of the fire sucks the reader in and only in the last couple of lines does one realize that the story is about an individual whose experiences that day changed medicine for ever. It is a fast-paced story, woven around Francis Daniels Moore explaining how medicine was practised then and what changed with him.

Any science story should convey the sense of wonder and discovery. It should carry the readers to new worlds: under the ocean, to the South Pole, deep into the rainforest, to the moon and Mars and far into space, to the inside of a cell or an atom; it should convey a sense of 'you are there', and give the readers an opportunity to experience people, places and events that they might otherwise never know.

Science, however, is not always of the 'Gee Whiz' variety. It can be pretty dry, mathematical and hard to break down at times. Not all scientists may sparkle either.

The job of a science writer is to decipher scientist-speak and translate it into English, even as she weaves a story colourful enough to hold the reader's interest. This does not require you to be trained in science; you only need to be inquisitive and eager to learn. Of course, with scientists who do not open up easily, you need a little extra charm to extract those special details, zinger quotes or character quirks that the reader will find fascinating.

A great tip from John Wilkes, director of the science writing programme at University of California, Santa Cruz—'...Resist the deep-rooted, often unconscious desire to be approved of by sources.' 'Be Cheeky,' he adds.[3]

'Science'-ing Your Story

Got your reader to start reading your piece? That is great. How do you keep him going? Couching the science within the story and making it palatable is the science writer's next challenge.

Use *your* words to explain the science—not those of the scientist you interviewed, the book you read or the journal you referred to. You can easily put off wary readers with textbook language they would rather forget.

In a story on neutrino astrophysics, trying to explain why South Pole ice is a good medium for detecting neutrinos, you can write: 'The absorption length in South Pole ice is large at Cerenkov wavelengths and hence the detection volume is much larger than the physical volume of the detector.'

Something like this will lose you readers faster than you can say 'neutrino astrophysics'. These are the hard facts of life.

So, simplify: 'Ice at the south pole is very transparent. Light from a muon (a product of neutrino collision with matter) 200 metres away makes it to your detector. So, the detector can see farther than its size implies.'

Here is an example of spooky science (cited by Philip Yam, a science writer and news editor with *Scientific American*): 'Would you have guessed,' he asks, 'that 'Lysomotropic Agents and Cysteine Protease Inhibitors Inhibit Scrapie-Associated Prion Protein Accumulation' refers to certain drugs that could treat mad cow disease?'[4] Huh?

To simplify for the reader, the writer needs to understand the science in the story—not just what you get through one read of an article in a journal, but the block-by-block deconstruction of the science you are trying to explain. The key is to ask all those questions ('Stupid questions are the birthright of science writers') you were too shy to ask—and keep asking till the answers make complete sense.

Having understood the science, the urge is to lay it on the reader—that is, to over-explain the technical details you have mastered with such effort. Abstain! The editor of the *Santa Cruz Sentinel* once told John Wilkes about Wilkes's students working as interns, 'They're very smart, but if you ask them what time it is, they tell you how the watch works.'[5]

The number of words you use to explain a topic should depend on the topic's importance in the story, not on the time and effort it took you to understand it.

'The question is not "should" you explain a concept or process, but "how" can you do so in a way that is clear and so readable that it is simply part of the story,' says Sharon Dunwoody,

Professor of Journalism and Mass Communication at the University of Wisconsin, Madison.[6]

Several strategies are used by good science writers for explanatory writing. Active-voice verbs that speak; analogies and metaphors that bring the science into the realm of the reader's experience; explaining scientific terms instead of defining them, using examples and writing logically.

In his story, 'Gravity in reverse', for *Natural History* magazine, Neil deGrasse Tyson explains how scientists discovered a mysterious energy that is tearing our universe apart and scattering celestial objects away from each other at ever increasing speeds. This was based on an observation of a type of exploding star (supernova) by a couple of scientists. Here is what he writes:

> To an astrophysicist, the supernovas used in Perlmutter's and Schmidt's studies are worth their weight in fusionable nuclei. Each star explodes the same way, igniting a similar amount of fuel, releasing a similarly titanic amount of energy in a similar period of time, and therefore achieving similar peak luminosity. Hence these exploding stars serve as a kind of yard-stick, or 'standard candle', for calculating cosmic distances to the galaxies in which they explode, out to the farthest reaches of the Universe. Standard candles simplify calculations immensely; since the supernova all have the same wattage, the dim ones are far away and the bright ones are nearby. By measuring their brightness (a simple task), you can tell exactly how far away they are from you. If the luminosities of the supernovae were not all the same, brightness alone would not be enough to tell you which of them are far from the Earth and which of them are near. A dim one could be a high-wattage bulb far away or a low-wattage one close up.[7]

This is a physics story, which are harder to write as they are more mathematical than most other science stories. Numbers (science is full of them), unless put in context, can harm a story more than help it. Using analogies is a way to tackle this. George Johnson, a physics writer, was faced with evoking the potential power of an invisibly small experimental device called quantum computer. One consisting of a string of 64 atoms would, in theory, carry out 18 quintillion calculations at the same time. For a conventional supercomputer to do that, he wrote, it would need millions of trillions of processors:

> And so, all things being equal, it would occupy 750 trillion acres—roughly a trillion square miles. It wouldn't fit on the planet. The surface of the Earth is just 200 million square miles, so a supercomputer as powerful as the invisible

64-atom quantum calculator would fill the surfaces of 5,000 Earths, assuming you could figure out a way to operate equipment on ocean-floating platforms.

Easy for the reader to visualize—mission accomplished.[8]
Simplify. But, there is a danger in simplifying too much. Albert Einstein is known to have said: 'Everything should be made as simple as possible, but not simpler.' The trick is to simplify without insulting the intelligence of the reader and without getting it totally wrong. A wrong analogy, an example that does not work, can be a crime. Trust is a fragile commodity in any reporting, especially so in science reporting, because when the reader uninitiated in science bravely picks up your story, he trusts you to give him the right information. You have failed in your job if you fail this trust.

Keeping the Pace

The hook is in. You have reeled the reader into the story, science and all. Now you need to set a pace. If the reader is able to read through the story quickly, the story was well-written. Ideas from fiction-writing can help in this.

A story in present tense in active voice and with telling verbs conveys the reader to the scene of the story. It is important to use colourful writing—descriptive details through which you show the reader rather than tell him about the person or scene in your story. 'COLOR is a matter of the right details—observed directly, elicited from witnesses, always with the breath of actuality,' says Rene J Cappon.[9]

Here is a story from the Associated Press after the Exxon Valdez disaster:

> Like a candy bar in the hands of a 2 year-old, crude oil from the Exxon Valdez has gotten into everything. Globs of mousse litter the cobbled beach. Rainwater beads up on rocks as on the waxed hood of a car. A clean-up worker digs into the sand and his hand comes up a greasy brown.
>
> A burly fisherman breaks into tears as he describes steering his boat through the slick: no water lapping, no birds crying, just the sickening silence of oil slipping past the hull.
>
> At a bird rescue center in Seward, some of the patients are failing. They have been washed clean, but not before swallowing fatal doses of oil. They don't cry out; instinct tells them not to advertise their distress to predators.

'They just get real quiet, sit in a corner and die,' says rescue coordinator Jay Holcomb.

Colour

Describing people, even scientists, helps too. It helps define the person in the reader's mind. Identifying with the person doing the science removes some of the fear and makes it easier to accept a description of their scientific work.

Imagine if there were no photos of Einstein, just articles. Who would not want to know about his crazy hair and moustache, his kind, gentle eyes? His appearance has come to personify the image of a scientist in the public's eye. So if your subject happens to be a clean-shaven, fit-as-a-fiddle, Armani-suited scientist, the reader would like to know. If nothing, you would be re-defining fashion.

In trying to colour your story, it is easy to fall into the 'cliché trap'. Rene J Cappon advises writers, science writers specifically, to avoid this. Clichés deaden the story.

Quotes are another way to brighten up your story. Tom Brady in his book *The Craft of Interviewing* describes quotes as 'those brief, brilliant bursts of life'.[10] Quotes give the readers the feeling they are talking to real people–scientists talking about their work, people in medical stories describing their ailments and reactions, animal right activists talking about the sight of caged animals to be used for medical research, and so on. Quotes used the right way can control the pace and rhythm of a story.

Writing a fast-paced story is hard. A science story that moves, with the reader tagging along for the ride–well, it is a challenge. But it can be done and the best of science writers do it consistently.

Get all the information you can, make sure you understand it, rank it according to where you want the story to go (deciding what to leave out is half the battle), and then start writing.

If your reader is still with you at the end, you have achieved your goal. The story has to end well too. You have to give the reader a sense of completion, says Gareth Cook (a Pulitzer Prize-winning science writer):[11]

I like to think of structuring a news story like hosting a party. When your guests arrive at the door, welcome them and tell them what is going on, but don't overload them with information. As they settle in, make sure that they get around to talk to the people they should meet. Look like you are having fun, even if you are stressed out. When it's time for guests to leave, say goodbye and maybe even give them a parting gift to remember the occasion by. Who knows, they might just want to come to your next party?

Notes

1. Jennifer Kahn, 'Stripped For Parts', *Wired*, March 2003. Available at: http://wired.com/wired/archive/11.03/parts.html. Reprinted in Dava Sobel and Jesse Cohen (eds), *The Best American Science Writing 2004* (New York, Ecco, 2004).
2. Atul Gawande, 'Desperate Measures', *New Yorker*, 5 May 2003. Reprinted in Dava Sobel and Jesse Cohen (eds), *The Best American Science Writing 2004*.
3. John Wilkes in Deborah Blum, Mary Knudson and Robin Marantz Henig (eds), *A Field Guide for Science Writers (The Official Guide of the National Association of Science Writers)*, 2nd edition (USA, Oxford University Press, 2006).
4. Philip Yam, 'Finding Story Ideas and Sources', in Deborah Blum et al. (eds), *A Field Guide for Science Writers*.
5. John Wilkes in Deborah Blum et al. (eds), *A Field Guide for Science Writers*.
6. Sharon Dunwoody, 'Explaining Science–Writing Well about Science: Techniques From Teachers of Science Writing', in Deborah Blum et al. (eds), *A Field Guide for Science Writers*.
7. Neil deGrasse Tyson, 'Gravity in Reverse', *Natural History*, December 2003. Reprinted in Dava Sobel and Jesse Cohen (eds), *The Best American Science Writing 2004*.
8. George Johnson, *A Shortcut Through Time: The Path to the Quantum Computer* (New York, Alfred A Knopf, 2003).
9. Rene J Cappon, *The Word. An Associated Press Guide To Good News Writing* (Associated Press, 1982).
10. Tom Brady, *The Art of Interviewing* (USA, Vintage Books, 1997).
11. Gareth Cook, 'Deadline Writing', in Deborah Blum et al. (eds), *A Field Guide for Science Writers*.

12

The Arts Beat! Feel the Heat!

Aditi De

The arts beat. Does it exist? What is its significance in a contemporary media world where politics, sports and entertainment pay their way for page space but the arts seldom do?

The arts have never been at the heart of mainstream media, whether in India or abroad. Notable Indian exceptions to this perception would include specialized journals on music, dance, the fine arts or even theatre, such as the now-defunct *Shruti* from Chennai, *Art India* from Mumbai, and Kolkata's *Seagull Theatre Quarterly*, now in an e-*avatar*. Yet, until about a decade ago, most Indian dailies did devote token space to the arts, though their focus was mainly on reviews.

Then came a conscious dumbing down of the Indian media since the early 21st century, as professional editors gave way to proprietor-editors, and the balance sheet became the bottom line. Both paintings and restaurants alike were gauged through a five-star rating. Book review pages gradually metamorphosed into hyped reports regarding which author got a mega-advance after a bidding war, or what a glamorous writer's favourite recipe was. Theatre pieces were shaped by whether film stars were participating in the exposition or if a famous playwright had penned the script. New talent was seldom discovered or nurtured, while paper applause greeted the mere appearance of a Neena Gupta or Hema Malini on stage, no matter the merits of their performance. A Gangubai Hangal or a Bismillah Khan was sidelined, even when in dire straits, in favour of reports about Pandit Jasraj's take on national civil honours bestowed on Pandit Ravi Shankar, or on whether Anoushka Ravi Shankar's love life was scintillating in comparison to her performance on the sitar.

But Indian arts' writing has not always played to the gallery. Nor, from the 1950s to the 1990s, did it bury itself in the superficial, the mundane and the formulaic. It was an open space that supported a cross-section of intelligent writing, such as Chidananda Dasgupta on films (didn't he initiate one of India's first film clubs in Kolkata, along with Satyajit Ray?), or Shanta Serbjeet Singh on Indian classical dance, or in-depth critiques of books in publications like *Biblio* or the *Indian Review of Books*.

Around the arts pieces, the mainstream media spun its constant refrain of natural and political calamities, sports highlights or stock market scams. But until recently, there was a lingering sensitivity that without music, dance, theatre and art, there could be no song in life, or the means to wing above the prosaic, to see a pulse of life throb beyond the reports of accidents, deaths, rape, ministerial speeches (and now Page 3 socialite evenings).

Why, then, do I make a case for writing on the arts? Because I have found from personal experience in the media since June 1976 (that is, midway through the Emergency) that bad news is headline news. Prolonged exposure to the Kanishka crash, the Soweto riots, the Gujarat pogrom, the Kutch earthquake, the Orissa cyclone and other 'big news' can cause even the most sensitive individual in the profession to subconsciously develop a skin as tough as rhino hide.

That is where the less hardcore aspects of journalism can significantly alter the overview for both the practitioner and the eventual reader. So, a feature could be about why a dancer like Chandralekha has shaken the Indian dance firmament to its core, re-inventing classical forms, infusing them with feminist perspectives within a contemporary mindset. Or, as a corollary, why younger contemporary dancers like Navtej Singh Johar and Tripura Kashyap, breaking away from pioneers like Narendra Sharma or Astad Deboo, are emerging from the classical forms that originally moulded them.

Writing about their lives, their triumphs over enormous social and economic constraints, the feature writer/reporter realizes some salient facts. That a life in the arts can prove as fascinating and as fantastical as upheavals in politics or the hero-for-the-day scenarios in sports. That, like TV journalism and its condensed bytes, the arts are rapidly losing ground in the print media in our age of sensationalism and 300-word pieces. This is attributed to lower reader attention spans, a fact not yet scientifically proved, or the onslaught of video and online media. Yet it seems irrefutable that a brilliant theatrical production by a genius like Manipuri director Ratan Thiyam (think *Ritusamharam* or 'Nine Hills, One Valley') can outlast the impact of low spirits sparked by news of an Indian loss at cricket or a man poisoning his family over a devastating business crash.

Why, then, has space for the arts in the Indian media shrunk since about 2000? Does this reflect a lack of public interest in these creative spirits? Or a decision by business interests, as commerce rears its head, that culture does not pay its way as journalism?

Or could it be that young blood coming into journalism is more interested in video values and TV cues than in the centuries-old foundations of the Gwalior *gharana*, the *dhrupad* style and the Dagar family, or the *Koodiyattam* of Kerala, the last bastion of Sanskrit drama? These value systems, not necessarily to be seen in black-and-white terms, could reflect a generational divide or a crossover media phase where the market is tested for what sells by the easiest route, where capsule journalism—in easily digestible nibbles—is on offer throughout the Indian print market.

But that has not always been the main story. Even recently, the life and times of a M S Subbulakshmi did make the front-page headlines. But then, she was truly unique, both as an individual and as a singer nonpareil. Similarly, Bangalore dailies as diverse as the *Times of India* and the *Hindu* splashed news of performances by Sting and Mark Knopfler, both golden oldies as performers, on their front page.

The obverse face of the current cultural phenomenon vis-à-vis the media is equally radical. The print media goes to town when Arundhati Roy turns down a Sahitya Akademi award for *The Algebra of Infinite Justice*, a collection of her essays. Her letter is highlighted in great detail. But the media refuses to engage in a campaign when *shehnai* maestro Bismillah Khan is in dire straits. Why do we in India not elevate our arts' greats and nurture them as 'Living National Treasures'—as Japan does, even for its master potters? No easy resolutions here.

Since I have chosen to concentrate on arts journalism as a practitioner, what values have kept me going? A focus on the small as beautiful, such as giving the outstanding Madhubani painter, the late Gangadevi, as much time and space as a mega-selling artist like M F Husain. Gangadevi was just back from the Festival of India in the US when we met for an interview on behalf of the *Indian Express* in Chennai in December 1985. Small, frail and gap-toothed, her charm lay in the feisty spirit that took her to America with her senses wide awake. What was the result? The Padma Shri awardee rendered the US in her art as few contemporary artists ever have.

What did Washington look like to her, following conducted tours during her months there. As her *desi*-nibbed pen touched handmade paper, the vividness of memory springs to life. A tower spirals down the centre, with a top-hatted man at the entrance, queuing up for an elevator ride to the top. What does he see there through Gangadevi's eyes? Queues for tickets; sightseers in a bus; cars and people in immaculate rows; a seated man munching an apple; flags atop masts aplenty. The attire and locales are all American, the faces pure Madhubani.

In that encounter, long before globalization set in, we discovered that the world was shrinking at an amazing pace. That art was not an urban preserve, and that traditions as old as the 3,000-year-old Madhubani art can re-invent themselves, given the right impetus. That prices can soar as supply keeps pace with demand, once the Krishna Leela traditionally rendered on the plastered walls of the *kobar ghar* (nuptial chamber) was transplanted to the Crafts Museum in New Delhi and climes overseas.

The interview with M F Husain of 9 May 1981 in the *Indian Express* was similarly an eye-opener, which puts in perspective the buzz in corporate India when the Mumbai-based Swarup Group of Industries bought 125 of the 89 year-old artist's paintings for Rs 100 crores in 2004. This raised issues that are debate-worthy. Does the Indian media give Husain more than his due because of his colourful personality and because he is frequently in the eye of a storm? Or is it that the corporate sector considers him a solid investment because his talent is really phenomenal?

In 1981, Husain was in the throes of reinventing himself through an exhibition of his photographs (not paintings) of the Madras cine-hoardings at the Sarala Art Centre. Shooting over two days with two rolls of Kodak colour film in 1980, what did his lens record? Women queuing up outside a marquee that features an outsized Tamil mega-star, Rajnikanth. Two giant faces from Richard Attenborough's *Gandhi* looming large over a family sipping tea on the footpath. A set of erotic film posters, some peeling off the wall, as a forlorn mother wanders by with her child over her shoulder on the road.

Is this man, then, an artist, no matter whether he chooses to express himself on film, through the camera, or with the brush? Does this show indicate nostalgia for his past as a billboard painter? Perhaps it does. For, in a revealing answer, Husain responded with a social slant, 'The film industry treats them [the poster painters] shabbily. Their plight is similar to that of the artists of the ninth and tenth century in Europe, before Giotto. They are considered as artisans, not as individuals or creative entities.'

That spurred Husain on to reminisce about his early days. Recalling his hoarding painting phase, he said, 'Yesterday, I went to see the hoarding painters here. They had huge boards and buckets of paint. I had an impulse to pick up a brush and join them ... I began as a poster painter in Bombay. I painted hoardings for four years. It gave me tremendous confidence. You have to work very fast. There is no time to be afraid. No time to sit and think.' Ruminating, he continued, 'That old habit remains. I still sit down and paint on the floor at one go. It gives me a different optical perspective'[1]

Is that not a whole new take on India's most iconic contemporary artist today? This is a man who makes news every time he picks up his brush (or even his paintbrush-shaped walking stick, for that matter!).

Interviews are a primary conduit to some of the most brilliant creative minds in the arts. But an interview seldom works without some essential inputs, such as in-depth research into the subject and evolved interpersonal skills, including a genuine ability to listen. Unlike TV, where aggression seems to be the norm when a face-to-face bout occurs, in print, despite deadline constraints, a more rounded picture should emerge, allowing for some introspection on the writer's part. That, of course, is if space allows for the sharing of an intelligent interface.

A little bit of luck goes a long way on the arts beat, as I know from experience. How else did I happen to share the same space and time slots as some movers and shakers of this sphere? These include American folk music legend Pete Seeger (he is the one who made 'We shall overcome' hugely popular through the world); the *enfant terrible* of global contemporary dance, Merce Cunningham; John Cage, who often composed according to the laws of chance; and Paul Theroux, before he had his newsworthy spat with future Nobel laureate V S Naipaul.

On home turf, it helped that my very first interview was with a living legend: Kamaladevi Chattopadhyaya. This was a woman who lived life according to her own rule book, one to whom we owe accolades because, without her commitment in the field, none of our homes would be adorned with stunning embroidered pieces from Kutch or Punjab, *kalamkari* art from Masulipattinam, or even silk-fine straw mats from *Pattamadai* in Tamil Nadu. That is a story to which our media has still not done justice.

An arts writer can, if culturally enabled, recast the public vision of what constitutes the arts. For instance, is there any reason not to consider R K Laxman, the defining Indian post-Independence cartoonist, as an artist? He has rendered brilliant wash drawings of crows at shows that were sold out at Mumbai, Chennai and even Dubai. Should we not lend an ear when artists like Mumbai's Navjot and the late Altaf voice their concerns over communal disharmony through installations, or when they passionately feel that there can be no art without political consciousness? Could that be the reason why Navjot chose to go to Bastar for years in the 1990s, to work with tribal artists on an equal footing, sharing their collective output at galleries in Mumbai and Japan, dividing all income equally with them, thus bridging the urban–rural divide? Is there any reason why Dashrath Patel, India's first internationally recognized designer, is not given his due either as an artist or as a photographer?

The media, in retrospect, seems to have neglected major talent while reorganizing its priorities in the light of market studies. What are these priorities? They include the focus on Bollywood, even Aishwarya Rai's private life, rather than the Jehangir Art Gallery; the insinuation of figures on advances received by new authors in bidding wars, with few cues to the real talent of a

Vikram Seth, a Vikram Chandra or a Lavanya Sankaran; the creation of an artificial buzz about Naipaul's glamorous love life, in lieu of recognizing his literary saga through *Magic Seeds* and what it means within his oeuvre.[2]

That brings us to another vital aspect of arts writing: the review. At its most superior, it was practiced by Pauline Kael, the film critic of the *New Yorker* from 1967 to 1991. Her reviews of films like *The Godfather, The Sound of Music* and even *A Passage to India* are relevant today because she pushed the envelope on reviewing with her knowledge, her strong opinions and her individualistic personality. So much so that her reviews are today studied in film schools and writing classes alike. For, as Kael once wrote, 'In the arts, the critic is the only original source of information. The rest is advertising.'[3]

How true this is—whether the statement applies to painting, films, music or even fashion. For a star rating system or hyperbolic expression or a mere retelling of a story does no justice to these art forms. And yet that is the way the large mass of the Indian media practices this art form within journalism. In the absence of any practitioners of the calibre of Kael within the Indian profession, we might as well take our cue from this grande dame of American cine criticism, 'I believe that we respond most and best to work in any art form (and to other experience as well) if we are pluralistic, flexible, relative in our judgments, if we are eclectic.'[4]

Any critic worth her ink (or column centimetres) could spend a few minutes mulling over that. For aren't films like *Rang de Basanti* or *Black* or *Hum Aapke Hain Kaun....!* worth critiquing in terms of cinematic values, acting potential and innovation (or lack of it)? Is not a theatrical exposition like Naseeruddin Shah's *Katha Collage* worth dissecting from multiple perspectives besides performances onstage? Do the stories he chose make the transition to performance pieces? Does the staging stumble because many members of the audience in south India do not understand Urdu? Or does sheer theatre craft see it through?

But reviews of art are an even tougher terrain. Most critics—with exceptions like Charles Fabri—tend to mask their regional or art movement loyalties with jargon, doublespeak and dense verbiage, through which the sunlight of shared perception rarely seeps. Why do audiences today shy away from art galleries, though they flock to the cinema and the theatre, even to the circus?

Why do they buy art at auctions with an eye to future big bucks, without the faintest clue about what constitutes good art?

If the public at large is not cued into the pain and the passion that imbues the arts, is the media to blame? If pages devoted to debates on the history, the issues and the creative personalities who enrich our lives have vanished from the mainstream media, whose loss is it? If popular gossip from filmdom, if footnotes from celebrity lives, if mega advances to rising literary stars are seen as more worthy of space than reviews of their work, does this signal a new arts order in the media? Or is this just a realigning of perspectives on what constitutes page-worthiness in print?

As a practitioner, I cannot deny that writing on the arts has proved more challenging to me than reporting or subbing copy, no matter how earth-shaking the news focus. Beyond the constraints of who, why, where, when, how, my colleague Sandhya Rao and I at the *Indian Express*, Chennai, found that when writing up an interview with an actress and a director from the Trinity theatre repertory company from Rhode Island, US, in 1981, we could find our own voices.[5] We transformed 27 pages transcribed off our tape into a play-like script, with stage instructions to boot. This was a piece that found reverberations among readers of the 'Saturday Page' of the *Indian Express* in Chennai in the early 1980s. Can news copy ever match this kind of thrill?

The arts beat brought into my path people who have illuminated what constitutes a life of viable beliefs to me. These include Badal Sircar, who ushered in the contemporary Indian theatre revolution late in the last century, along with his peers like Vijay Tendulkar, Mohan Rakesh and Girish Karnad. Why did he choose to move beyond proscenium theatre? Why did this non-conformist choose radical reforms? Even in this day of instant communication, his response rings true:

> Feedback from the audience is essential. That's why I came out of the proscenium theatre because I felt it had too many barriers. Barriers of artificial distance, of labels, of light and darkness ... I wanted to be near the audience. I wanted it to be man-to-man communication. That is also why I believe in free theatre. Because I don't think this commercial arrangement of buying and selling tickets is conducive to human action. And I hate that arrangement whereby the audience is classified according to paying capacity. I would much rather beg for money or pass the hat around later.[6]

In our outrageously commercial times, is not that worth thinking about?

Arts writing in the Indian media is besieged today, with news space being sold to boost the coffers; and politics, business and sports being highlighted as prime fare (each with a profitable bottom line, no doubt). The popular is being recycled for mass consumption, instead of explorations into the alternate, the rare and the brave who seek to render an explored ideational world. No wonder young readers today have so few icons to look up to—sports, pop music and movie stars apart.

Perhaps the last word on the ongoing arts media crisis should be left to the legendary Pete Seeger. During our encounter in Bangalore on 13 November 1996, this is how he summed up a world view that offers hope for our media in crisis:

> If there's a world in a hundred years, it will not be because of any big organization. It'll be because of millions of little organizations. And we'll disagree about so many things, it'll be hilarious. But we'll agree about two things. It's better to talk than to shoot, right? And bombs always kill innocent women and children .... When words fail, and they will fail from time to time, well, I say: Try the arts, pictures, rhythms, dancing ....[7]

Is anyone listening in the big media world beyond the fragile realm of the arts?

Notes

1. Aditi De, 'The Camera, His Brush' (Interview with M F Husain), *Indian Express*, Chennai, 9 May 1981.
2. V S Naipaul, *Magic Seeds* (New York, Knopf, 2004).
3. Pauline Kael, *Newsweek*, 24 December 1973.
4. Ibid.
5. Sandhya Rao and Aditi De, 'Where Movement Beats Sound', *Indian Express*, Chennai, 17 October 1981.
6. Aditi De, 'Footprints in the Sand' (Interview with Badal Sircar), *Indian Express*, Chennai, 13 September 1980.
7. Aditi De, 'Deep in my heart ...' (Interview with Pete Seeger), *Deccan Herald*, Bangalore, 13 November 1996.

13

Writing on Art

Geeta Doctor

Art remains one of the last surviving mysteries of the modern world.

Writing about it can be as exhilarating an adventure as sky-diving, or as prosaic as brushing and flossing one's teeth at night, or as demanding as a love affair. You can make it as rigorous as a scientific document seeking to unravel the secret lives of voles, or as woolly as a fair isles cardigan knitted by an amateur. In short you can make it whatever you like as long as you keep in mind one basic quality—you have to be passionately involved in the subject.

Art has been a part of the earliest language of human beings. It has been used by them to communicate ideas about the world in images that have taken on magical qualities in the form of signs and symbols that have through repetition conveyed a sense of belonging and identity to the people who have used them. The earliest forms of this pictorial writing have been pressed on the walls of caves, with colours made out of the blood of animals that have been killed during the hunt, or from a mixture of animal fat and pigments ground from the plants and earth around them. It has been scratched on bone, imprinted onto clay and, as technology progressed, woven into fabrics that have been dyed and painted, knotted with beads, shells and feathers, embroidered and embellished with abstract patterns and regular geometric shapes, and filled with forms of animals, birds and human beings in action, as though to remind the people of a particular tribe or region, so that they may at all times remember who they are and where they belong.

It has been used to celebrate and record events. In times of plenty, art has been a badge of prosperity, designed to create an aura of glory and pomp around the image of a person—in the old days a king, a church or a community; and today a city centre, a business magnate or a corporation. It has been used to forge a bond between people, or as we may say today, give them an identity. In the process, art has also become a deeply satisfying and creative form of self-expression—a 'this is who I am' way of describing a person's feelings about herself or himself and that person's view of the world.

The mind looks for patterns. It searches for repetitive forms that can then be counted and assimilated into a mathematical order as a means of getting a sense of being in control of the world. There is a certain soothing effect that is conferred by the idea of a harmonious pattern that can be created by the human mind and hand. Art caters to these instincts. The need to recognize the texture, colour and shape of things during the hunter-gatherer phase (no less than the later agricultural phase) was an essential part of survival. In these primitive societies, the artists were often shamans or persons endowed with the ability to read signs and predict the future. At the same time, it is interesting to note how the most striking pieces of art that come to mind are those that deal with subjects such as death or destruction.

If not images of the Agony of Christ that forms the core of Christian iconography, or paintings such as Picasso's 'Guernica' that was made after the horrors of the Spanish Civil War, such examples from the past are always with us: *Mahishasuramardhini*, or images of the goddess killing the demon with the head of a buffalo, or even Shiva in his magnificent dance—'Shiva *Tandava*'—stamping out the demon of ignorance while celebrating the idea of a universe filled with his energy. Equally, we have images of fertility that suggest the cycle of life in all its splendid variety, whether as the sun, the moon and the verdant landscapes, or portraits that depict a 'Mother and Child', or in representations of the bounty of nature in the 'still life' studies of fruits, vegetables and bottles of wine and hunks of bread, fish and poultry, which indicate how artists through the ages have always kept close to nature.

In a very different way, artists continue in this role by creating new ways of looking at the world. The manner in which an artist manipulates different kinds of materials through his or her imagination creates blueprints for the future. With the discovery of the 'subconscious' and the idea that there could be a type of unconscious thinking that links all the people of the planet together in a common way of responding to certain stimuli, artists were amongst the first to explore these very subtle states of experiencing the world around them in a visual manner that could be shared with others.

Writing about art can touch upon any and all of these aspects. It depends on where you are writing and for what kind of an audience. To an artist the work is the message. The art historian or critic makes the message easier to grasp by looking for a context in which to understand and appreciate the work of art. There are many different ways in which a work of art may be understood. There are the aesthetics of art; the history of art; the unique qualities that different people across the world have interpreted through their art and which could lead to a comparative study of art; and all the different movements in art that have given rise to the dramatic methods and techniques that have transformed and continue to challenge the ways in which artists perceive the world.

In today's world there is also the commercial aspect of art. Art reflects the society in which it is produced. In a capitalist-dominated, materialist society, art too becomes a celebration of these values. In a scientific and technological society, art automatically looks for the new inventions created by LEDs (Light Emitting Diodes), for instance, or fibre optics, or transmitted at increasingly fast speeds through the digital highway in sound bytes and gigabytes. The writing will obviously have to keep pace with these developments.

It was during the time of the Industrial Revolution in the West that people began to look at art as being separate from society. Phrases such as 'Art for Art's sake' and 'A rose is a rose is a rose' delinked the experience of art from its traditional role as glorifying a certain religious group or royal family. The rise of the individual artist as against the collective experience of the group created the image of the lonely genius struggling to express himself or herself in an alienating world; and this has created its own mythology. There is an equal amount of interest in the artist as in his or her work, particularly soon after the person's death. One has only to mention the name of Van Gogh, the tormented Dutch artist, who was so traumatized by his struggle to keep painting that he lopped off one of his ears; this is as well known as his own portrait of this incident. Equally fascinating is the knowledge that an artist who was so unsuccessful in his life time that he could barely manage to sell one of his works is now not just one of the most reproduced of painters in the world but that his individual pieces such as 'Irises' and the portrait of his personal physician, who was treating him for his bouts of manic depression, have fetched the highest prices on the art market. There is now as big an industry devoted to the lives of the persons who produce the work as to the work itself. The art historian is also a biographer.

While there are many reasons for writing about art as art itself, one could summarize them under a simple formula. A for appreciation—without a basic affinity for art, it would be useless to write about it. B for beauty—the purpose of most artistic endeavour is to create an instinct for that which is beautiful and eternal; a person writing about it should have the same sense of searching for this quality. The manner in which it is written should also reflect the need for beauty of expression, balance and harmony. C for context—every art is a product of a certain time and place; it helps if a writer can place it in its right setting. D for description—even if there are visual accompaniments, it helps if a writer also provides a commentary on what the painting or work of art is all about.

Art may be about seeing the world in a totally new and fantastic way. Writing about it clarifies the picture.

14

Pun Job, Sind, Gujarat, Maratha: Humour in Indian Journalism

Baradwaj Rangan

A common pledge in Indian schools is the one that goes 'India is my country ....' It could have well been 'India is my comedy ....' Our great nation is nothing if not a daily catalogue of every imaginable kind of humour–irony, slapstick, satire, farce, black comedy, toilet humour, and surreal or even absurdist comedy. Look at our traffic, our roads, our infrastructure, our politicians, our maidservants, our neighbours, our parents, our relatives, our film stars, our everything else. It is a wonder babies still cry when born in our country; you would expect them to slide out with smiles, a ready-made joke on their lips. (Knock, knock. Who's there? Baby. Baby who? Baby C D E F G H ...)

Yet humour is the one thing that is used only occasionally when we write about our nation. (That is, without considering unintentional humour of a spelling or grammatical mistake, say, or the sort of pompousness that spurs otherwise competent writers to substitute 'pulchritude' for the perfectly simple, perfectly valid, and much more understandable 'beauty'.) We get indignant, apoplectic, caustic, and a lot of other things, but if you are looking for a funny commentary about the state of our country, you will have only the cartoons to contend with. Otherwise, you will see humour columns–special spaces allotted to discuss the events of the day, week or year, with a dose of the comic. They are two almost separate, monolithic entities: To your left, ladies and gentlemen, you have the serious writers; and to your right, you have the funny men (and women).

The intent of this chapter is not to propose a new style of writing for the print media–'Funny Facts,' or 'Jolly Journalism'. There are surely stories that are meant to be treated seriously–and only seriously. I do not intend to say that when there is a devastating earthquake in the Middle East, for instance, we are in dire need of an article that is headlined 'Sheikh, Rattle and Roll'. That is a tragedy, the opposite end of comedy. But how about a story detailing the ban of mobile phones on college campuses being headlined 'Students, Don't Buy a Cell!' That would be coverage of a serious issue, but with a sarcastic touch–the idea being not to make readers roll with laughter as much as alert them into recognizing the absurdity in the situation. Along with the headline, maybe the text too could, at points, nudge into the ironic, the satirical.

Television seems to do this more and more (a news segment extolling the virtues of the Value Added Tax was titled 'VAT's the Good Word'). The journalism there is more chatty, more informed by the need to entertain (as opposed to merely educate), perhaps because the medium is that of moving images, and when we think 'moving images', we think 'movies', i.e., entertainment. (That, along with a lack of time, could be why more and more people are getting their news from television.) In contrast, the Indian print media takes itself very, very seriously. That is because the average Indian writer takes himself very, very seriously, and that in turn is because our society takes itself very, very seriously.

The reason the average Indian writer takes himself very, very seriously is perhaps that the average middle class Indian who is not a writer is either a lawyer or a doctor or an engineer or a scientist or a businessman or an MBA. These are all people in professions that are reflexively seen as more valid, more substantive, more worthy than being a writer. To explain this better, we could look at one of the great Indian traditions: the arranged marriage. 'My son is a financial analyst with Anybank' versus 'My boy is hacking it out as a correspondent with the *Daily News*.' You don't need to be an investigative reporter to figure out the answer. Could that be why our writers are so serious, because they are already at the lower end of the professional hierarchy and because being seen as some kind of joker would be their one-way ticket to lifelong bachelorhood? Or have our readers, over the years, been so trained to look at news as didactic blocks of information, whose sole purpose is the delivery of information, and not the delivery of information in a manner that sometimes–when the context permits–also entertains.

We do not trust humour, period. Take any field–advertising, for instance. There is the hilarious television commercial for Fevicol where an angler by the riverside, and with all kinds of paraphernalia, has presumably spent all day waiting in vain for a bite, when a local upstart sneaks up beside him, dabs spots of the advertised glue on to what looks like a twig, immerses the contraption into the water, and walks away with the fish he has thus caught. Now, this is an established brand, and this commercial merely played up a message that everybody knew. But had it been a new entrant in the market, the commercial would have surely gone along these lines: screen gets divided in two; left half shows a broken vase being mended with 'ordinary glue'; right half shows said vase being mended with Fevicol; the vase on the left hand side breaks again; the vase on the right does not, because it has extra-strength GREIPNFC or POQWAKL (you never really know what these acronyms really mean) molecules that ensure lifetime binding. The assumption is that if the message is new, give it to them straight. Applying this analogy to journalism, since most news is 'new' it is given to them straight. And because it is straight, it is not cheerful or humorous.

Another reason could be the deadlines. With stories coming up every hour of every day, with headlines to be written, copy to be edited, people to be met, data to be researched, it is sometimes easier to just dish it out without any frills or fancies. It is very easy to fall flat while trying to be funny–not everybody agrees on what constitutes good humour, and the worst ego deflator, especially for a 'serious' writer, is to be told that what he has just written does not work. That may well be the case–one of the most difficult commands to issue to the brain is 'think funny'–but that does not make it any easier to take, especially when the juniors are sniggering behind your back about what a joke (the wrong kind) the story is. It is hard enough to craft a story that conveys all it has to and does so simply and solidly, so why complicate things by over-reaching?

A lot of it is also cultural. In school, we grow up with Tom Sawyer and Robinson Crusoe and Shakespeare; and humour, if any, is only in the odd poem by Ogden Nash. Why, even the comics we grow up with are not exactly comic: Phantom and Mandrake and Bahadur and Flash Gordon and *Amar Chitra Katha*. Ah, *Amar Chitra Katha* did have funny stories, but even there, as when the issue dealt with stories from the *Panchatantra* or the *Jataka* Tales, the humour was tied to a homily. In other words, it is okay to laugh, but only if there is a life lesson attached. (Perhaps our movies illustrate this best. We make very few outright comedies. Most of what passes for humour exists as a laugh track that pops up periodically to punctuate the main, serious story.) And after growing up, when aspiring to be writers, we are shown the examples of the *New York Times* and the *Washington Post*— sound, but hardly silly.

Is that why the silly stuff is all in the silly columns? 'How I Learnt to Drive While Clutching a Newborn and Simultaneously Rattling off the Recipe for Paneer Butter Masala to my Sister Do- ing her Master's in the University of Nebraska'—that sort of thing. Slice of life, it is called. It is the journalistic equivalent of a 'Sardarji' joke—the one community we have that seems to have a definite sense of humour, God bless them! The papers are full of such outpourings, all stacked neatly in the last few pages. The progres- sion is presumably to indicate that the reader is done with all the serious stuff, and is therefore now permitted to unwind a bit (either that, or as a reward for all that unrelenting grimness, get yourself some grins).

The other thing is that our society, for all its Westernization, is essentially Indian—especially beyond the metros. We are taught from a young age to respect elders, to be nice, to not make fun of others. In the United States too, parents surely teach their children these core growing-up ideals, but the society there is much more irreverent. There, an entire culture of humour thrives on making fun of the people in office. Nothing is sacred. Here, almost every- thing or everyone is. Offend a film star and he may never speak to you again. Offend a sportsman and those free VIP passes may just end up in someone else's hands. Offend a politician and you may never work in this town again. That is why it is a likely bet that even a story about something as innocuous as a morning interview with the Prime Minister will not be headlined, 'A.M. Session With PM.' What you will likely see is a quote from the meeting, or 'Prime Minister Meets City Journalists'.

The other cultural aspect is that we are taught that it is just not right to laugh at people. So while we–serious writers that we are–do not want to become the butt of a joke, neither is it nice to make someone else the butt of a joke. Occasionally, certain characters crop up on the cultural landscape who become acceptable targets: Laloo Prasad Yadav or Mallika Sherawat or Parthiv Patel. But catch someone doing the same with Sonia Gandhi or Amitabh Bachchan or Rahul Dravid. Those are the untouchables. They have done great service to the country, and how dare we even *think* of belittling their greatness by using humour in a story about them!

With all these constraints and conditions, is there any practicality to the notion that humour could–and perhaps should–make greater inroads into journalism? Some newspapers have a long-standing image of seriousness, of respectability. It is a chicken-and-egg question: are they deemed respectable because they are serious, or are they serious because they want to be deemed respectable? We would probably see them shut shop before they consider adding jokes to their journalism.

But in a way, print journalism has become some kind of a joke. There are instant writers on the Web, for instance, who consider the print establishments about as relevant to the times as their fuddy-duddy forefathers, and who are capable of writing–or blogging, as in the case of Internet publications–thoughts and opinions that are cutting and comical, enlightening and entertaining, all at once. Many of them do not have the kind of training or background that would make them suitable for jobs at the offices of newspapers, but perhaps it is this very lack of relevant education–their not knowing about the right way to write (versus the wrong way), assuming that they do know how to write, and well at that–that is making readers tune in to their lively, heartfelt subjectivity.

But is journalism not supposed to be objective? Are facts not more important than the funnies? Is it not enough that the news is involving; does it also have to be interesting? Surely every reader is not defecting to the Web or to television or–shudder, shudder–to the tabloids! Are people still going to wait till the next morning for their dose of the news instead of opting for the easy right-here-right-now option of these other media? With Abhishek Bachchan and Rani Mukerji reading the news–as part of a promotional strategy for their film *Bunty aur Babli*–and apparently having a whale of a time while doing so, will traditional forms of newscast ever be the same again? Should headlines also be punch lines? With newer and more entertaining forms of media breathing down our backs, there is no better time than now for these questions to be asked. Good luck–and may the farce be with you.

Part III

MEDIA IN PERSPECTIVE

15

The Information Revolution and the Emerging Media Ecology[1]

Sashi Kumar

Since the early 1990s the spectre of a new revolution has been haunting us. Variously called the Information Revolution or the Information and Communication Technology (ICT) revolution, it assumes a paradigmatic shift in production processes and relations, the emergence of a new knowledge-based economy, and a quantum leap from an industrial society into an information society. It is an epochal change anticipated as far back as the 1970s in Alvin Toffler's metaphor of a Third Wave,[2] in Daniel Bell's evocation of an emerging white-collar workforce replacing blue-collar industrial labour,[3] and in MIT Media Lab founder Nicholas Negroponte's dizzying vision of a digitally determined world.[4] It has sparked a combative post-industrial discourse that came to a head with Francis Fukuyama's dire predictions of an 'end of history' and a 'great disruption'.[5]

In the first flush of this revolution there were tantalizing opportunities conjured up for developing economies like India. Here was our historic chance to bridge the North–South divide that the Industrial Revolution had left us chafing under. Since the principal and popular instruments of the information revolution— the electronic media and the computer—came to us close on the heels of their application in the West, we could, suddenly, transcend the technological lag of the industrial epoch and move forward abreast of the developed world. In any case 'endism' in history and rupture rather than continuity in the political economy (au Fukuyama) meant that we could all start afresh with a clean slate.

A later variant on the same theme, and particularly in fashion now, is 'flatism': the theory that the entire world is a level playing field with easy enough exits and entrances. Thomas Friedman's history in a hurry 'of the globalized world in the 21st century' seeks to reconfigure the world as flat in this sense.[6] It is a queer mix of anecdotal empiricism and suspended disbelief, which seems to make out that the bonding of exclusive IT enclaves in different countries at different stages of development into a global supply chain makes the world one big happy family. It would be a harmless, idiosyncratic proposition if it were not so callously indifferent to the lived lives of the masses of real people outside this virtual flatland.

Stretching the 'flatness' figure of speech to the media of our times takes us into post-modernist territory, especially in terms of the flattening of heights and depths into one surface sweep. Susan Sontag has pointed out that in the post-Nietzschean tradition 'there are neither depths nor heights but only various kinds of surface, of spectacle.'[7] Roland Barthes too, like Nietzsche, rubbishes the idea of 'depth' as a repository of any concealed meaning,[8] and Jean Baudrillard's take on television as a mirror metaphor reinforces the surface-spectacle dimension of the media.[9] Depth has yielded to breadth and we 'surf' TV channels across a shallow expanse. Seeking our way through the dense clutter of images, we find ourselves stumbling upon the prescient aphorisms of Guy-Ernest Debord. In his *Society of the Spectacle*, Debord observes that in societies where modern conditions of production prevail, all of life presents itself as an immense accumulation of spectacles.[10] Everything that was directly lived has moved away into a representation. Scholars like Pierre Bourdieu have noted how Debord, whose work has remained relatively obscure, was way ahead of his time and how relevant he is to our understanding of the organic role of contemporary media.[11]

The peculiar manner in which the tension between the *represented* and the *real* is abstracted by the represented subsuming or *becoming* the real is not a new problem. As far back as 1841 we have Ludwig Feuerbach, in his preface to 'The Essence of Christianity',[12] pointing out that his era 'prefers the image to the thing, the copy to the original, the representation to the reality, appearance to being.' In our own context, Dushyanta, in Kalidasa's *Shakuntala*, laments the trick memory plays on him:

Like one who doubts the existence
of an elephant who walks in front of him
but feels convinced by seeing footprints,
my mind has taken strange turns.[13]

Post-modernist empathy with the media takes a new turn with the shift from analogue to digital technology. In the new pixellated media environment, McLuhan's soothsaying finds fresh meaning, as when he talks of a dispersed media structure 'whose centres are everywhere and margins are nowhere.'[14] The constructs and methods of the analogue world are jettisoned as we plunge head-long into this digital realm. In the process, the hierarchization of text and the logical cause-and-effect sequencing of content give way to a simultaneity and multiplicity of information bites. In the dominant medium of television this change is manifest in the altered role of the screen as a site where *montage* and *collage* combine at the same time. Live and taped talking heads; inter-vening fast-cut visuals and reportages; layers and tiers of discrete information delivered as charts, financial text or animated graph-ics; insets on the stock or commodities market; news update scrolls; commercial pop-ups and a medley of sound and musical effects … all vie at once with one another for our attention. That is the look of the new-age TV screen, and it demands fairly de-veloped multi-tasking and non-linear ingestion capabilities from the viewer.

The digital-driven speed of the media has converted what used to be seen and experienced as a seamless 'flow' across channels into what Todd Gitlin calls a 'torrent'.[15] The sheer pace of it is self-defeating because there is less and less time and space to even pay attention to it, let alone assimilate the barrage coming at us without let or pause. Attention spans have dwindled to ridiculous lows and the turnover of media generated celebrities seems to keep pace with the rapid rate of obsolescence of the technology itself. The future that Andy Warhol spoke of, when everyone will be famous for 15 minutes, may well be here.[16]

Celluloid cinema too seems reconciled to a makeover, where the depth, resolution and tone of film negative stock all defer to the speed, malleability and, above all, cost saving of digit-ization. The distribution and exhibition ends are likely to conflate with the prototyping of digital release, whereby satellite-fed signals of a new film are tapped and simultaneously screened by appointed cinema theatres.

The Information Revolution, then, with the media as its shifting eye of the storm, is in the melting pot, constantly redefining and reframing even the objective conditions in which it plays itself out. Coming to terms with this evolving media ecology can at best be tentative and open-ended. As first- and second-generation beneficiaries (or victims, depending on how you look at it) in the thick of it, we do not have the benefit of distance to assess how it will all turn out. But it does appear that new dynamics are at work in the information sector, which, combined with the impetus to globalization and the free market, put us on a course whose direction we need to have some sense of.

Two determining features riding tandem in this media situation in a flux are convergence and corporatization. Convergence, in the MIT's Media Lab definition of the term, implies a coalescing of what were hitherto three separate segments—viz., (a) broadcasting and the movie industry, (b) the print and publishing industry, and (c) the computer industry—into a single electronic delivery screen of the future. As it turned out, this became a model for business consolidation, with forward and backward integration. The turn of this century saw a frenetic spate of mergers and takeovers, the first half of 2000 alone recording deals totalling 300 billion dollars. When the dust settled, nine transnational corporations were in control of the global media market: General Electric, AT&T and Liberty Media, Disney, AOL-Time Warner, Sony, Newscorp, Viacom, Vivendi and Bertelsmann. They were, for the most part, also vertically integrated to combine related businesses and convergent technologies. They are a formidable oligopoly with, as media scholar and activist Robert W McChesney points out, cross-holdings of one another's shares and interlocking boards of directors, and are therefore not really in competition with each other.

In his work with the telling title *Rich Media, Poor Democracy*, McChesney points to the converse relationship between the prosperity of the media and the prospect of democracy in the US in a context where the hyper-commercialized content limits the ability of Americans to act as informed citizens.[17] Ben H Bagdikian, in his classic study *The Media Monopoly*, shows how, with the control of the media market by primarily American MNCs, the US sets itself up as a supervening 'ministry of information' in the world.[18] International and multilateral institutions like UNESCO and ITU which, by law and convention, dealt with the media, have been sidelined and their role appropriated by US-controlled mechanisms like the WTO and ICANN. While the aggressive role of WTO in telecommunications and intellectual property rights issues is by now well known, it is instructive to find that ICANN (Internet Corporation for Assigned Names and Numbers), which assigns names and numbers for Internet and Domain Name Systems (DNS), is registered as a not-for-profit private sector corporation under Californian law, bringing it under the control of the US Department of Commerce.

Paradoxically, it was the Direct Broadcast Satellite (DBS) technology of the mid-1980s that liberated television from the control of national governments, and also abetted the process of the dismantling of communist governments in Europe and paved the way for a unipolar world of American supremacy. The collapse of the Berlin wall, and much of the erstwhile Eastern bloc, was hastened as much by DBS signals from the sky as by the internal contradictions on the ground. The American serial 'Dallas' and its received message in the former German Democratic Republic is a case in point. Beamed across the wall from West Germany, the serial had a wide, if surreptitious, viewership in the East. Unfortunately, with the limiting exposure of a closed society, those who watched the ostentatious lifestyle and lavish consumerism depicted by the soap thought that what they saw was what they would get in the West. And even as Marxists saw in the excesses of 'Dallas' a critique of capitalism, for the East Germans–the benefit of subsidized or free housing, gas, mass transportation, health care and education notwithstanding–they constituted the good life in the West denied to them in their system. 'Dallas is cultural imperialism,' the French Culture Minister Jack Lang had declared in 1982. The revolution of rising expectations that brought the Berlin wall down soured, of course, when the bulk of East Germans found themselves refugees in the new unified Germany.

Successive US administrations in the period since the Second World War have consciously promoted American ascendancy in the information sector as a central plank of their foreign policy, spending as much as a trillion dollars till the end of 1990 towards this end. As early as 1946, Assistant Secretary of State William Benton made it clear that 'the state department plans to do everything within its power along political or diplomatic lines to break down the artificial barriers to the expansion of private American news agencies, magazines, motion pictures and other media of communications throughout the world .... Freedom of the press–and freedom of exchange of information generally–is an integral part of our foreign policy.' That this was a specious concern for free flow of information–an American-centric version of it–became obvious when the Reagan administration quarrelled with UNESCO over its espousal of the New World Information and Communications Order (NWICO) and quit the organization, followed dutifully by the UK. The US even elbowed its ally, the UK, out of the race by setting up the communications satellite undertaking, COMSAT, which effectively neutralized the British command of undersea cable.

Behind the rhetoric of freedom of information, as Nye and Owens noted, was the ambition to preside over an information superstructure which would place the US in a position that was 'better than any other country to multiply the potency of its hard and soft power resources through information.'[19] By the same token, behind the corporate control of the media in the US is the pro-active presence of the US administration. Contrary to the popular perception, the multinational media corporations have not flowered out of the free market but are products of state-led growth. The nexus between the state and the firm, which in any other market would be decried as protectionism or interventionism, becomes in the US a compact as much of liberty as of profit. The media that results cannot but carry this qualification.

Noam Chomsky and Edward Hermann in their incisive work *Manufacturing Consent*[20] describe how the mainstream US media constitute a 'propaganda model' defined through a series of five filters: (*a*) size, concentrated ownership, owner wealth and profit orientation of the dominant mass media firms; (*b*) advertising as the primary source of income; (*c*) the dependence of the media on information provided by the government, business and 'experts' funded by these primary sources and agents of power; (*d*) 'flak' as a means of disciplining the media; and (*e*) anticommunism as a national religion and control mechanism. Irrepressibly buoyant and bold on all domestic issues, the American media tend to consensually freeze when it comes to US foreign policy or the American way of life, irrespective of whether the rest of the world wants or needs it.

The Indian media have, happily, acquitted themselves better on this score. Virtually nothing is taboo to the press; a good section of it is not squeamish even on sensitive issues like Jammu and Kashmir, and even excesses by the media are excused as a small price to pay in the cause of democracy. The few overt attempts by the state to control the press, most notoriously during the Emergency imposed by Indira Gandhi, have ended as misadventures and actually made it stronger and more resilient. But over the last few years one cannot help feeling that the market is running away with the media. Apart from the pressures of globalization and liberalization, the advent of the independent cable and satellite regime may have played a significant role in driving the media into the arms of the market.

Cable and Satellite (C&S) Television, enabled by Direct Broadcast Satellite technology, came to India almost by default. The first Gulf war of 1991, fought as much on camera as for the camera, was offered to the world as DBS signals up there, ripe and ready to be picked. A number of low-budget entrepreneurs set up receiver dishes and conveyed the CNN images of the war to subscribing households along cables strung across high-rise buildings in cities and towns. The cable revolution had begun, just like that. Each of these cable operations mushrooming across the country catered typically to not more than a hundred homes. By the time the government began to sit up and take note, it was already a changed scenario.

With the proliferation and rapid spread of cable networks it was only a question of time before alternative channels, programming initially in Hindi and south Indian languages, made their appearance. Since they could not uplink to their satellites from Indian territory, they used uplink stations abroad, from as far away as Russia to facilities in the region in Hong Kong, the Philippines and Singapore. From those ad hoc beginnings cable and satellite has today grown into a mammoth industry. The anonymous *cablewallahs* who first showed the way have, for the most part, been taken over by bigger players. Many of them now find themselves handling the last-mile operations for the big cable companies. As the competition for eyeballs among the satellite channels began hotting up and as television began to stake a claim for a larger share of the advertisement spent, the print media went into a spin trying to reinvent itself. In the ensuing race to the bottom between tabloidized print and dumbed-down television, the net loser is the reader and the viewer.

Although between the two, television must appear more irredeemable, it is in fact print that seems to be in a tailspin from which there is no escape in sight. With price wars having reduced cover prices of most newspapers to token amounts, the reliance on advertisement revenues is fostering a dependency syndrome which may be difficult to break free from. Also, in a situation where the reader as subscriber is not the main or even a substantial source of revenues, his right to be informed as a citizen vies with his role as a consumer in the market for the paper's attention. That the advertiser is more interested in the reader as consumer than as empowered citizen does not make things easier.

This fatal attraction of the market and the consequent alienation from civil society has serious implications for the future of the media themselves. Although in India the freedom of and for the media are not specifically stipulated in the Constitution (unlike the United States where the First Amendment forbids Congress from making any law that abrogates the freedom of the press), they are a derivative right by Article 19 in the Fundamental Rights chapter guaranteeing freedom of expression. Courts have repeatedly reaffirmed this right and civil society has stood shoulder to shoulder with the media whenever they were under threat, whether from the executive, the legislature or the judiciary. Should the media place itself purely at the mercy or bidding of the market, it would forfeit its right to the moral and statutory high ground it has enjoyed all along as a fourth pillar of democracy. It therefore devolves upon the media to reconnect with the public as more than consumers, just as it is a challenge for the people to reclaim the media for themselves.

In television, technological renewal makes the essential difference. After two decades of DBS technology we are already into DTH (Direct to Home) transmission in India and may soon be turning another corner into broadband distribution through the optic fibre grids (of Reliance or BSNL) that crisscross the country, or video streaming on Internet once the bandwidths open up. Subscription revenues in the DBS regime accrue to the distributor as cable operator rather than to the programmer as the television channel. Subscription management in this system has been a blind man's buff with rampant under-declaration of customer lists by cable operators and payment irregularities and losses through the network chain. DTH could change all that and establish a more direct relationship between what the viewer pays and what she gets. With both technology and the advertiser sorting the vast amorphous viewership into tiered and profiled purchasing power segments, a fragmentation takes place which may actually work against dumbing down or least-common-denominator programming, with fare that seeks to meet the different levels of expectation, and sophistication, of different target groups.

In the process, however, television becomes less and less a mass medium or broadcaster and more and more a narrowcaster. It is a model of the medium that runs counter to its normative 'national' role of an integrating social agent. Already we have less and less of each other in our regional language C&S channels. Television is no longer a site for multicultural expression as it was in the heyday of Doordarshan, when, for example, it was possible to get to see films in different Indian languages, subtitled for a cosmopolitan viewership, on the same national channel. On the other hand, the structural devolution has debunked the Delhi-centric paternalistic model and set in motion a regional idiom of the electronic medium, which is an enterprising mix of the local and the global. In this new axis the nation state is no longer the primary framework of reference. The global village has come full circle.

Notes

1. A slightly modified version of this essay was earlier published under the title 'In the melting pot' in *Frontline*, Volume 22, Issue 22, 22 October–4 November 2005.
2. Alvin Toffler, *The Third Wave* (New York, Bantam, 1984).
3. Daniel Bell, *The Coming of Post-Industrial Society: A Venture in Social Forecasting* (New York, Basic Books, 1973).
4. Nicholas Negropnte, *Being Digital* (New York, Vintage Books, 1996). Also see Stewart Brand, *The Media Lab* (USA, Penguin Books, 1988).
5. Francis Fukuyama, *The End of History and The Last Man* (New York, Avon Books, 1992).

6. Thomas L Friedman, *The World is Flat: A Brief History of the 21st Century* (GB, Penguin–Allen Lane, 2005).
7. See Susan Sontag, 'On Roland Barthes', in Susan Sontag (ed.), *Against Interpretation* (New York, Farrar, Strauss and Giroux, 1966).
8. See Roland Barthes, 'Myth Today', in Roland Bathes (ed.), *Mythologies* (New York, Noonday Press, 1972), pp. 109–11.
9. See Jean Baudrillard, 'The Ecstasy of Communication', in Mark Poster (ed.), *Jean Baudrillard: Selected Writings* (Stanford, Stanford University Press, 1989).
10. Guy-Ernest Debord, *Society of the Spectacle* (London, Verso Books, 1998, published in French in 1967).
11. I refer here to Pierre Bourdieu, *On Television and Journalism* (London, Pluto Press, 1998).
12. Ludwig Feuerbach, *The Essence of Christianity*, English translation (Amherst, NY, Prometheus Books, 1989).
13. A K Ramanujan, *Uncollected Poems and Prose* (USA, Oxford University Press, 2005).
14. See Marshall McLuhan, *Understanding Media: The Extensions of Man* (Boston, The MIT Press, reprint in 1994, originally published in 1964).
15. See Todd Gitlin, *Media Unlimited: How the Torrent of Images and Sounds Overwhelms Our Lives* (New York, Metropolitan/Owl, 2003).
16. The actual quotation is 'In the future everyone will be world-famous for 15 minutes.'
17. See Robert W McChesney, *Rich Media, Poor Democracy: Communication Politics in Dubious Times* (Urbana and Chicago, University of Illinois Press, 1999).
18. Ben H Bagdikian, *The Media Monopoly* (Boston, Beacon Press, 1997).
19. Joseph S Nye was former Assistant Secretary for Defence for International Affairs, and William A Owens was former Vice-Chairman, Joint Chiefs of Staff.
20. Noam Chomsky and Edward Hermann, *Manufacturing Consent: The Political Economy of the Mass Media* (New York, Pantheon Books, 1988).

16

In Your Face!
Teaching Broadcast Journalism

Amanda Harper

The subject of teaching broadcast journalism should be set against the backdrop of television in 2006. Mass-produced format television pervades. A successful format devised by the so-called 'creatives' is syndicated worldwide to an audience not hungry but curious about new genres. Those in the 18–30 age group are served a diet of freak shows where the participants, for money, fame or both, are encouraged to act and behave in a way previously considered simply vulgar. Whether it is a talk show, or an Orwellian progeny, the viewer is now the voyeur of an on-screen circus where sex and debasing language are packaged as entertainment. Producers have argued that this is some sort of sociological exercise, proof if it were needed of their scant regard for the viewers' intelligence. Audiences may not be commercially savvy, but even those who barely made it out of the 'Jack and Jill' school of learning must sense something is afoot, and it is not social science! It isn't even a stab at *cinema verite*. As the *Observer* in the UK commented as long ago as 8 September 1963: 'The trouble with *cinema verite* is that it all depends how interesting your *verite* is.'

Subjects that were formerly taboo are now slipped into late-night schedules with the regulator's blessing. My mother in an unguarded moment happened upon a programme late one evening on a UK channel. Although 79 this year, she still has a charming innocence about certain things. 'Amanda,' she announced one evening on the telephone, 'can you believe what they do with animals in America?' Perhaps it was a film about animal rights, performing camels or LA pooch houses, I pondered. I asked her to explain, which she did in graphic detail. Thinking my mother had quietly bought a satellite dish and stumbled on a porn channel while searching for her usual fare of news, history, art and documentaries, I asked where she had seen the programme. She told me that she had been watching the late night feature on an otherwise respectable terrestrial channel in Britain. So into which genre did this particular feature fall? My mother had obviously been out of the room when the 'clear verbal and visual warning' about the film's content was given before it was transmitted.

Jammed in between the *faux* soul-bearing and titillation is the one constant, the news. Like some cantankerous ageing aunt who is grudgingly invited to a family function, she sits uneasily at the scheduler's dinner party muttering her *raison d'être* to inform. She is moved from one part of the scheduler's room to another– perhaps she'll look better at 10.30 PM, and here at least she won't interrupt another grubby edition of *Torture Your Soul*.

News and current affairs are becoming increasingly marginalized. The problem, or so we are led to believe, is that audiences do not have the same appetite for news and programming and television must increasingly appeal to a younger audience. This, in the parlance of television scheduling, means that news gets in the way of the real money generators. The drive for ratings-winning programmes that draw advertising revenue and profits has resulted in news being squeezed. At the same time little has been done to address the thorny issue of public service. So, like the rest of the programming, news too must battle it out for audience share. How is this achieved? The recipe is quite simple. Take one video wall, super-size the set to Hollywood Bowl proportions, buy in some high cholesterol graphics for opening titles, mix liberally with crashing drum and bass music, preferably loud enough to wake the entire mainland of Europe, and garnish with attractive anchors. To this add helpings of celebrity gossip, lifestyle, and sometimes unctuous and sanctimonious storytelling and you have a winner–or do you?

You might think that broadcast journalism has already crossed and drunk from the Lethe, having sold its soul on the way to a passing scheduler. Thankfully there are plenty of excellent, committed journalists who still believe the cause is worth fighting for. Of course a dumbed-down audience filled with popcorn consumerism, where acquisitiveness is the *mantra*, living vicariously through small-screen soaps are ideal fodder for our esteemed leaders and the world's money men who would like to remain unaccountable. After all who wants a questioning audience, let alone a questioning media?

This is how the world wannabe television journalists now find themselves. But it wasn't always so.

As a teenager I remember sitting uncomfortably in my career master's office. 'So what sort of profession are you thinking about entering, Amanda,' he enquired with all the earnest concern of a lay preacher. 'Journalism, sir,' I replied without hesitation. Having decided at the age of 14 that this would be my calling, I was a little unprepared for his response. 'Mmmmm,' deep sigh, 'but journalism isn't a very stable profession.' He looked pained, paused for a second and then asked, 'What about banking?' I stared back blankly, and with growing indignation replied, 'But sir, I am not numerate.' I think the irony was lost on him.

As a youngster I would sit glued to our black-and-white television at home in the UK watching news and current affairs programmes. *Panorama*, *World in Action*, and *This Week* told audiences things they didn't know but which empowered them to demand answers. Journalists John Pilger, Duncan Campbell and the late Paul Foot, with whom I was privileged to work briefly, were granted airtime by broadcasters and column inches by newspaper proprietors to investigate and uncover political scandals and social injustice. It was never an easy co-existence. Investigative journalists are by nature obsessive and meticulous, they devote sweat-stained hours bringing us news the powerful don't want us to see. Journalists are frequently threatened with legal writs, harassed by television regulators, and sometimes receive personal threats. The BBC, which has over the years had various run-ins with government, saw the departure of its Director General, Alasdair Milne, in the 1980s over the *Panorama* programme, 'Maggie's Militant Tendency' which sought to expose right-wing extremists in the party. *This Week* and *World in Action* departed from British television screens some time ago. *Panorama* teeters on the edge, having lost its cherished Monday evening slot, and is now sidelined to Sunday evenings where, with dwindling audiences and without intervention, it will be left to wither on the vine. So with no commitment to current affairs, who exactly is going to ask those awkward questions? Well, we hope the current crop of graduates and postgraduates tumbling out of the many thousands of journalism colleges across the world will do so.

With 20-odd years in print, radio and television trailing me like a forgotten tax demand, I stand once again before an audience, staring not into the black aperture of a lens to deliver a faultless piece to camera (more irony), but this time to a classroom of trainee broadcasters. Television reporting prepares you for a lot; not least talking to small and large audiences. Hair checked, teeth cleaned, nose powdered, script in head, bubbling with enthusiasm, one sets out to teach an afternoon class of postprandial students in various stages of sleep deprivation.

The 'getting to know you' session which kicks off the course usually comprises who I am, where I am from, what I am going to teach, why we are covering certain subjects, and when and how the course will be delivered. 'Any questions?' Silence. 'OK so let's talk about you.' Unusually worried looks are returned, they might have even woken up. So what attracted you to a course in television broadcasting? Sadly too many will answer money first, then fame, or perhaps both. 'What's wrong with wanting to earn money?' ventures a brave soul, so perhaps there is hope after all. 'Nothing,' I say, 'so long as this isn't your only motivation.' Then I go for the killer question, 'What about wanting to change the world?' I get some guffaws and shaking of heads, others just look blank. Such hopeless idealism from one so old must make these fledglings wonder what I have in store for them. It doesn't take them long to find out!

Stepping into a classroom for the first time can be unsettling. The temptation to rush at breakneck speed through a syllabus is very reminiscent of a young television reporter doing a piece to camera for the first time. The words are garbled, the vernacular unclear, the message lost, and all delivered with the expression of a condemned man. There is a saying, 'you can be a good journalist and a good trainer, but you cannot be a good trainer and a bad journalist.' It is important that you have practised at least some of the skills you are about to teach (not preach, please!). The most common problems to afflict the unsuspecting teacher are a sudden attack of nerves, which appear variously as a dry mouth and stumbling or sudden forgetfulness; which country am I in; and the fear of an awkward audience, although I particularly relish the latter!

Passion, enthusiasm, dynamism and humour are some of the virtues which mark out the truly great teachers. I remember one particular teacher at school who was variously strict, funny, sarcastic and just that little bit different. He commanded respect, his students attained good grades, and he in turn gathered plaudits.

Trying to recreate the bustle, stress and sheer adrenalin of a television newsroom standing in an airless classroom devoid of natural light, while speaking to an audience for whom English is not always the first language, might appear a little daunting. But it's not, and a little humour goes a long way. From day one I speak to them not as teacher talking to student, but as an Editor-in-Chief holding a morning editorial meeting with a team of journalists. Bad time management being one of the worst offences, I point effusively to my watch, 'Twelve hours of unbroken sunshine may be your ally but time, or rather lack of it, is your enemy.' Only when they start producing daily news programmes working to strict deadlines does this become clear. On punctuality and attendance I am strict to the point of being tyrannical. Well, perhaps that is overstating it, but do you get the idea?

I liken making television programmes and interviewing in particular to cooking a Chinese meal, long in preparation but short in the delivery. Students often underestimate the importance of good preparation. As any television reporter will tell you, there are times when you have to rely on your own onboard database. Good general knowledge and awareness of the current news agenda is important for any journalist, but vital for a broadcaster who, because of breaking news, often doesn't have time for hours of research. Teaching is much the same. Being prepared with thorough notes and visual aids, knowing your subject matter, anticipating any awkward questions or answers, researching your audience, familiarizing yourself with the room and equipment, and doing breathing exercises to calm your nerves is not unlike the preparation for a television news report. A broadcast journalist uses powerful visuals, strong sound-bites, and clear, conversational writing to produce a television report to hold the interest of his viewer. So a broadcast teacher can't assume students are locked on to every word like heat-seeking missiles, or that they are either listening or understanding. You may hold the attention of your television audience for three minutes, if you are lucky!

Television news writing is an area where students often struggle the most. Writing for broadcast means doing away with literary conventions, including the rules of grammar. To illustrate my point I regularly ask members of the team to describe something they have witnessed in the past week, just as they would talk about it to a friend in a café. We tend to tell a story more simply than we write it. Out go the purple prose, clichés, hyperbole (novelist John Galsworthy once described hyperbole as 'headlines twice the size of the events'), quotes and redundancies. In comes clear, uncluttered, conversational English with contractions, where the voice adds light and shade and where the words complement the pictures. No confabulations please, otherwise the interview is not fructuous! Viewers cannot re-read the pages of a television report as they might in a newspaper, so you have one chance and one chance only to get your story across.

Watching students variously hunched and stooped as they trudged into class one day, I decided to pull up one of the worst offenders. With a broad grin I pointed out that he had the deportment of an ageing septuagenarian and asked what message I should deduce from his body language. As he tried to work out the first bit, I cut to the chase. 'Body language accounts for 55 per cent of communication,' I ventured. With his brain still untangling sept-something, I moved on. 'What if you were doing an interview with a senior politician?' He, still perplexed, shrugged. 'I think they would see you as someone lacking in confidence and self-esteem, who they could probably run rings round, right?' So it is with teaching—bad body language in any classroom can and does send out the wrong signals, as does fidgeting and chair rocking. Keeping eye contact and a smile help to build up a warm rapport, whether you're a teacher or a reporter.

Role-play, question-and-answer sessions, playing devil's advocate, topical references, quizzes and tests are vital if your nuggets of information are to be absorbed. One of the most effective ways is to draw on your fund of personal anecdotes. In my case this ranges from a fairly eclectic mix of stories which include being arrested airside at Heathrow airport, kissed by actor Tony Curtis, interviewing Nelson Mandela and being sprayed with pig slurry (not on the same day, you understand), as well as others too numerous to mention.

All too often students are happy to accept a government press release or corporate handout as truth. A trainee journalist must know what to look for in order to see the real story; or, as I like to say, the headlines behind the headlines. This is particularly apposite in a world of spin and counter-spin where media-trained executives know how to avoid answering tough questions, and where the real story is deliberately hidden.

Television newsrooms need journalists who can assess a situation quickly. This often involves scanning large documents and assessing the contents, knowing whom to contact and where to get the information, and then producing a television report clearly, fairly, accurately and to a deadline. The core values of accuracy and fairness, impartiality, objectivity, balance and straight dealing are constantly under threat. These subjects may be as dry as the Gobi to most students, but by citing examples of how the media has encouraged violence through biased reporting, whether in the Balkans or Rwanda, brings home the message of what can go wrong when the media forgets it has responsibilities as well as power.

If this were not enough, today's news broadcasters are expected to be able to film and edit their own stories. News studios are packed with the latest hi-tech equipment, and anyone who does not understand even the basics will feel like as if they were drowning. Nowadays many news broadcasters are competent at some form of video journalism and some, including myself, have already extended that to documentary film-making. At the same time, audiences are interacting much more with the broadcasters. The London bombings of 7 July 2005 saw the emergence of citizen journalists armed with camera phones, who, in seconds, sent pictures from the scene to news-desks. Both the BBC and commercial channels are localizing more of their news, with the audiences being encouraged to become film-makers. Disintermediation, the new buzz word for audience interaction directly with people who run television, means the public can be consumers and producers, whether this is downloading new shows, broadcasting homemade news stories, or starting a Website or blog. Increasingly the viewer calls the shots, or so we are told. More than ever before, journalism, and broadcast journalism in particular, is under threat from enthusiastic bloggers and non-media Websites that report and publish stories, while at the same time being squeezed by shareholders who want higher returns. But will the new citizen journalists be as rigorous and objective, will the blogger uncover fraud and corruption, can the current crop of Websites mushrooming from the Web be trusted?

My question remains, who will ask the difficult questions? If a television viewer's biggest crime is to be passive, then a journalist's biggest sin in my view is the failure to challenge. Over the years I have seen fawning and sycophancy worthy of Dickens' Uriah Heap. Journalism and overt deference are uneasy bedfellows. Being polite is one thing, but accepting a non-truth because it is spoken by someone in power is quite another. If we as journalists fail to challenge and question, then who will? To question is to err? I sincerely hope not.

17

My Days at Sun TV

A S Panneerselvan

It goes in great swoops, it goes in spirals or in loops, it every so often reiterates something that happened earlier to remind you, and then takes you off again, sometimes summaries itself, it frequently digresses off into something that the story-teller appears to have thought of, then it comes back to the main thrust of the narrative. Sometimes it steps sideways and tells you about another, related story inside a story, then they all come back you see.

–Salman Rushdie

It is imperative that I explain my relations with the *Kungumam* group, the parent organization of the Sun Network in Tamil Nadu, to understand my three years' stint as Managing Editor of Sun TV.

I started writing in 1981, and was determined to be a bilingual journalist. I never looked at journalism purely as a careerist pursuit. I believed, and still believe, that media is a site for democratic mediation of ideas. It is important for any politically sensitive person (but who is not a politician) to reach out to the public directly, to bare open his ideas and views through the dynamics of the media to ensure a place for those ideas to germinate into something more concrete in the domain of public sphere. Not for a minute, did I have any delusions about the media being free from ideas and political orientations. I never subscribed to the concept of neutral, sanitized media and the myth of being 'neutral' repulsed me.

I must add a caveat here: this does not mean distorting facts or creating myths. Furthermore, the sacrosanct line that divides the news and views must be fully respected, even to take forward a viewpoint or an ideological argument to its logical fruition. I believe that anyone who wants a space in the public sphere comes in with a worldview, and with a clear motivation of pursuing that worldview and arguing for it, and is therefore constantly engaged in the process of refining, redefining and enriching that worldview based on empirical evidence and sharpened by intellectual input. The crucial component of my political belief is that there is not a single public sphere, in a Habermasian sense, but multiple public spheres. A journalist can play the role of a mediator of these public spheres only when he operates in more than one public sphere; hence my decision to be a bilingual journalist.

In 1982, I got a call from Paavai Chandran, who was then the editor-in-charge of *Kungumam*, asking whether I would like to write for them. I agreed immediately and that was the beginning of my relations with the Kungumam group. In those days, Kalanidhi Maran, who now heads the Sun Network, was still in school. His father, the late Murasoli Maran, ex-Union Minister affiliated to the Tamil Nadu Dravida Munnetra Kazhagam party, was looking after the media house. Neither I nor anyone else had imagined that India would be freeing its broadcasting and that a young Kalanidhi Maran would emerge as a media mogul. In fact, my interaction was only with Murasoli Maran until 1989.

In the interregnum, the year 1984 turned out to be a genuine Orwellian nightmare. Mrs Gandhi was assassinated, former Tamil Nadu Chief Minister M G Ramachandran was critically ill and undergoing treatment in the US; there was a constant influx of Tamil refugees from Sri Lanka; and the year ended with the worst-ever industrial disaster, the Bhopal Gas Tragedy. These events made such a powerful impact on me that I quit the discipline of science to pursue journalism. It was also a moment when my political belief of being a bilingual writer got an economic vindication. It was very clear that Tamil writings would not fetch me enough money to pursue all my interests and that the salary levels were indeed much better in English language journalism. This is a sad reality in the case of most of the sub-continental languages even today.

While I continued to work in English, I never stopped my involvement with *Kungumam*. In fact, I relished every minute I spent in that compound. Paavai Chandran was a great editor. Murasoli Maran encouraged new ideas and fresh approaches.

One of the lasting achievements of that era was a two-part series: the first series was titled '*Nangavathu Puthaka Kan Kathichiyil Kidaitha Kathaigal*' (the stories found in the Fourth Book Fair). It ran for nearly a year. Almost every important contemporary writer was included in that series. For the first time in Tamil mainstream publications, important painters and artists did the illustrations for stories. These included K M Adimoolam and Trotsky Marudu, who brought in new sensibilities to the visual renditions. Paavai had the energy and persuasive power to get most of the concerned literary figures involved in the series. The second series introduced some of finest Tamil novels of the age to readers. Nearly a score-and-ten major novels were abridged with amazing literary sensitivity and even some of the most finicky critics admitted that the shorter versions did not injure or harm the originals.

The group's other publications were equally engaging. I wrote in *Vannathirai* on major international film-makers. From Ritwick Ghatak and Mrinal Sen to Andre Tarkaovsky and Wim Wenders, these film-makers found a place in that publication. In *Mutharam*, I did a series on the Bhopal Gas Tragedy and later wrote a series on major industrial disasters, including the Three Mile Island nuclear disaster. In fact, this series helped me a few years later to write another science serial for *Junior Vikatan* on nuclear issues.

In 1989, the National Front government came to power and Murasoli Maran was inducted into the Union cabinet. Kalanidhi Maran started his direct involvement in running the *Kungumam* group. Kalanidhi's contribution to Tamil journalism during this period is comparable to G Kasturi's (of the *Hindu*) contribution to English journalism. In the preceding decades, Kasturi modernized the publication scenario in English. Kalanidhi did the same in Tamil, brought in state-of-art machines, and reduced the production time lag considerably. Kalanidhi also took the lead in bringing out supplements for magazines. Until then, only dailies had supplements. Paavai and he asked me to handle a weekly supplement for *Kungumam*, in the size of the now defunct *Illustrated Weekly of India*, a *Times of India* publication.

There are three distinct political narratives in Tamil Nadu: Indian nationalism, the Left, and the Dravidian movement. Indian nationalism, like the Indian media, is not a monolith. It has strands of secularism as well as bigotry. In Tamil Nadu, right-wing Hindutva has always masqueraded as Indian nationalism. I had two problems with the Left: it was highly centralized (and remains so) and it never recognized the power of discrimination when it came to the caste question, though its formulation of the class question was more defined.

The Dravidian movement and its understanding of the caste dynamics inspired me. Its notion of state autonomy and its fight for language rights proved that it showed a wonderful way forward for the entire sub-continent. Imagine Sri Lanka having a federal political structure. There would have been no ethnic crisis and the teardrop-shaped island would have been the pearl of the sub-continent. The Rajamannar Committee Report on centre–state relations remains one of the finest documents on the subject and that report was a direct result of the Dravida Munnetra Kazhagam coming to power in 1967.

It took nearly half a century for the rest of the country to understand the egalitarian import of this movement. In 1990, when the National Front government came to power, it drew heavily from the ideological support of the DMK. At that time, Prime Minister V P Singh told me (in a private communication) that the DMK's support was more crucial to him than even that of some of his own party men. 'In numerical sense it may be insignificant because the DMK had no presence in the Lok Sabha. It stood by me when I decided to lose the government in order to implement some irreversible structural changes to fight inequality and establish social justice. I would not have been able to implement the Mandal Commission's recommendations without the support of DMK. After Independence, this is the most significant political development.'

In 1991, the discredited Chandrashekar government dismissed the Tamil Nadu DMK-ruled government and paved the way for Jayalalithaa's ascendancy. Rajiv Gandhi's assassination in May and the emergence of the P V Narashima Rao–Manmohan Singh duo in the political and macro-economic scene at the centre forced me to continue my career with the *Business India* group. I was recruited for *India Week*, a political magazine from the group, but it folded up and I had an option of either continuing with the group as a correspondent for *Business India* or opting

out. I thought it made immense sense to be with a business magazine when the Indian economy was going through a major shift.
I knew that I would learn a lot about corporate India and its
worldview, which I instinctively knew would dominate the course
of political economy over the next two or three decades.

This was also the period in which the Pink Paper revolution
happened; satellite TV started making its deep penetration; a lot
of lateral induction was happening in the media; and the salary
levels were constantly on the upswing. Samir Jain of the *Times
of India* group emerged as the undisputed media leader; and while
others were critical of his approach, they soon tried to imitate
him. In 1992, Tamil Nadu Assembly Speaker Sedapatti Muthiah
invoked the privilege of the Legislative Assembly against a journalist, K P Sunil, for an article written by him in the *Illustrated
Weekly of India*. But Sunil had left the *Weekly* and joined the
Reliance Group's head Dhirubhai Ambani's short-lived newspaper, the *Business and Political Observer*. Neither his old employer nor his new employers were forthcoming to take up
his case.

I took upon myself the task of defending Sunil. Instead of
meekly surrendering to the powers that be, there were still institutions in the country that would defend his fundamental rights.
It was a heroic struggle. We succeeded in securing a Supreme
Court stay on the speaker's order. One person who stood totally
with me in this case, and had spent many a sleepless night in
planning, strategizing and getting the legal luminaries of the
country to take up our case was the *Hindu's* present editor-in-
chief, N Ram. It was Ram who introduced advocate K S Natarajan
to me; and it was Ram who also secured the support of advocates
Indira Jaisingh and Soli Sorabjee in this mega legal battle—widely
described as the battle between the legislature and the judiciary.

The legal battle also exposed the shifting priorities within the
media. Newspapers were reduced to mere products; magazines
had become brands; and the notion of media as the site of democratic contention was becoming weak. However, there were some
heroic exceptions. Sunil had acquired a halo and we thought it
was the right time to invest that halo in the creation of a new
media organization which would be close to our concerns. I was
extremely impressed by the style and the functioning of the
Alacrity Foundations in Chennai. It had a set of value systems

and ethical practices that was not common among the corporates, especially in the construction and real estate business. Apart from Alacrity's founder Amol Karnad, it had other interesting people at the top. We worked out a blueprint for a weekly magazine and a detailed budget for a weekend newspaper on the lines of Vinod Mehta's *Sunday Observer*, and asked Amol to fund our project. Though Amol and Dr Vijay Nagaswamy, who was then a director with Alacrity and who was instrumental in giving this idea some shape, were determined to support the venture, the Harshad Mehta-led stock market scam derailed the project at that time.

Then we decided to launch our own television company and thus started Telezoom. My friends from the Tamil film world– Ananthu, the erudite scriptwriter and a long-time associate of veteran film director and producer K Balachander, actor Kamal Hassan and music director Illayaraja–were extremely support-ive and gave us the initial leg up. However, within six months it was evidently clear that my notion of the media–be it news or entertainment–differed widely from that of Sunil. It was also a moment of realization that though both of us watched the match with equal interest and admiration, we were supporting two op-posing sides. On All Fool's Day of 1993, I quit Telezoom. I also paid a huge price for this misadventure. I had interviewed Illayaraja for nearly three hours in Colombo, and also filmed his concert in Colombo. Illayaraja was at his eloquent best; he spoke at length about his musical journey. I had this grand idea of pro-ducing a musical biography of the maestro. But everything came to naught and I did not see even a single frame of that exhaustive interview.

Fourteen days after I had quit Telezoom, Kalanidhi Maran launched Sun TV. And, 14 months later, my former employer *Business India* decided to launch a national channel, BiTV. Kalanidhi was a meticulous planner and a hands-on manager. His success lay in the fact that he was never reluctant to apologize for his mistakes and effect a mid-course correction. He first went in for a Russian satellite, with disastrous results, but quickly aban-doned that satellite and shifted to one that had a very good foot-print in the region. There was no major splurge, and the resources were used very carefully. He had a small core team–most of them were either his college friends or his employees at *Kungumam*. There was cohesiveness in his approach. However, the market was not smart enough to understand his genius. It pinned more hope on the channel started by the Tamil Nadu liquor baron Ramaswamy Udayar–Golden Eagle TV–with playwright and *Tuglaq* editor Cho S Ramaswamy as the head of the content. The only outcome of Cho's adventure into television was the opening up of the south Indian media to Rupert Murdoch, as eventually it was Murdoch's Star which bought the channel and renamed it Star Vijay.

The market had pinned high hopes on Business India TV and on Ashok Advani who headed it. Ashok had been a pioneer in his own right, as the first man to anticipate the markets for niche publications. He always managed to get the total respect of his staff, was a liberal and generous to a fault. In 1994, BiTV organized a week-long television training programme in Delhi conducted by Frank Magid Associates of the United States. To my knowledge, no other television company had such a meticulously planned training and induction programme in South Asia. BiTV had everything right: the right attitude, the willingness to spend money on capacity building, the desire to have an inclusive narrative–the only channel which had a culture editor, an environment editor and a development editor. But BiTV remains one of the biggest failures in the 250-year history of the Indian media.

Thanks to Kalanidhi, I realized that BiTV was heading for a major disaster. He pointed out three major flaws in Ashok Advani's business plan. First, Ashok was spending enormous energy and resources to create an earthstation in Nepal. Kalanidhi considered this entire move as one trapped in Mrs Gandhi's model of economic growth and did not reflect the new Narashima Rao–Manmohan Singh economic dynamics. 'If India has to sustain the present boom in the media market, it has to open up its uplinking facilities. It's a matter of time. Please ask Ashok and Mala (Malvika Singh) to refrain from pursuing the earthstation idea,' said Kalanidhi in a private communication to me. Second, there was some confusion and overlap between the entertainment segment and the news segment of the channel. Third, *Business India* was squandering its head-start advantage of being the best business journalism house in South Asia, by not building upon its core strength and permitting CNBC and other players to walk away with its natural client base. After trying in vain for a year to impart to this venture Kalanidhi's more far-sighted understanding of television economics, I moved on to join Vinod Mehta's new venture, *Outlook*.

Many were sceptical about the future of the weekly magazine format. The *Illustrated Weekly of India* had been shut down; *Sunday* was on its last legs; and the leader in the magazine market was a fortnightly, *India Today*. The space for dissent was already occupied by another fortnightly, *Frontline*. Media pundits declared that the featurization of dailies and the rapid strides made by television had made weeklies redundant. It was also the time when editors were vacating their places to accommodate managers, and to have a strong editor like Vinod Mehta was itself seen as an anachronistic move. How we succeeded is a subject matter for another essay. Vinod did provide a wonderful space for us, and the first five years of my stint as Bureau Chief of *Outlook* remain the best days of my journalistic career. The new millennium was not the best news for the media. The Bharatiya Janata Party-led government started not just intimidating journalists but also targeting the owners of media houses. *Outlook* was no exception. The entire senior team could actually sense the pressure from the government and its cohorts.

My days with Sun [TV] started the day the DMK lost power to the AIADMK (All-India Anna Dravida Munnetra Kazhagam) in 2001 and ended the day the DMK-led alliance pulverized the AIADMK-led front 40–0 in the 2004 Lok Sabha polls. Those were three eventful years. Though I had been in journalism for long, I had always worked for a fortnightly or a weekly. I had not even worked for a daily. Television is a 24 × 7 job. The best aspect of running the news section of Sun was its extraordinary network of grassroots reporters across south India. There were more than 400 journalists—some part-timers, some stringers and the rest full-time reporters. It had an excellent delivery system with more than a dozen points for feeding the footage to the central newspool through SNGs (Satellite News Gathering facilities) and a well equiped outdoor broadcast van. It now has news operations in five languages: Tamil, Telugu, Kannada, Malayalam and English. Kalanidhi never thought twice when it came to the issue of investing in technology. Sun Network had a full-fledged, digitized non-linear system for processing and broadcasting news that gave maximum flexibility in terms of putting the news capsules together.

I would like to deal with five specific aspects and one particular episode to explain my days at Sun. The first is the question of dealing with an adverse government and using the network as a platform to protect the rights of journalists and journalism. The second is the question of protecting the integrity of news in the era of corporate sponsorship. The third concerns the political affiliations of the owners, while the fourth is connected to devising the right mix of local, national, regional and international news for an essentially south Indian network. The fifth is linked to the economics of news.

Before explaining the larger five issues, let me explain the single episode for which Sun TV has been rapped on its knuckles quite often. Within a month of my new assignment as Managing Editor of Sun TV, Tamil Nadu Chief Minister Jayalalithaa ordered the disgraceful midnight arrest of the former Chief Minister M Karunanidhi. Our crew managed to film a short footage of the barbarity of the state police before being thrown out of the place. Though we had the footage by early morning, 1.30 AM, we decided that we would not disturb people with the footage right away and deny them their sleep. We went on air only at 6 AM. Many people were shocked by what they saw on television, although a section of media remained hostile. For the first time, a journalist crew was accused of being present at the site. 'How did Sun TV manage to get the footage?' was the most ridiculous question posed to us. Instead, the right question would have been why others failed to be at Karunanidhi's home when a former chief minister was pulled out of his bed at the dead of the night and arrested in total violation of the Supreme Court directives in this regard.

We were accused of overplaying the arrest footage. Who decides what the ideal duration of any news capsule is—the editors of the channel or its bitter critics? The BBC went on with the single event of Princess Diana's death for four days; the US networks went on and on for nearly two years covering the O J Simpson episode; the 11 September attack was on air for nearly four weeks; but six hours of sharp and effective coverage of a blatant human rights violation was projected by a section of media as overplay. What would have been the reaction of this section of media, which was, and is, hostile towards Sun, if we had treated Karunanidhi's arrest as yet another news event? We would have been damned for carrying on with our usual business. We realized that we were damned either way in the eyes of these critics, and we decided to go ahead and do what we thought was right and just.

The state repression that started with Karunanidhi's arrest continued till the electoral reverse in 2004. It was during this phase that Sun TV had become the platform for rallying support for journalists, writers, human-rights activists and others from the resistance movement. *Nakheeran* suffered the worst fate and I am pleased to recall here the central role Sun TV played in defending the journalists of this subaltern Tamil publication. I spent many nights discussing the issues with journalists' organizations, lawyers and editors, and I am grateful to Kalanidhi for giving me the space to continue this fight. The last straw in the war against the media was the breach of legislative privilege motion against the *Hindu* and *Murasoli*, a Tamil publication. It was a moment where past, present and future coalesced to create grey. While N Ram was in the forefront defending the editors and the journalists of the *Hindu*, I was handling the problems at *Murasoli Selvam*. Journalists of every hue—starting from cub reporters to editors and newspaper owners—joined us in our struggle. It got the support of major political parties of the country. In one of my in-house reviews of Sun Network's current affairs and news content, I discovered that during the first two years of my stint as the Managing Editor, we had devoted nearly 22 per cent of our airtime for the protection of the freedom of expression.

Sun Network has 13 channels and the major source of revenue is from advertising. But that did not deter us from taking on the corporate giants. Due to lack of space, let me confine myself to just two major cases that happened during my tenure. The first direct conflict with the corporate world was with the soft drink majors: Coca-Cola and Pepsi. The soft drink majors are substantial sponsors for the network. But that did not deter Surya TV, a Malayalam Channel of the Sun Network, from breaking the Palachimada water extraction controversy against Coca-Cola. And when this was followed by the Delhi-based Centre for Science and Environment Report on pesticide residue in its products, the current affairs team in all the languages of the network were highly critical of the corporates. Kalanidhi's position was that the corporates come to Sun because of its reach and popularity. The reach and popularity comes from the fact that the team is doing a professional job. 'If they want to pull out their advertising, they will be the losers,' he declared in a private communication to me. During my tenure, Hindustan Lever was the single largest advertiser for the network. One of my young recruits from the Asian College of Journalism, Satya Reddy, did a feature on mercury dumping by the Lever's Kodaikanal plant. In retrospect, it emerged that we were the only television network to take on Hindustan Lever, despite their being the single largest advertiser for our company.

The tricky question for any employee-editor of a media house that has obvious political affinities is: how to deal with politics? During the greater part of my stay as an employee of Sun, the DMK was part of the Bharatiya Janata Party-led National Democratic Alliance government at the centre. But this did not deter any of us from taking on the BJP on its Hindutva programme. Our coverage of the Gujarat riots, our stinging critique of the saffronization of education, and our well-mounted critique on the Sangh Parivar were totally independent actions. Never once did Kalanidhi, or for that matter anyone else, ask us to tone down our criticism. There was a specific instance where Sun TV's current affairs discussion was at total variance with even the DMK. While the DMK, PMK and MDMK voted for the Prevention of Terrorism Act, 2002, we opposed it totally from the word go. I had personally led at least a score of debates against POTA.

One of the methods I evolved for creating an optimum mix for the local, national, regional and international news was harnessing the in-house resources with those of international feed and the huge Indian academic and journalistic diaspora. The biggest in-house resource was the enviable grassroots reporting team in the four southern states. We decided that every language would feed in their top five stories to the newspool, from which the other language editors were free to choose and select the capsules that were appropriate for their audience. This newspool structure eliminated the danger of in-house contradictions in covering news and developments. I also brought in a South Asian perspective to the channel and I hosted a weekly programme titled 'In-Focus:

South Asia'. We became the only regional channel to cover major South Asian developments.

I went to Agra to cover the Indo-Pak summit in 2001; V Raja, editor of Sun TV's Tamil news accompanied me to cover the first press conference of LTTE leader Prabakaran from the Wanni jungles; I lead a team of reporters to the LoC to cover Operation Prakaram; and we also extensively covered the Sri Lankan elections of 2004. In 2003, we were the only channel from South India to cover the Iraq war. Some of the other exciting developments during my stay included creating a space for writers and ideas: we had interviews with many interesting personalities of our times, ranging from David Davidar and Ramchandra Guha to Shiv Viswanathan and Noam Chomsky, all of whom featured quite prominently in Sun.

While creating this oeuvre of a multitude of voices gave me professional satisfaction, it also helped to hold the mirror closer to myself. I realized that my fiction writing had suffered a major setback, and the instant analysis of television had denied me time to reflect on men and matters. My engagements with arts and literature were totally subsumed by the demands of a 24×7 hunger of the television screen. The urge to move on was strong. But the country moved into election mode. I decided that it would not be fair to resign from Sun TV when the elections were around the corner. I stayed on till the elections were over.

I had spent nearly two decades in mainstream journalism and had switched jobs the moment I felt the urge to move on. But I was never subjected to an interrogation about why I was leaving one job for the other till I decided to quit Sun Network. There were five theories about my resignation. One, there was a clash of ideas with Kalanidhi Maran, Chairman and Managing Director of Sun Network. Two, I was frustrated because the promised English newspaper from the network was not happening. Three, the DMK had swung an international posting for me, using its clout as a leading partner of the newly formed UPA government. Four, I was not happy being confined to a peninsular network and was looking for a sub-continental profile. The fifth theory was the most interesting one: I was in an emotional bind about how to run a rival newspaper when my mentor N Ram had just returned as the editor-in-chief for the *Hindu*, and as a resolution to my emotional crisis, I decided to leave the country. I must confess I was both delighted as well as exasperated by these speculations: delighted because I never knew that I was a focal point in media discussions; exasperated because they failed to catch even a glimmer of the truth of what prompts a full-time journalist to opt out of the profession.

18

Prescribed Truth, Licensed Freedom: The Press in Post-Mahathir Malaysia

Mustafa K Anuar

Expectations of social reform ran high when the majority of Malaysians gave incumbent coalition party Barisan Nasional (BN), under the new leadership of Abdullah Ahmad Badawi, a resounding victory in the 2004 general elections. The BN won 198 out of 220 seats in Parliament. This was especially so when the general public was consistently fed with 'feel good' sensations that was embodied by Abdullah during the electoral campaigns mounted by the mammoth BN campaign machinery. There was promise of good governance, transparency and accountability from the new kid on the block, so to speak. Abdullah even remarked during the election campaign period that he and his government would listen intently to the voices and criticisms of the ordinary Malaysians, people whom he cajoled to 'work with him, not for him'.[1]

More than three years have passed by since Abdullah was anointed prime minister in October 2003 by his predecessor Mahathir Mohamed, and yet the status of press freedom in Malaysia remains practically the same under the Abdullah administration as it was under the previous Mahathir regime. (Mahathir was placed by international press watchdog *Reporters Sans Frontieres* in the 2003 international list of 'predators of a free press' because of his well-known mistreatment of the press.)[2] Abdullah's style of leadership may be less abrasive than his predecessor's, but he is no less restrictive in his handling of the press and other mass media in the country. It is thus unsurprising that the coverage of the mainstream press and other media during the 2004 general election campaign period was as unabashedly and wholly supportive of the incumbent BN as it was in the previous general elections when Mahathir was the leader of the coalition.[3]

Like his predecessor who ruled the country for 22 years, Abdullah has thus treated the mainstream mass media in a manner that suggests that he too dangerously believes that the media are ideological apparatuses for the maintenance of political power and the promotion of the ruling party's hegemony. As a result, the credibility of the mainstream press still suffers, although not as severely as during the height of the so-called *Reformasi* days, when ordinary Malaysians took to the street to demand social reform from the Mahathir administration in the wake of the Asian financial crisis and the unceremonious dismissal of Mahathir's former deputy premier Anwar Ibrahim in the late 1990s.

This chapter examines the present status of the Malaysian press in particular and of the mainstream mass media in general. In so doing, it also attempts to link it to the legal restrictions and political intervention that give rise to the contemporary state of press freedom in the country. Additionally, the chapter also assesses the relationship between the mainstream press and the Internet, and subsequently attempts to extrapolate the future of press freedom in the country.

The Malaysian Multicultural Mosaic

Comprising peninsular Malaysia, the east Malaysian states of Sabah and Sarawak, and the Federal Territory of Labuan Island cover a geographical area of approximately 330,000 square kilometres. Peninsular and east Malaysia are separated by about 450 kilometres of the South China Sea. Peninsular Malaysia, which spans over a land area of 132,000 square kilometres, shares its borders with Thailand in the north and Singapore in the south. Sabah and Sarawak, on the other hand, share their frontiers with the Indonesian region of Kalimantan.

The Malaysian population, which is multi-ethnic, multicultural and multi-religious, is mainly composed of the dominant Malays (also categorized as *Bumiputera*, the indigenous group), ethnic Chinese and ethnic Indians, and numerous other ethnic groups in the various parts of the country. According to the 2000 Census,[4] there were approximately 21.89 million Malaysians. Of this, *Bumiputera* comprised 65.1 per cent, ethnic Chinese 26 per cent and ethnic Indians 7.7 per cent. In Sarawak, the biggest ethnic group in the census was the Ibans, which comprised 30.1 per cent of the state's total Malaysian citizens, followed by the ethnic Chinese (26.7 per cent) and Malays (23 per cent). Similarly, Sabah had the predominant ethnic group of Kadazan Dusun (18.4 per cent), followed by Bajau (17.3 per cent) and Malays (15.3 per cent). The population now stands at 26,885,658 (http://www.statistics. gov.my, accessed on 12 December 2006).

Such diversity in cultures and ethnic backgrounds can be a pride and asset of Malaysia—and this has been a selling point, at least in the tourism brochures. On the other hand, this very diversity can and has become a factor exploitable by parties with vested interests, which often yields divisive, and at times destructive, consequences in society. Politics of ethnicity permeates almost all levels of society, which explains, for example, why most of the political parties, the ruling BN coalition included, are ethnic-based and can consequently be problematic in certain situations as far as ethnic relations are concerned.

The Malay-based United Malays National Organization (UMNO) party, the dominant partner in the ruling BN coalition, champions the interests and rights of the Malay majority; the Chinese-based Malaysian Chinese Association (MCA) party, another BN coalition partner, advocates the rights and interests of the ethnic Chinese; while the Indian-based Malaysian Indian Congress (MIC), yet another key partner of the coalition, promotes the interests and rights of the ethnic Indians in the country. There were times when the interests pushed by one partner of the ruling coalition severely clashed with those pursued by another partner of the ruling BN, thereby causing tension and anxiety, if not minor fights, between the ethnic groups as well as within the larger Malaysian society. Inter-ethnic tension can also arise if and when a component party in the BN champions the interests of one ethnic group that conflict with those of another ethnic group, which another ethnic-based opposition party (such as the Chinese-based Democratic Action Party [DAP] and the Malay-based Islamist Parti Islam SeMalaysia [PAS]) promotes.

And yet it is ironic that Malaysians have often been reminded by the state of the importance of avoiding articulation of views that could give rise to ethnic hatred and distrust. Equally insidious, so-called ethnic and cultural sensitivity can be and has been exploited by the powers that be to justify the use of undemocratic means of social control, and this includes the control of the mainstream mass media. In other words, the state exercises control over, among other things, the mainstream means of communication and freedom of expression, all in the name of preserving and protecting harmonious ethnic relations and national security, and ensuring uninterrupted socio-economic development in the country.

It is also instructive that unlike a number of alternative publications in the country such as *Aliran Monthly*, most of the mainstream press, with the exception of the English-language dailies, is divided along ethnic lines, particularly the vernacular Chinese- and Tamil-language newspapers. The Malay-language newspapers, although using the national language, also tend to target and serve primarily their Malay constituencies.

Binding Laws, Bounded Press

The Malaysian Constitution confers certain fundamental rights, particularly in relation to freedom of expression, of association, and of assembly, which are provided for in Article 10 of the Constitution. However, at the same time Articles 10(2)(a), 10(4), 149 and 150 authorizes Parliament to impose certain restrictions on free speech if it deems necessary or expedient on the following 14 grounds.[5]

1. Security of the Federation or any part thereof (laws such as the Internal Security Act [ISA], Official Secrets Act [OSA], Printing Presses and Publications Act [PPPA] and the Sedition Act come under this rubric);
2. Friendly relations with other countries;
3. Public order (Sedition Act, Police Act, PPPA and Broadcasting Act);
4. Morality (Film Censorship Act, PPPA, Finas Act, etc.);
5. Privileges of Parliament or of any Legislative Assembly;
6. Contempt of Court;
7. Defamation;
8. Incitement to any offence;

9. Right to Citizenship under Part III of the Constitution;
10. Status of the Malay language;
11. Position and privileges of the Malays and the natives of Sabah and Sarawak;
12. Prerogatives of the Malay Sultans and the Ruling Chiefs of Negeri Sembilan;
13. Legislative action designed to stop or prevent subversion, organized violence and crimes prejudicial to the public (the ISA is derived from this provision); and
14. Legislative action required by reason of emergency.

Such iron-clad provisions only demonstrate that the Constitution 'has been so devised as to give the government in Parliament virtually unfettered powers to do whatever it wishes to do to regulate speech, assembly and association.'[6]

It is therefore hardly surprising that, in a response to the recommendations made by Malaysia's Human Rights Commission (Suhakam) in 2004 to improve press freedom in the country, the government insisted that printing licences and publishing permits be granted as a privilege and not as a right.[7] Such a reaction indicates the government's lack of concern for press freedom and, worse, an executive arrogance that is spawned by the ruling coalition's overwhelming majority in Parliament and a battery of illiberal laws. It is no exaggeration to assert that the government, emboldened by this kind of political and legal strength, has at times treated the press with impunity when it so desired.

Specifically, the Printing Presses and Publications Act (PPPA, 1984) is a principal law that governs and shapes the press industry. It provides immense power to the Minister of Internal Security, i.e., Abdullah Badawi himself. The legal provision stipulates that he has the authority to grant, renew and revoke printing licences and publishing permits. The choice to reject an application is also available to him.

A British legacy, the PPPA, which was amended in 1988, precludes any judicial review of the Internal Security Minister's decision if the minister should revoke or suspend a publishing permit on the grounds that the publication was prejudicial to public order. Presently, the minister's decision is final and unchallengeable in any court of law, as stated under Section 13, sub-section (1); Section 13A, sub-section (1); and Section 13B of the Act:

> 13(1) Without prejudice to the powers of the Minister to revoke or suspend a licence or permit under any other provisions of this Act, if the Minister is satisfied that any printing press in respect of which the licence has been issued is used for printing of any publication which is prejudicial to public order or national security or that any newspaper in respect of which a permit has been issued contains anything which is prejudicial to public order or national security, he may revoke such licence or permit.

> 13A(1) Any decision of the Minister to refuse to grant or to revoke or to suspend a licence or permit shall be final and shall not be called in question by any court on any ground whatsoever.

> 13B No person shall be given an opportunity to be heard with regard to his application for a licence or permit or relating to the revocation or suspension of the licence or permit granted to him under this Act.[8]

Apart from this, Section 7(1) of the amended Act empowers the Minister to prohibit the printing, sale, import, distribution or possession of a publication. The Minister may do this if he believes that a publication can threaten morality, public order, security or national interest, conflicts with the law or contains provocative materials:

> If the Minister is satisfied that any publication contains any article, caricature, photograph, report, notes, writing, sound, music, statement or any other thing which is in any manner prejudicial to or likely to be prejudicial to public order, morality, security, the relationship with any foreign country or government, or which is likely to alarm public opinion, or which is or is likely to be contrary to any law or is otherwise prejudicial to or is likely to be prejudicial to public interest or national interest, he may in his absolute discretion by order published in the Gazette prohibit, either absolutely or subject to such conditions as may be prescribed, the printing, importation, production, reproduction, publishing, sale, issue, circulation, distribution or possession of that publication and future publications of the publisher concerned.[9]

The PPPA, with all its restrictive features, remains unchanged under the new Abdullah administration, despite calls from civil society and some members of the press to repeal it. As a result, fresh attempts to publish newspapers and even party organs were met with either a wall of silence or downright rejection by the authorities. Online newspaper *Malaysiakini*, for example, applied for a permit in September 2002 to publish a daily hard copy, but the government has so far only hinted that it was not likely to approve the application because it feared that *Malaysiakini* would 'be prejudicial to and jeopardize national security and public order.'[10] The government was referring to a clash it had with the online newspaper over a letter published by the latter on 9 January 2003, which, the government claimed, was seditious and could incite ethnic hatred. The incident subsequently provoked the police to mount a raid on the online newspaper's premises and confiscate a number of *Malaysiakini*'s computers on 20 January 2003—at a time when Abdullah was the deputy prime minister and minister of home affairs (the ministry that then handled matters of publication) under the Mahathir administration.

Another instance involves the permit application in 2004 by the opposition Parti Keadilan Rakyat (People's Justice Party) to publish a bi-monthly party organ called *Suara Keadilan* (Voice of Justice). The Abdullah administration was reportedly still dragging its feet over this urgent matter.[11] The democratic right of a political party to disseminate its views and party news to its members and the general public has been unjustly delayed by the minister via the PPPA.

In contrast, the permit application of Malay tabloid *Kosmo!*, by the Utusan Melayu press group was predictably entertained in a positive and swift manner by the Internal Security Ministry. This is because *Kosmo!*, which emerged in late 2004, is owned and published by the newspaper group that is closely related to the dominant ruling party, UMNO. This example reveals that the PPPA can be employed by the minister in a discretionary and discriminatory fashion. In short, double standards and injustice rear their ugly heads.

Organs of other opposition parties have, to be sure, had run-ins with the previous Mahathir administration. For instance, *Harakah*, the official organ of Islamist party Parti Islam SeMalaysia (PAS) had its frequency of publication slashed by half—from twice a week to twice a month—after the Mahathir government realized that its circulation had reached about 300,000 copies in the heydays of the Reformasi movement in the late 1990s. As stated earlier, that was the time when the credibility of the mainstream press, primarily owned by friends of the ruling coalition, was at its lowest. As if this ruling was not enough, the ministry concerned subsequently further tightened the rules of the PPPA so that the sales of party organs would be only confined to the membership. Obstacles are placed in the path of opposition publications as well as other smaller magazines critical of the government, especially if these publications have shown the capacity and tenacity to attract a large readership.[12]

Indeed, the PPPA is a sword of Damocles that hangs over the heads of publishers and editors of newspapers, often putting them at the mercy of the Internal Security Ministry. A case in point is the controversy involving Deputy Internal Security Minister Noh Omar, who allegedly remarked on 29 November 2005 that foreigners and tourists could go back home if they thought that Malaysian police were cruel. This was in direct reference to a recent incident in a police lock-up where a woman suspect, widely suspected of being a Chinese national, was forced to do repetitive ear-squats in the nude, with the purported objective of retrieving any hidden foreign objects from body orifices. This disparaging remark, which he later denied making, was splashed in the evening editions of the Chinese language dailies in Malaysia as well as in certain international newspapers such as Singapore's *Straits Times* and a few dailies in China. The next morning's editions of the local Chinese dailies and other newspapers did not however report those remarks, thereby giving credence to the allegation of the opposition leader Lim Kit Siang that there was a directive emanating from the Prime Minister's Department instructing the mass media to black out the remarks concerned.[13]

The government was ostensibly embarrassed and edgy about this whole affair because it had taken on an international dimension as the 'nude squats' incident apparently involved a Chinese national. Things got a bit pricklier, given the fact that the 'nude squats' scandal was recorded on a handphone video by an unknown party and the images had already been circulated among members of the general public and on the Internet, and in newspapers in the form of still pictures. Additionally, prior to this incident, four women who were Chinese nationals were also allegedly forced to strip by the Malaysian police when they were detained in a police station.[14] News of this nature was the last thing that the Malaysian government would want, as this scandal could, and did, reduce the number of tourist arrivals from China. The fear of losing substantial revenue from Chinese tourists saw the immediate despatching of Home Minister Azmi Khalid to

China, for the purpose of exercising damage control public relations there.

But, as it turned out, a special commission of inquiry that was swiftly set up to investigate this scandal revealed, among other things, that the woman who was forced to strip during the police body search was actually a Malay Malaysian, and not a Chinese national as was widely speculated. This twist of events in turn witnessed the turning on the screw by the Internal Security Ministry on the local Chinese daily *China Press*, whose evening edition first broke the news of the video clip of the 'nude squats' scandal. The daily was issued a show-cause letter on 19 December 2005 by the Internal Security Ministry, which sought an explanation for the misreporting of the identity of the woman in question,[15] which, so went the argument, had outraged Malaysians, caused a diplomatic tiff between Malaysia and China, and subsequently affected tourism. Consequently, under heavy government pressure *China Press* published in its evening edition an open apology for its admitted error in identifying the ethnicity of the woman in the 'nude squats' scandal, and at the same time announcing the sacking of its editor-in-chief Chong Choon Nam and executive editor-in-chief Wang Zhao Ping.[16] This led to accusation from media freedom activists that the two top editors were made sacrificial lambs to appease the Internal Security Ministry.[17] In a more liberal setting, a public apology from the newspaper's editorial board would have sufficed, as there was no malice intended.

The twisted logic in this episode, it appears, is that the messenger gets 'killed' by the ministry that is armed by the PPPA for merely having done what was journalistically expected of a newspaper worth its salt—viz., highlighting the violation of a woman's rights and dignity, irrespective of her nationality, ethnic background or creed. Anyway, tourism from China would have still suffered to a certain extent because in the other case its nationals (the four women) were allegedly forced to strip naked by the Malaysian police.

It is noteworthy that the Chinese language press in general and *China Press* in particular were resolved to publish, at least through their evening editions, the report about the 'nude squats' and the story about the blunder that the Deputy Internal Security Minister made. Most of the Chinese-language dailies had been known for their relative independent-mindedness, especially before many of them were taken over by groups closely associated with the ruling party whose primary intention was to 'tame' the newspapers. Nonetheless, these newspapers did occasionally display their measured independence thereafter, as in the case of the coverage of former deputy premier Anwar Ibrahim, whose ill-health was prominently covered by the Chinese language press but shunned by many other newspapers.[18]

In the case of the 'nude squats' scandal, there are at least four possible reasons why the Chinese-language press were determined to run the story: (*a*) the story was perceived to be newsworthy given that the Chinese dailies serve their respective Chinese constituencies in Malaysia; (*b*) to expose the scandal that involved a police force, which is incidentally Malay-dominated and whose public credibility is questionable of late; (*c*) there is, as mentioned earlier, a measure of ethnic consciousness among Malaysians and social institutions such as newspaper organizations; and (*d*) to exercise some degree of editorial independence. Indeed, the latest incident involving the *China Press* was an attempt by the government to rein in any supposedly recalcitrant newspapers and journalists, and subsequently to make it an example of 'bad journalism' for other newspapers.

Another major implication of the execution of the PPPA is that it is highly likely that a media organization that has invested so much money in hi-tech printing machinery, huge manpower, sophisticated computerization systems, and so on, would be extra-cautious in exercising any semblance of investigative and socially responsible journalism, simply because of the fear of permit revocation, suspension or rejection of permit renewal application. That is why senior editors (and, subsequently, many other journalists) exercise self-censorship,[19] especially towards the end of the year when most permits expire—which is even more dangerous because after some time self-censorship acquires a life of its own.

But, as implied, the PPPA is not the only law that impacts on the press, press freedom and freedom of expression. The Sedition Act (1948) is a law that proscribes public comment on issues classified as sensitive, such as citizenship rights for non-Malays, the special position of Malays, and certain aspects of religion. Section 4(1b) of the Sedition Act reads as follows: 'Any person who utters seditious words shall be guilty of an offence and shall, on conviction, be liable for a first offence to a fine not exceeding

RM 5,000 or imprisonment for a term not exceeding three years or to both, and for a subsequent offence, to imprisonment for a term not exceeding five years.'

However, the recent past has shown that the Sedition Act was also abused to stifle legitimate criticisms and dissent. For instance, Lim Guan Eng, former member of parliament and then deputy secretary-general of opposition Democratic Action Party (DAP), was charged in early 1995 under the Sedition Act and the PPPA for 'publicly criticizing the government's handling of the allegations of statutory rape against former Melaka Chief Minister Rahim Tamby Chik in 1994.'[20] In February 1995, Lim was charged under the Sedition Act for encouraging 'disaffection with the administration of justice in Malaysia' and was further charged under Section 8A(1) of the PPPA for 'maliciously printing' a pamphlet containing allegedly 'false information'.[21] In another case, opposition organ *Harakah* editor-in-chief Zulkifli Sulong was convicted by the Kuala Lumpur Sessions Court in May 2003 for having published a 'seditious article' regarding the trial of former deputy prime minister Anwar Ibrahim.[22]

The Official Secrets Act (OSA, 1972) was amended in 1986 to broaden the definition of government documents and puts the burden on journalists to prove that the information sought is not an official secret before it is published. This law also provides for a mandatory minimum one-year jail sentence on those found guilty of an offence under the OSA. Under these circumstances, very few journalists dare to practise investigative journalism. Zulkifli Sulong of *Harakah*, for one, was questioned in September 2003 by the police under this Act over the publication of 'secret' letters pertaining to Malaysia's Election Commission's thorny plan to hire part-time election workers from among members of the Puteri UMNO, a young women's wing of the ruling UMNO.[23] It was felt that the proposed plan would involve a conflict of interest on the part of the incumbent UMNO.

Although originally meant to combat the threat of communism in the country, the repressive Internal Security Act (ISA), which was enacted in 1960, has been used to detain opposition politicians, government critics, labour activists, intellectuals, academics, students, religious leaders, counterfeiters of identity cards, environmentalists, drug traffickers, armed robbers and, last but not least, journalists.[24] *Malaysiakini* columnist Hishamuddin Rais was detained under this preventive detention law on 10 April 2001, presumably because of his trenchant criticisms of the government. And in the 1970s, former *New Straits Times* editor-in-chief A Samad Ismail and *Berita Harian* news editor Samani Amin were both detained on suspicion of having been involved in communist activities. The ISA allows for detention by the police for up to 60 days for interrogation of any person suspected of acting or about to act in a manner prejudicial to the security of Malaysia or any part of the country. Subsequent to the initial 60 days, further detention for up to two years may be authorized in writing by the Minister of Internal Security. Furthermore, the right of detainees to challenge the legality of their detention is limited to procedural matters.

Media Moguls, Money and Control

Over the years, the media industry in Malaysia has witnessed a growing and troubling trend of media ownership concentration and consolidation. What is also worrying is the fact that the mainstream press outfits are in the hands of a few who are closely aligned with or friendly to the ruling coalition. Indeed, central to this unhealthy development is the state's use of the PPPA. A cursory look at the press ownership pattern in Malaysia would indicate the degree of involvement of the various component parties of the BN and their economic allies.

Media Prima, which is by far the largest media conglomerate in the country, has a large stake in the New Straits Times Press (M) Bhd (NSTP)—which publishes the English-language newspapers *New Straits Times*, *New Sunday Times*, *Malay Mail* and *Sunday Mail*, and the Malay-language newspapers *Berita Harian*, *Berita Minggu* and the fast growing *Harian Metro*—and also owns the Sistem Televisyen Malaysia Bhd (popularly known as TV3), the new channel 8TV, Channel 9, and the recently acquired ntv7. This group, which is said to be close to the dominant UMNO party, also owns the radio stations WAfm and Fly.FM.[25]

An investment arm of the BN component party MCA, Huaren Holdings, owns the English-language *The Star* and *Sunday Star*; the Chinese-language dailies *Nanyang Siang Pau* and *China Press*; and the radio stations Redi 988 and Red 104.9.[26] The acquisition of Nanyang Press Holdings Bhd, which publishes *Nanyang Siang Pau* and *China Press*, by Huaren Holdings on 28 May 2001 triggered strong opposition from the ethnic Chinese community as a whole, because this sale was perceived as 'the final nail for press freedom in the country'.[27]

Utusan Melayu (M) Bhd group, which is closely linked to UMNO, owns the Malay-language newspapers *Utusan Malaysia*, *Mingguan Malaysia, Utusan Melayu Mingguan* and the tabloid *Kosmo!*. Apart from newspapers, the group also publishes magazines, namely *Wanita, Mangga, Saji, Rias, URTV, Hai, Mastika, Harmoni, Al-Islam, Kawan, Pemikir* and *Umph*.[28] The group's oldest daily, *Utusan Melayu* (which has been changed to a weekly, and hence the present name, *Utusan Melayu Mingguan*) was the first newspaper in Malaysia that faced a takeover by the ruling party UMNO in 1961. Editors, journalists and other newspaper workers, who were concerned about the daily's editorial independence, resisted the state's intrusion and staged a 93-day strike, but it ended with the triumph of UMNO.

Timber tycoon Tiong Hiew King, who owns Sin Chew Media Corp Bhd, publishes the popular *Sin Chew Daily* and *Guang Ming Daily*, apart from having other media interests in Cambodia, Indonesia and Papua New Guinea. This Sarawakian media magnate, who is well connected to the Sarawak state's political elite, had reportedly increased his stake in Nanyang Press Holdings Bhd, fuelling suspicion that he was a step closer to fulfilling his ambition to establish a 'global Chinese media network'.[29]

Another Sarawakian, timber tycoon Lau Hui Kiang, was given permission by then premier Mahathir to operate the Chinese *Oriental Daily* as a way of checking the growing influence of Tiong in the Chinese community.[30] The daily's birth was filled with pangs of pain as its permit was suspended on the very day it was launched in September 2002, only to be reinstated after three months of negotiations with the Ministry of Internal Security. The emergence of *Oriental Daily* had raised hopes among the Chinese community that it could provide democratic space for criticisms and dissent soon after the Nanyang takeover. But these hopes were dashed as the newspaper increasingly practised self-censorship and, buckling under the pressure of the Internal Security Ministry, terminated certain columns of critical writers.[31] Many of the writers who were eventually axed by *Oriental Daily* were those who staged a boycott of the other Chinese-language newspapers in the wake of the Nanyang acquisition in 2001.

Yet another example of close ties between the state and the press is the media outfit Nexnews Bhd. Former prime minister Mahathir's close allies, Vincent Tan Chee Yioun and Tong Kooi Ong, jointly control Nexnews Bhd, which owns the *Sun*, a free paper (that is distributed freely via selected outlets), business weekly *The Edge*, and *Asia Inc.* Vincent Tan also launched satellite TV station MiTV in late 2005 to compete with the satellite TV Astro, which is owned by another Mahathir associate, Ananda Krishnan.

Not quite in the same league as the above media conglomerates in terms of capital and corporate size, Tamil newspaper *Tamil Nesan* is published by Indrani S Vellu, the wife of Samy Vellu, the current president of the Malaysian Indian Congress (MIC), a component party of the ruling BN. Another Tamil daily *Malaysia Nanban* is also closely allied with the MIC.[32] The ties between the papers and the MIC are unmistakably close.

The growing media ownership concentration and consolidation has also meant that the media industry has become increasingly commercialized over the last decade or so.[33] The major newspaper organizations have become big businesses, always seeking ways and means to enhance corporate profits so as to please the shareholders. That is why readership and circulation ratings have become of great concern to all the major players in the media industry in the last few years. In their desire to attract and capture more readers, particularly the younger generation, many of these dailies have resorted to offering contests that promise material rewards, such as motorcars and handphones. This, in a sense, suggests the collusion between the newspapers and business conglomerates. The net result is that the interests and concerns of the rich and the powerful take precedence over those of ordinary Malaysians, the poor and the disadvantaged. In terms of content, in the mainstream press there are more pages allocated for business news and analyses, share market reports, advertisements of consumer goods aimed at the upmarket readership, and supplements on higher education, information communications and technology, photography, fashion and popular music, than for other issues like labour disputes, eviction of the landless or street demonstrations.

Additionally, the pattern of media ownership in Malaysia presents the ruling party the opportunity to engage in 'close cooperation' with the mainstream press and other mass media, particularly when the ruling coalition is confronted with fissures in its political hegemony, a crisis of national magnitude, or the need to boost its public profile in a general election. The media machinery is expected to provide ideological support to the ruling party, and not offer resistance to this form of 'camaraderie'.[34]

Embedded Journalism and a Net of Hope

The close relationship between media organizations and the ruling coalition has given rise to a situation where many journalists, especially the senior ones, have developed a symbiotic relationship with government politicians to the point of compromising their journalistic independence. These journalists have put themselves in a dubious position, where the line between professionalism and friendship has been drastically blurred. Often this kind of relationship develops into deference to authority, so that journalists become fearful of asking ministers probing questions.[35] This also means that the journalists' view of the world is substantially and increasingly informed by the thinking and political preferences of the politicians concerned. As a result, the ruling politicians, apart from other important individuals and social groups, have become primary definers of events and issues. In other words, the newsroom agenda has been largely determined elsewhere. The media and journalists have in turn been reduced to being secondary definers.[36]

Journalistic independence is also compromised by the manner in which the PPPA has been applied, the OSA vaguely defined, and the Sedition Act casually interpreted. This has all generated a culture of fear, over-cautiousness, self-censorship, unethical journalistic practices and even sycophancy among journalists in the mainstream press. Such a political and professional environment assails the very importance of investigative journalism that is required of all journalists worth their salt. If the present content of the major newspapers is of any guide, many journalists have apparently shied away from or totally abandoned investigative journalism. Now as then, most stories that 'grace' the front page and the first few inside pages usually pertain to state-ments, actions, events and issues involving the ruling elite. And there is a likelihood that crime stories are peppered in between these pages, often with a tinge of sensationalism. It is the sort of news reports that try to offer momentary titillation, without caring too much about the underlying causes of crime or links to the larger society.

Another form of journalism that has become quite popular in the mainstream press is the use of 'advertorials', i.e., a form of writing that attempts to camouflage its advertising element and at the same time pretends to be a journalistic write-up. Put another way, it is a forced marriage between advertisement and editorial. This has come about with increasing commercialization of the mainstream press that causes advertisements to crowd out the editorial content in the newspapers. What were once strategic or important pages of the editorial department have been slowly usurped by advertisements. Worse still, some newspapers seem to avoid issues, or dare not delve deeply into certain issues, that might hurt certain private concerns–e.g., the proposed plan of the government to privatize the public health care system of the country.

Equally serious, as implied earlier, the mainstream press adheres to official and unofficial directives from ministers to impose news blackouts at a time when the news in question is vital for public consumption. Or, half-truths are consciously dis-seminated by the mainstream press in order to protect the inherent interests of the ruling elite, as happened in the days of *Reformasi*.

The professional credibility of the press suffers, especially in these days of the Internet, when issues and events in Malaysia that are sidelined by most mainstream newspapers find a pro-minent place on the Internet. Users of the Internet in Malaysia are riding on the guarantee made by the previous Mahathir admin-istration that the state would not indulge in Internet censor-ship. This was promised as a way of enticing foreign investors to Mahathir's extravagant pet project: the Multimedia Super Cor-ridor. (It needs to be emphasized here, though, that other laws of the land, such as the Sedition Act, the OSA and the ISA, still ap-ply to Internet users, thereby indicating the legal and political vulnerability of the users themselves.) In certain cases, the main-stream newspapers could not afford to ignore certain issues or events completely, let alone lie about them, as these would have been highlighted by online newspapers, Websites and Weblogs. A case in point is the financial losses that the national car-maker Proton had incurred in a number of its foreign investments or commercial activities.

In a sense, the mainstream press has come under the gaze of the alternative media on the Internet. Over the years have emerged a number of Websites that not only provide alternative news and viewpoints but also monitor the performance and coverage of the mainstream media. For instance, Merdekareview. com (http://www.merdekareview.com/main.asp), a Chinese-language Website, reports as well as analyses issues and media coverage, particularly of the Chinese-language press. *Malaysia Today* (http://www.malaysia-today.net/index.html) is an English-language Website that provides incisive analyses of issues of the day in Malaysia, while Malaysia's Centre for Independent Journalism runs a Website (http://www.cijmalaysia.org/default.asp) that, among other things, monitors press freedom in the country. Charter2000-Aliran, a citizens' media initiative, runs a Weblog (http://www.aliran.com/charter/monitors/index.html) that monitors the state of media freedom in Malaysia and also media coverage of issues and events.

This explains the uneasy relationship between the press and the Internet in the recent past. For example, in December 2004 popular Website *Malaysia Today* was accused by Malay-language dailies *Berita Harian* and *Harian Metro* of 'having bad intentions for conducting an open debate on a Friday prayer sermon and allowing postings that "accused Muslims of ridiculing other religions".'[37] The government had expressed concern over this matter. In another instance, famous blogger Jeff Ooi was threatened in October 2004 with the ISA because of an allegedly blasphemous comment posted by a reader, 'Anwar', on his Weblog *Screenshots*. He continued to be attacked by ministers, UMNO politicians, and the mainstream media, particularly *Berita Harian*, even though he had quickly reprimanded 'Anwar' and also banned any of further postings by him in his Weblog.[38] Cases such as these give the impression that the mainstream newspapers indirectly 'pry' on certain websites on behalf of the state.

Despite the emergence of the Internet, Websites and Weblogs, Malaysia's mainstream newspapers have managed to boost their circulation since the days of the *Reformasi* movement in the late 1990s. The newspapers took a number of steps to increase their circulation, including concentrating on human interest stories, crime reports, sports, entertainment news and information; providing prescribed parameters of commentaries in, say, the letters column; and promoting consumer culture through advertisements and commercial supplements published in the press.

Still desperately looking for ways to boost their sales and to remain relevant, newspapers such as the *Star* and *Utusan Malaysia* undertook, in the beginning of January 2006, some cosmetic changes. They changed their respective logos on the front page, and also played with bigger photographs and existing editorial space, among other things. In the case of the *Star* and the *New Straits Times*, they started to welcome journalistic contributions from readers via e-mail or SMS (Short Message Service) under the rubric of citizens' journalism. So far, it appears that the papers encourage brief discussions that are largely 'politically safe'. Photos that have been sent by readers via handphones have so far confined themselves to the unusual, the accidental and the trivial. The readers are of course assured of some monetary rewards.

To be sure, cosmetic changes had taken place a number of times before in many of the mainstream newspapers, which desperately seek to look different in a political environment that essentially does not allow for meaningful journalistic changes. It happened during the rule of Mahathir;[39] it also occurs under the Abdullah administration. But, as mentioned earlier, that is not the only negative feature that prevails in both administrations. The mainstream press is governed more by the discretion of the prime minister and his government than by institutional structures and democratic practices. Put another way, critical reporting that occasionally appears tends to get its cue from the political masters.

Indeed, the state's grip on the mainstream press is very much in existence and stifles any meaningful endeavour on their part to make a qualitative journalistic change. This journalistic inertia within the mainstream press is made more apparent due to the advances made by some of the Websites and Weblogs. It is thus conceivable that the relatively fast pace of the alternative media on the Internet may be 'checked', as and when necessary, by the mainstream press—and with a little help from the state.

Notes

1. *The Star*, 20 March 2004.
2. Cited in SUARAM, *Malaysia: Human Rights Report 2003* (Petaling Jaya, SUARAM Kommunikasi, 2003), p. 97.
3. Mustafa K Anuar, 'Defining democratic discourses: The mainstream press', in Francis Loh Kok Wah and Khoo Boo Teik (eds), *Democracy in Malaysia: Discourses and Practices* (Richmond, Surrey, Curzon, 2002), pp. 138–64.
4. Malaysia Department of Statistics, *Population and Housing Census of Malaysia 2000* (Kuala Lumpur, Government Printers, 2001).
5. Shad Saleem Faruqui and Sankaran Ramanathan, *Mass Media Laws and Regulations in Malaysia* (Singapore, AMIC, 1998).
6. Ibid.
7. *Malaysiakini*, 2 June 2004.
8. International Law Book Services, *Printing Presses and Publications Act 1984 and Deposit of Library Material Act 1986* (Kuala Lumpur, International Law Book Services, 1998), p. 11.
9. Ibid., p. 5.
10. *Malaysiakini*, 8 June 2004.
11. Ibid., 8 November 2005.
12. SUARAM, *Malaysian Human Rights Report* (Petaling Jaya, SUARAM Kommunikasi, 2000), pp. 11–15.
13. *Malaysiakini*, 30 November 2005.
14. Ibid., 23 November 2005.
15. Ibid., 30 December 2005.
16. Ibid., 5 January 2006.
17. Ibid.
18. Ibid., 16 July 2004.
19. Personal communication with an editor of a major daily, 30 December 2005.
20. SUARAM, *Malaysian Human Rights Report* (Petaling Jaya, SUARAM Kommunikasi, 1998), p. 225.
21. Ibid., p. 226.
22. SUARAM, *Malaysia: Human Rights Report 2003* (Petaling Jaya, SUARAM Kommunikasi, 2003), p. 107.
23. Ibid., p. 108.
24. Swee Yong Koh, *Malaysia: 45 Years Under the Internal Security Act* (Petaling Jaya, SIRD, 2004).
25. *The Edge*, 21 November 2005.
26. Ibid.
27. SUARAM, *Malaysian Human Rights Report 2001* (Petaling Jaya, SUARAM Kommunikasi, 2001), p. 90.

28. http://www.utusangroup.com.my/.

29. SUARAM, *Malaysian Human Rights Report 2004* (Petaling Jaya, SUARAM Kommunikasi, 2004), p. 72.

30. Edmund Terence Gomez, 'Politics of the Media Business: The Press under Mahathir', in Bridget Welsh (ed.), *Reflections: The Mahathir Years* (Washington, DC, Johns Hopkins University Press, 2004), p. 482.

31. SUARAM, *Malaysian Human Rights Report 2004*, pp. 72–73.

32. K Ramanathan, 'The Tamil press in Malaysia', *Aliran Monthly*, 1992, vol. 12, no. 4, p. 11.

33. Francis Kok Wah Loh and Mustafa K Anuar, 'The Press in Malaysia in the Early 1990s: Corporatisation, Technological Innovation and the Middle Class', in Muhammad Ikmal Said and Zahid Emby (eds), *Malaysia: Critical Perspectives. Essays in Honour of Syed Husin Ali* (Petaling Jaya, Malaysian Social Science Association, 1996), pp. 96–131.

34. Mustafa K Anuar, 'The Malaysian 1990 General Election: The Role of the BN Mass Media', *Kajian Malaysia* [Malaysian Studies], 8 (2), 1990, pp. 82–102.

35. Eric Loo, 'Filipino journalists speak out and pay the price', *Media Development*, 2005, vol. LII, no. 4, p. 57.

36. Tim O'Sullivan, John Hartley, Danny Saunders, Martin Montgomery and John Fiske, *Key Concepts in Communications and Cultural Studies*, 2nd Edn. (London, Routledge, 1994), pp. 242–43.

37. SUARAM, *Malaysian Human Rights Report 2004*, p. 80.

38. Ibid.

39. Francis Kok Wah Loh and Mustafa K Anuar, 'The Press in Malaysia', in Said and Emby (eds), *Malaysia: Critical Perspectives*, op. cit., pp. 96–131.

19

When the News Desk Makes the News

Subhashini Dinesh

The memories of that Wednesday night are deeply etched in my psyche. At 4.30 AM. I was returning from my night shift with my colleague in the office car when a mob stopped us. Seeing the 'Press' sticker on the car windscreen, the men wanted to know the newspaper we worked for. They first asked us where we were from. I went cold with fear.

It was December, and winter in Kolkata is reasonably severe. In panic, I seemed to be wrapping my shawl tighter and tighter around myself, to the point of being fidgety. Then my friend suddenly noticed some crude weapons and hockey sticks in their hands. He was answering all their questions with a shaky confidence, even while asking me in English to wind up my windows. But some people in the crowd knew English, and began pawing my window panel. I was terrified. My heart was pounding. What were they planning to do? 'We are only guarding our area,' said someone who seemed to be their gang leader, and then they let us go.

A few yards from there, another mob stopped our car. Terror revisited. I was now trying to be calm. I realized panic was getting me nowhere. So I gathered my nerves and tried to be calm as my friend went through the interrogation again. When we left that place and drove on, I asked him in a broken voice (I had lost my fluency due to fear) how he managed to remain calm. As he was telling me that he would make a better actor than a sub-editor– he confessed that he was a nervous wreck behind that cool veneer–a third mob confronted us! I was shattered. My nerves went out of control as the men launched their set of questions. I was exhausted and rigid with fear, but tried to talk to them in an attempt to help my friend. But I could not hear my own voice. Finally, in desperation, I told the crowd to just let us go, as we wanted to get home after the night shift. The mob parted to let the car continue its journey. Strangely, I was not relieved but uneasy. The crowd had not asked us our names. If they had, either of us might have been a prize catch. One was a Hindu, and the other a Muslim!

The year I am talking about is 1992, and the month December. After the saffron brigade had reduced the Babri Masjid to dust on 6 December 1992, the nation went up in flames. Humanity was stained. Death and destruction took over. And the press was lapping it all up. I was one of the few desk persons who tasted the bitter aftermath of the demolition, which would, in normal circumstances, be the reporter's 'privilege'.

I started the night shift that black Sunday at 8 PM. I was a sub-editor on the political desk of a national English language daily. Anyone who aspires to be a 'serious' journalist wants to be a reporter; a 'desk person' is generally referred to in derogatory terms by 'serious' journalists. Those that land up on the desk do so because they did not find a place at the reporting desk or bureau. Very few journalists take to the desk by choice, but I was one such. Newspaper production—planning stories, editing them, displaying them—fascinated me. There was a challenge in attracting eyeballs to the story with captivating headlines, attractive layouts and an appropriate choice of pictures.

The two leading dailies in Kolkata covered the demolition in two different ways. As a letter to the editor published in one of the newspapers said, 'While one covered the Babri demolition like it was the World War II, the other covered it like it was a small street clash!'[1]

The city (like many other cities and towns in India) was placed under curfew for a few days from the evening of Sunday, 6 December 1992. With the situation apparently on the mend, the curfew was relaxed on Wednesday (9 December). Riots erupted later that night in Metia Bruz, Khiddirpore and Ballygunge Phadi areas. Curfew was re-imposed all over Kolkata. An evening newspaper carried explosive reports on places of worship being demolished, in addition to those on the usual rioting and lynching. Did these reports fuel the riots or did the newspaper merely report the incidents? Or was it the flawed news sense of the desk person to have presented the news in that provocative manner? The onus is almost always on the desk person to present news in an acceptable way. She has the option to sensationalize it in print or bury it in some innocuous column, or even kill it.

Most news organizations avoid sensationalism but not sensational stories. The word 'sensationalism' in journalism implies an emphasis on or an exaggeration of stories dealing with issues like riots, crime or sex. News stories relating to these issues are not in themselves sensational. However, newspapers display them as a big package because of their importance.

Journalists who evaluate a potentially sensational story must weigh several considerations:

- How newsworthy is the story?
- How will this story harm the persons it mentions?
- How will readers react to this information?

Thus, even if the reporter brings in her sensational piece of information, it is the person on the desk who should weigh the possible consequences, before giving it any kind of 'display'. The reaction to such news is likely to match the specific interests of the person handling the desk. Some desk persons react to sporting events passionately, while some might get excited about novel scientific breakthroughs. Environment, economics, education, and rural–urban deprivation–these are all issues that pertain to a desk person's interests.

Reporters choose their beats according to their interests. But the desk person (the chief sub-editor on duty), who is usually 'denied' that chance, chooses stories that coincide with her interests! Although most newspaper leads on most days are political stories, the desk person gets the other slots (like the anchor at the bottom of the page with an eight-column headline, or the second lead) to play around with and highlight her areas of interest. So a stock market story that could have been relegated to the inside pages may be interestingly rewritten and make it to the front page. An offbeat cricket story that could have been boxed on the sports page could become an anchor. (In fact, Greg Chappell's controversial 'middle finger' incident went across seven columns in a leading newspaper.)[2] Even a Bollywood/life-style story (that usually attracts the maximum readership) may be dressed up as a box item to share space with a Manmohan Singh story on page one. In spite of following the broad guidelines of news presentation, keeping in mind the policy of that particular newspaper group, the desk person can use her judgement to choose the way she wants to shape up the edition.

On news stories based on rumours, the news-desk person has to exercise very sharp judgement. Usually news organizations are reluctant to report rumours, especially harmful ones. Yet failing to report some rumours may confuse, frighten or alienate the public. As a rumour spreads through a community, more people are likely to become interested in it and believe it. Furthermore, those who are aware of the rumour but see no coverage of it are likely to believe that journalists are deliberately suppressing the story.

Some rumours involve important issues, such as communal tension, and may cause anxiety. Normally, responsible editors investigate the rumours, and, if they find no evidence to corroborate them, conclude that there is no worthwhile story. Editors will consider the rumour's effect on a community, especially on innocent people. They may decide that deeming a rumour to be untrue will be more beneficial to the people involved.

One such incident was the 1996 episode relating to the deity Ganesha's supposed consumption of milk. The rumours started in a random manner and then became a rage nationwide, even globally. There were reports of overcrowded temples and serpentine queues of believers sampling the elephant god's 'miracle milk consumption'. Consequently, a few of us on the desk devoted the day's edition (except the business and economic pages) to this episode, citing instances across cities and towns. To maintain the balance, we carried scientists' and rationalists' views on the incident on page one. So this bizarre event was splashed on the newspapers at the cost of holding back a number of important news stories.

The desk person is also responsible to guard the soul of the paper, viz., pictures. Pictures add character to the news pages. A stand-alone picture can elevate a dull page and grab the reader's attention. Many newspapers hold a meeting to choose the day's page one picture. The page one picture is as central to the newspaper as its lead story. Both scream for attention from the stands, and it is usually the picture which arrests the attention of the reader. There was once an intense debate in our newsroom about carrying a picture of a couple who got married in a tub of chocolate. Repulsive, said some. This will perk up readers more than their cuppa, felt others. The 'yes' brigade won and the picture was blown up in five columns. Next week, there was a barrage of letters disapproving the desk's choice of the picture. There could be brickbat or bouquet for the final choice of pictures. Usually, most newspapers try and abstain from publishing vulgar pictures for fear of being dubbed a shady tabloid. Again, many newspapers have a lacklustre approach to visuals. However, in some cases, a good photograph might prove mightier than the sword in getting a point across to the reader.

The news-desk acts as a responsible filter. Even if the reporter's diary has the name and other details of a rape victim and these slip into the story, the desk can scrutinize the story and delete the gory details that might hurt the sensibilities of the readers. Some news organizations refuse, as a matter of policy, to identify rape victims, as they believe that publishing the names of victims may discourage women from reporting rapes. So the desk persons rewrite the story accordingly.

Being an alarmist can affect readership. The newspaper may lose its credibility if every piece of news is blown out of proportion. There is an ongoing argument on carrying banner headlines with large point sizes for news stories. The traditionalists feel that treating every other story with a large-headlined splash could affect the seriousness of a genuinely important story. But a modern desk person feels that the newspaper lives for no more than 24 hours, and it is therefore better to create that splash to capture the readers before they reach for the remote.

But, there is another way of looking at a piece of news—that of cautioning our readers against an incident through some measure of exaggerated display. Here is an example from my own experience. I was on a link-shift, sandwiched between the morning and night shifts. Most of the editing and page planning is done during this shift. One evening, my news editor noticed this one-liner (not even a datelined story) on an agency ticker which read: 'Man dies of plague in Surat.' That was it! He sensed a major story. In a split-second reaction, he was already talking to our correspondent in Ahmedabad. Soon, we were on the job; collecting facts from our library (no Google search-engine was available then) on the disease, complete with past outbreaks, warning signs, symptoms, treatment and precautions. We also managed to collect pictures from the photo library for a photo-essay. The newspaper was going to town with this news. The next day, the newspaper carried a seven-column banner headline (in 72-point type) on the plague outbreak in India, helping readers navigate into the inside pages for the major package on the crisis.

No other newspaper in India had any news in their editions. But other newspapers followed later with follow-ups. The West panicked. A quarantine period was fixed for those travelling abroad. The issue even rocked Parliament. So who made the difference? Was it the one-liner put out by the agency? Or was it the alert desk person, who felt the pulse of the news without going to the field? Was it sensationalism? Or was the desk person an alarmist, displaying news that would lose the credibility of the newspaper? Or was it good journalism?

Personally, I thought that it was great journalism.

Notes

1. The anonymous letter to the editor was published in the *Statesman*, Kolkata, on 9 December 1992.
2. Did Chappell have a sore middle finger or was he making an obscene gesture at the media persons? This was the issue at the core of the controversy.

20

Covering Photojournalism

Desikan Krishnan

The debate on the difference between the photographer and a photojournalist has always been inconsistent and inconclusive. There is only a very thin line dividing the two, and attempting to define the specific roles played by the two would be rather difficult. Broadly, for the sake of definition, a photographer produces an image using a camera, but what does the photojournalist do? A photojournalist also produces an image using a camera, but he produces an image that tells a story. Going by this definition, is it right to assume that only photographers who work for newspapers and magazines can be called photojournalists, and the rest are photographers?

There seems to be no major difference between a photographer covering a wedding and a photographer covering a political event or development. Both try to tell the 'story' through their photographs. The term 'photojournalist' is only an elitist name for a photographer. But let us assume for the record that a photojournalist is one who can also write a little more than the caption, and a photographer is one who just shoots photographs.

Between 1871–when the first half-tone photograph was published in the Canadian *IllustratedNews*–and today, photography or photojournalism has grown beyond recognizable limits. The sheer volume of photographs shot today has necessitated newer and more efficient storage and indexing systems all over the world in every newspaper or magazine. This increase in the volume of photographs shot today is directly proportional to the technological advancements made in photography.

In the beginning, photographers had to make their own negatives using glass plates. This was known as the 'wet plate', as the photograph was to be shot before the plate dried. This was a very tedious process and so not many exposures were made. Then we had the dry plates or the factory-manufactured pre-coated glass plates. The cameras used for taking these plates were large and cumbersome to operate. In fact the early cameras had to be carried on horse-drawn carriages with a team of 20-odd persons to set them up! Glass was replaced by cellulose and cellulose by polyester to hold the light-sensitive material which we call film. At every stage of development, the size of the cameras and films was getting smaller, while the speed of lenses and emulsions was getting faster.

This brought about a change in the photographers' method of working, from changing their film after every shot (as in the plate camera days) to having to change film once after every 10 or 12 photographs (120mm camera and film), to only once after 36 photographs (35mm camera and film). The photographer now began to shoot more, sometimes much more than what was required; there have been several instances where several rolls of film have been exposed to get just one image! The advancement in the camera has been from a fixed slow F6.5 lens and a 24 ISO film to a 1600 ISO film and super-fast and long focal-length lenses. The photojournalist of today is equipped to shoot in most situations—something that was not possible earlier. At every stage of development of the camera and the film, the number of photographs that were taken all over the world, not only by professional and press photographers but by amateurs as well, increased due to the ease of operation and 'user friendly' equipment. The equipment or the camera also got progressively smaller and easy to carry around.

The digital revolution has made the task of the press photographer easier and definitely faster, but poses a major challenge to photo index departments all over the world—to come up with an effective storage and retrieval system to store the images that have multiplied manifold in number!

Technological advancements apart, it takes a rare type of commitment to be a successful press photographer or, to use the accepted definition, photojournalist. The photojournalist is the eye of the reader and his job is to visually communicate to the reader, through one picture or a series of pictures, the event or the story of the day, sometimes taking great risk and in some cases braving physical discomfort or injury. There are no fixed office timings for him, as news breaks around the clock and he should be in a position to cover it. Being in the right place at the right time matters a lot, since there is no action replay for events that must be recorded. Long hours in not so comfortable surroundings or conditions are part of a photojournalist's occupational hazards and conditions of work. The commitment is the same, whether he is covering a local cricket match or the World Cup, as he is the eye of the readers and his duty is to get them to the spot.

The precious skill–'seeing the story' and therefore providing meaningful content–is developed in a variety of ways. It requires education, experience, knowledge, insight and, the rarest factor of all, talent. Most important, the photojournalist must be able to use all those factors in one instant to provide a picture that tells us more than we knew before. It takes a lifetime to learn that. No one masters it completely, because there is always a bit of serendipity in every situation the photojournalist faces.[1] Nobody asks a gardener for his tools or a doctor for his stethoscope when they are not on duty, but a press photographer is expected to carry his camera wherever he goes and even keep it by his bedside when he goes to bed!

The photojournalist of today needs to acquire various skills apart from photography. He has to acquire computer and software skills. He should be in a position to provide a basic caption which satisfies the five 'W's of journalism: Who, When, Where, Why and What. A photograph is said to be equal to a thousand words but without the basic information (the five 'W's) it may mean nothing.

With the advancement in communications and with competition from the online visual media, the photojournalist has to produce an image which would hold the readers' attention at least for a brief second or two. He may shoot hundreds of images on his digital camera using a motor drive, but the trick is to anticipate and capture the 'The Decisive Moment', to use the apposite term coined by the famous photojournalist Henri Cartier-Bresson.

Photography or photojournalism in India has made very slow progress. There are several causes for this retarded growth. The first and major one is the lack of a proper school or institute to teach photography. Even today, in most colleges where visual communication is offered as a major, photography is limited to a few guest lectures. There are very few places or none at all where one can learn the basics of photography.

Again, photography has never been either an elitist or popular profession. Many people have been discouraged from taking up the camera as a profession. The image of a photographer was of a person who would hang around weddings and other functions doing his job unnoticed. Society never offered him the status of a technician or an artist. Very few people from established and educated family backgrounds took this up as a profession due to the stigma attached to this activity. It was also a very poorly paid vocation.

We have several amateur photographers or persons with a great flair or interest in photography who are discouraged by their parents and well-wishers from taking up the camera full-time. Most of them have settled down as bankers or engineers or into other recognized and approved professions. The educated are forced to take up other professions and they look on photography only as a hobby. Photography has been taken up as a profession mainly by the less educated, and this, coupled with poor returns and unavailable or very expensive equipment, lack of access to information on the latest developments, and the low social status afforded to the photographer, have contributed to the slow growth of photography in this country.

Today even though most editors realize the influence that visuals have on the reader, they do not treat the photographer on par with the reporter. The photographer has to produce a picture that satisfies the reporter, however junior, ill-informed or ignorant he may be of the basics of photography or the possibilities of a photo opportunity in a given situation. A photographer has very little say, or none at all, in the photograph that is published and often has to sacrifice his creativity and ego to function as a photographer in the media.

The situation is now fast changing, with more and more young-sters from better social backgrounds taking up photography as a profession. Parents have realized that it can be a very viable pro-fession, with successful commercial photographers earning as much or more than engineers or doctors. Photographers now specialize in various fields such as industry, fashion, food, wildlife and nature; news photography has also had a steady growth.

In the last few years, many international news agencies, which were only covering events of international interest, have expanded their clientele and coverage to include important and not so important local events as well. Their photographs have an edge over most others, basically due to superior equipment and superior pay scales, which has resulted them in being able to attract the best in the field. Most of all, the photographers functioned independently and were encouraged to use their imagination and creativity.

The adage that a prize-winning or good photograph depends more on the photographer than the camera may not be true in every situation. For a photographer to produce good or even acceptable images consistently and continually on a day-to-day basis in any situation, he has to be backed by good equipment. At the same time, good gear in the hands of the unskilled will not produce the desired images. Most newspapers have realized this and are now equipping their photographers better. Leading newspapers take pride in using images taken by their own photographers despite subscribing to various agencies.

The photographic or photojournalistic scene is set to change rapidly in India, with the availability of the latest equipment at reasonable cost, and with better opportunities and returns, which has attracted more educated youngsters towards pursuing this as a profession.

Photography or photojournalism is a way of life, and one needs a certain amount of passion and fire to be in it and compete with the very best on a day-to-day basis. Very few professions afford the job satisfaction one gets as a photojournalist. Finally, a photojournalist never rests on his laurels, as he is only 'as good as his last photograph' and leaves nothing to chance, as 'chance favours the prepared mind'.

Note

1. Brian Horton, *Associated Press Guide to Photojournalism*, 2nd Edition (New York, McGraw-Hill, 2000).

21

The Relevance of the Metro Section

Shonali Muthalaly

Lipstick is not the only thing on our minds. Honest!

Unfortunately, over the past few years, the Metro section of a newspaper—usually comprising cheery local stories with bright, zesty writing—has come to be seen as the province of airheads, the domain of people who languidly swap notes on hair colour and facials (probably buffing their nails all the while), while the rest of the newspaper's reporters strenuously wade through pungent casualty wards at the government hospital, or ask well-researched questions at heated political meetings.

Whereas the most exhausting work a Metro reporter has to do is decide whether Shah Rukh Khan was wearing an orange or ochre linen bandanna at the latest cocktail party.

And our readers are not exactly regarded as intellectual heavyweights either.

This may come as a shock to all you 'serious' types out there, but the feature pages function as more than just frivolous eye candy. Even the ones that seem to feature little besides eye candy, usually turn out in strappy hot pink, pouting prettily beneath obscenely large headlines.

And almost everybody who reads the newspaper reads the Metro pages. Even, or maybe especially, the people who love to hate them.

For the Metro reporters tell important stories too. The stories that are not strictly important, in a conventional sense, are generally absorbing, to say the very least. And they are almost always gripping. Even if they do not always change the country or make politicians go hot under the collar. (Well, unless they are of the 'a little birdie told me glamorous Madam X was dining with powerful Mr Y' variety.)

Very often, however, these stories are news-related, supporting and complementing the all-important hard-news section of the paper.

Sometimes they are follow-ups on news stories, examining issues in detail, monitoring public opinion or championing causes. Carrying them in the Metro feature pages provides emphasis, giving important issues, such as protests against moral policing, far more mileage that they would normally garner by appearing in just one section of the newspaper.

The Metro section's symbiotic relationship with the news pages also means that the feature pages carry stories that the main paper cannot, owing to a shortage of space. After all, a number of stories compete for slots everyday in the local news pages.

Besides, hard-news stories are, by definition, required to be short and snappy, meaning they should ideally end by the time you hit the 300th word. This does not leave much room for description, whether to set the scene or include a handful of quirky quotes, both of which are features that readers enjoy.

If a flamboyant ship bearing high-profile ecological warriors docks at a city port, or ancient ruins are suddenly discovered by scuba divers, the Metro section is a perfect vehicle for the stories. Writers have enough space to be creative, as they are not bound by the 'pyramid' style employed in the news bureau, where reporters are required to have furnished the when, what, why, where and how of a story by the time they hit paragraph two. Feature pages also allow writers, sub-editors and photographers to support stories with boxes, tables and pictures, all put together in an eye-catching format.

So, for a writer, stories often get the best display in the Metro section where the layout is relaxed enough to allow the pagemakers' and artists' creativity free rein. And for a reader, all the frills make information far more palatable.

The best thing about the information the Metro supplies? It is about places you know, and maybe it even features people you know.

Local news is increasingly gaining in importance as the world shrinks. Today, finding out how David Beckham is wearing his hair, or studying the latest in Russian rocket science (and probably hooking up with a sizzling Russian scientist while you are at it) involves just three steps: switching on your computer, clicking on Google, and opening a bag of potato chips.

Ironically, it is much more difficult to find out what is happening right next door.

Maybe you want to know how safe the roads are at night for women drivers, so you can rest easy when that multi-pierced, meticulously gelled rebel you raised starts pestering you for a car. Or perhaps you are thinking of buying a new phone or laptop when prices drop in your city, and would rather have some resourceful reporter do the market research since you get dizzy when faced with large numbers. Either way, you will probably get this information from the Metro section of your newspaper, because its reporters' brief is to gather news that the locals can use.

Like food reviews, where a food critic is sent out day after day to sample new restaurants, interview flamboyant celebrity chefs and get the low-down on passing food festivals, so readers can pick where to eat and what to stay clear off. Or it could be movie reviews that warn readers well in advance about what to expect from the latest movies in town. (Once you sit through an excruciating three-hour story, with random beheadings and gyrating potbellies, you will realize how valuable a good movie critic can be.) Then there are the music critics, who will tell you what tracks are burning up international dance floors, so you can be hip and 'with it', even if the last time you saw a dance floor was during Woodstock. And do not ever underestimate the value of a good fashion reporter who will sincerely call or visit or e-mail every designer in town for the low-down on high heels, so that you do not embarrass yourself by going out in platforms when you should have been in wedges.

And let us not leave out the tabloids at this point. Yes, they are often cheesy, with their 'gasp, gasp, shriek, shriek' stories, and PYT overdo ('Look, we spotted a Pretty Young Thing talking on her Nokia at Nightclub Swank!'). But, they have certainly gained a following, even if it is largely made up of people who love to hate them. Celebrity journalism and catty commentary (sample headline: Look who's wearing the same dress twice in a month) might be frowned upon sternly and self-righteously, but it does get attention and draws a large number of readers, some slightly reluctant and many positively salivating in delight. Considering the fact that a number of young people today do without newspapers altogether, getting news they are interested in from pre-programmed Websites every morning, a tabloid that gets them reading again—even if it is just to see which of their friends made it to Page 3—is still doing the newspaper world a favour. For, once they are done with the spaghetti straps and the 'babe of the day' section, they are likely to turn the page and read the rest of the newspaper.

Besides, a newspaper's Metro section has at least one major advantage over every Website, news portal or TV programme working to edge out the traditional coffee, breakfast and news routine that has become a habit with families across the globe over the years: it monitors the pulse of the city, telling you where to go, what to do, whom to see and how to get there. Established newspapers, like the *Hindu* in Chennai and the *Times of India* in Mumbai, are always the best way to get to know a city, whether you live in it or are just visiting for a couple of days. For not only do the papers have teams of seasoned reporters who understand the cities and know all its key people, but the cities also identifies with the papers, so every newsmaker and anybody organizing anything of importance—whether it is a huge AIDS benefit concert or a brownie-baking competition—will make their way to the paper's offices for publicity. It is a 'you-scratch-my-back-I'll-scratch-yours' policy that ensures that the Metro section hardly ever misses anything important or interesting in a city.

So a large section of any Metro supplement will consist of news that is directly useful to a reader. These include stories telling you which roads to avoid during a cricket match; or lists of the best parties at for New Year's Eve; or a schedule of events during a big music festival; or stories on the best places to learn to salsa during the summer vacation.

Local stories also help a newspaper create a bond with the local community, strengthening loyalty and trust and making a city feel that the paper is truly the voice of its citizens. This bond proves especially useful at times when a city needs to be nudged into action. Or citizens need guidance, but do not know where to look. For instance, when Chennai was hit by the 2004 tsunami, large sections of the population wanted to help, but were confused about how to channel their money and energy. When the *Hindu* began its relief fund, streams of people, ranging from businessmen waving fat cheques to grubby schoolboys clutching a month's worth of pocket money, made their way to the newspaper's offices to make donations, and more than two-and-a-half crore (25 million) rupees were raised in about one-and-a-half months.

The Metro section of the newspaper also carried stories on the relief work, giving names and numbers of reputable groups and NGOs working in devastated villages and desperate for volunteers. And it gave lists of materials required, so people could buy specific items, like milk powder or blankets, and stop continually dumping agencies with old clothes.

An emergency of this sort is not the only way the local section of a paper can make itself useful. There are hundreds of ways in which the pages are vital to a city: running a column for homeless puppies, hiring a legal expert to answer readers' questions on anything from rent to divorce, getting a self-defence expert to write a column telling people how they can stay safe, supporting a citizen's run, putting foodies in touch with each other, encouraging local theatre—the list is as endless as it is versatile.

In small-town America the local feature pages will tell you when Farmer Brown's cow, Daisy, has a delightfully knock-kneed baby moo. In Chennai, they will discuss clumsy restoration of local heritage buildings, or fight for the re-instalment of a public swimming pool with the same enthusiasm with which they will inform you that pink is the new black.

After all, at a time when information is hurled at an average person from every corner, via the mobile phone, radio, Internet and television, with everyone from suited and booted newscasters to lissom, lisping VJs getting into the act, a newspaper needs to dish out potatoes and gravy, besides just the meat, to be perceived as totally comprehensive.

So its feature writers have to find stories that force people with short attention spans to read. This is tough. These, after all, *r ppl who spel lke dis coz s tuf 4 dem 2 rite ful wrds.* And while at least most people still read the news everyday, even if it is just so they do not look ignorant at scotch-soaked cocktail parties, the Metro section has to have both sass and style to gain new readers and keep its old ones from lining their cupboards with its reporters' blood, sweat and tears as soon as they are done with the Calvin and Hobbes strip.

These are challenges they have risen to in very different ways, ways that obviously work, considering the amount of feedback reporters get on random articles, ranging from a wave of moral policing sweeping a city to information on a hair doctor (an article after which, by the way, the entire reporting team had to endure three months of calls from gloomy women giving graphic blow-by-blow accounts of their approaching baldness.)

The trick is finding stories that touch a chord, which is not always easy, because a typical Metro audience is unbelievably diverse: elderly women who want tips on dusting potted plants, teenagers in ripped jeans who want to know how to convert DVD movies into iPod videos, and ladies-who-lunch who want to know how to get rid of dark circles before the next kitty party. And that is just a random sample.

So besides generic stories on city trends, news features and columns on subjects as varied as gardening, pet care, beauty, movies and music; a typical Metro section will also include stories featured because they are likely to appeal to readers. Often these are personality-based stories: maybe featuring a local snake charmer who stuffs vipers into his nose and pulls them out through his ears, or a hot and happening poet who has just popped his dreadlock-laden head into a school to teach kids how to slam. Small people doing big things—whether they are philanthropists, heads of NGOs or talented poets, writers or artists—need the local section, because that is often the only place they will get promoted. After all, they cannot afford slick copywriters, glossy advertisements or towering billboards.

And let us not leave out the advertising. Newspapers are dependent on their local Metro pages for economic reasons too. The feature pages attract the most advertisements, perhaps because they deal with leisure and everyday life in the city and thus draw the advertiser's favourite target group, 15–40-year olds, a good number of whom earn like investment bankers and spend like sailors.

In cases where the local Metro section is split into separate sections, advertisers get to target specific sections of the public. So a cruise liner, for instance, will use the paper's travel section to advertise its all-you-can-eat midnight buffets, and a *sari* boutique will make use of the women's pages to increase business. Often the rates in these pages are cheaper than those in the main paper. So, for small businesses and local manufacturers, the Metro pages are essential for publicity.

Besides, when you crawl to the breakfast table, grouchy, dishevelled, and groping blindly for a cup of coffee, you have to admit that it is nice to have a bright, upbeat section of the newspaper to turn to begin your day. Terrorists, a plunging stock market and fodder scams just don't cut it before breakfast.

Part IV

FUTURE TRENDS

22

Journalism: The Practice and the Potential

Subramaniam Vincent and *Ashwin Mahesh*

Is a discussion on the practice, values and constraints of journalism important in the India of the early 21st century? A number
of reasons lead us to think that the answer is 'yes'.

First, India is witnessing plenty of growth in its newspaper
markets–both in large cities and in towns, and in both English-
language and vernacular papers. While this growth is resulting
in more news and information for citizens, it is driven almost
wholly by commercial interests. It is interesting to ask, therefore,
how this particular focus impacts our profession, and what implications it has for the lens with which we journalists see the nation
around us.

Second, news media creates our public sphere, and our newspapers' growth is taking place at a time when our 'federal' governance and the public sphere remain severely fraught with enormous
challenges. There is growing public expectation today that the
nation should make tangible progress through improvements in
economic opportunity, public education, health, transportation
and local quality of life, and that all these goals should be pursued
without risking any further environmental and ecological de-
gradation. Journalism is supposed to report regularly on all this
to society, and thus the values that journalists themselves bring
to their profession will bear on the potential achievement of the
ends sought.

Third, public decision-making processes themselves–starting
with the undemocratic division of power between multiple levels

of governments–continue to be very non-participatory. Consequently, doors are often closed for consensus to evolve, whether on labour issues, regionalist threats, water-sharing conflicts or environmental clearances. Adversarial engagement between citizens and government has been the norm for a long time now. In addition, our heavily politicized system of government and law enforcement does not always protect the law-abiding. In this scenario, journalists bear a heavy responsibility as the relayers of news and views to citizens.

It is against this background that the discussion of journalism and the media's role must take place. The goals and challenges are significant enough that media cannot merely perform its role–we must additionally hold *regular* discussions on the values and constraints represented in the profession.

Still, it could be asked, 'What could two serious online journalists and e-publishers write about the practice, values and constraints of journalism itself, especially when most readers in India still get their news from print publications?' The quick answer is that we are practitioners of journalism too. The storytelling, reporting and opinion-making at the heart of journalism are important in all forms of media, not just in the print or broadcast worlds. Each medium in its own way certainly shapes and contours what people know, but there are also many parallels across each of the methods by which citizens choose to inform themselves. This being the case, while our experience as journalists is nearly all from online publishing, the inferences are valid in other media too.

Moreover, while we have always recognized the limitations of being an online publication, our editorial stewardship of *India Together* has been consciously informed by what the print media publications are doing or not doing, both in their printed dailies as well as in their online editions.

Values, Ideals and Morality

Journalism's first key value comes from its very purpose. As produced, shaped and carried by the news media, journalism must reflect society fully, and inform citizens so that they may be free and self-governing, and thereby able to navigate society better. In order to inform, journalism must first be read, and for this to happen, writers must report in interesting and relevant ways. Their narratives must connect the news they report to the society readers live in.

Besides this, there are other values most journalists will recognize and cherish. Journalism is supposed to be independent of faction. Journalists are meant to be independent monitors of all forms of power, be it governmental or business or special interest groups in civil society.

Many will point out that finding these ideals in the media industry today is a futile quest, and encouraging the industry to take these up is equally hopeless. There is some truth to this; the news media industry globally—and in the West in particular—has seen much market-driven consolidation and 'dumbing down'; its practices have come under sharp criticism and even scathing indictments from the West's citizens themselves, in opinion polls as well as from scholars ranging from Robert McChesney to Noam Chomsky. Despite this, however, few will disagree with the ideals themselves. Much of the support for a 'free press' comes from the premise that the good society may not be able to flourish without its journalism striving for these values.

But a mere statement of generalities will not do for journalism in complex, democratic and developing nations such as India. There are more particular ideals that Indian journalists must be alert to, deriving from, but also going beyond, the generalities.

First, journalists in India must believe that their work's original purpose is inherently pro-development in spirit. Reporting in depth and informatively on public matters has, prima facie, serious developmental implications. If an informed citizenry is necessary for citizens to be truly self-governing, then journalists' obligation to continually inform the citizenry is an inherently pro-development one in a developing country.

Second, the news media must strive to be comprehensive and proportionate in their coverage of society. Citizens' ideas about key matters in the public sphere often develop from news media envelopes of what is news and what is not, intersecting with their own sense of self-advancement. We live in a nation where entire communities—be they low-caste scavengers, sex workers and their shunned children, or colonies of migrant labourers—stagger through lives of denied opportunity right next door to the better-off. The media needs to reflect this India accurately to its citizen readership. Otherwise reporting creates a distortion in the public sphere, where entirely disjointed and inaccurate views of society can simultaneously exist in the minds of different segments of readers; as a result, citizens and the media both risk losing touch with reality.

Underlying all that we have outlined so far is a moral standard that is older than the media itself and is a central premise to our discussion about journalism in a developing society. By way of recognizing that, let us ask the following question: *While many agree that media organizations digress greatly from serving the public trust, this has nonetheless not diminished the expectation that this principle should be adhered to. Why is this?*

The answer to this lies in the domain of morality, and the fact that we seek this morality from many different sources, not just the media. Virtually all societies have developed lists of ideals— 'Good Samaritan' values, neighbourliness, courtesy, benevolence and compassion—that long predate the arrival of the media. Our ideas of what needs to be communicated between members in any society are much older than the methods eventually chosen to facilitate this communication. And these ideals are deeply rooted. Even obvious disregard for the public good from today's corporatized media has not dented the expectation that journalists should serve a nobler purpose than the commercial bottom-lines of their employers. Many citizens are thus aware that we cannot treat poverty and hunger as development failures alone, but must accept as failures of our democracy.

The Indian Development Journey

As in other democracies, in India too we cherish the freedom of the press. This satisfaction is, however, largely derived from theoretical considerations of how news organizations can build informed citizenship, and not in its actual achievement. Thus while we demand the right to be informed by an unhindered media, the evidence of our senses reminds us otherwise. We do not mean to be pessimistic, for there is much good that has happened in the last 50 years to which we must accord importance, but in many ways our development journey appears to have just begun.

Freedom for our people as well as justice for the majority are both a distant throw from reality. Constitutional propriety, the defence of women's rights, the eradication of poverty and malnutrition, lowered income disparity—all these theoretical details seem remote when viewed alongside the image of a partially clothed, emaciated child lying on a muddy street. Nor are such images anecdotal; the statistics all point to a poor and corrupt country. Literacy, health, food security, shelter—on all important counts the country lags far behind the ideal, and usually in the bottom third of the world's nations. In countries with as much widespread poverty and bad governance as India, the press's responsibility to act as guardians of the public good and provide an accurate reflection of society to the people should be pursued with even more vigour than in the more developed parts of the world.

Readers of English language papers—usually at the upper end of society and largely the income tax-paying class of the country—tend to be out of touch with the reality of poverty, oppression, indignity and deprivation suffered by vast numbers of their fellow citizens in both rural and urban India. Ousted in 2004, the NDA government's mindless 'India Shining' campaign, which was echoed in many newspaper columns and English media channels, was one indicator of a media that had lost touch with vast regions of the country.

In our cities and towns, citizens hardly ever get the full view of local decision-making in elected councils and town planning authorities, or of the vastly deprived communities in their own neighbourhoods. Journalists often complain that their superiors make them feel that readers prefer Page 3 pin-ups of semi-clad women and that local news should be limited to times when celebrities visit their cities. News about city and metropolitan public matters that greatly impact local quality of life does not get more than a report or two per day. The short-term growth in the formal sector seen in some cities in the 1990s has led to an inevitable increase in newspaper circulation—despite the lack of noticeable improvement in the journalism itself—prompting some editors and publishers to become overconfident about the need for soft stories.

How then should we judge our journalism and the media?

Before we proceed to answer that, we must throw in a caveat. Even assuming that all media organizations did the right thing, would that automatically lead to a more equitable and just public sphere, and hence to real development? In other words, can the media—by purposeful pursuit of the principles outlined earlier—perform a catalytic role in fostering a good civil society? Possibly, but we must not place too much faith in the media doing this by itself. Good news media may be necessary for good governance, but is by no means sufficient. There are plenty of obstacles to development within civil society outside of the media. An entire range of institutions in India—for instance, the law enforcement system, the judiciary, the health system, the education system and the civil administrative system—are in desperate need of pro-development reforms. Our nation has, in addition, among the most hierarchical and unjust social structures in the world. Even as journalists must continue to report relentlessly, it is not that progress in these areas can be the outcome of a progressive media agenda alone.

Are we being unfair in our criticism of the practitioners? We do not believe so. For many years now, commercial media houses have been functioning as profitable corporations first and holders of the public trust only thereafter. Reporting space in the commercial media in particular is controlled by publishers, not journalists. The publishing function is responsible for revenues and business growth, and editors are responsible for reporting and opinion-making. With profits acquiring the dominant focus, there is a predictable decline in serious reporting.

India Together[1] is a first-hand observer of this phenomenon; we receive a steady stream of letters from purposeful writers who want to report and comment for this publication because they feel limited by the space available for their work in the commercial print media. This is startling, given that the typical print publication runs between 12 and 40 pages of broadsheet a day, compared to the one or two articles we publish daily!

Still, even newspapers that are not alert to the public interest nonetheless maintain some limited coverage of development matters, in part because of their widespread acceptance. After all, the values we outlined earlier are usually recognized and cherished by journalists and often referred to by publishers themselves, when they refer to their newspapers as 'courageous', 'fair', 'the people's voice', and so on. Why is it, then, that despite the general acceptance of journalism's values, news organizations are failing those standards? In addition to the general diagnosis that our journalism is only reflecting the falling moral standards in other public institutions in our society, what else can be said?

Holding Back the Promise of Journalism

The first explanation has to do with 'process' failures. Stepping back from the media itself, let us look at a typical scenario often played out in our public sphere.

Although pro-people public policy often begins from virtue–that is, the view that fighting poverty and injustice is the moral obligation of all decent people–there is a tendency for 'effectiveness' and 'necessity' to very quickly overshadow the moral premises of such action itself. In a democratic society, government-led action in response to deprivation must still go through the legislative or executive processes by which the problems can be addressed, and even these are subject to politically and ideologically motivated examination over matters of cost and efficiency.

We witnessed a very good example of these recently, in the events leading up to the establishment by Parliament of the National Rural Employment Guarantee Act. Everyone appeared to agree that the desperately poor need jobs, but, amidst growth that would not provide them jobs, spending on a public employment guarantee for them was nonetheless assailed as 'unaffordable'. But what does this mean? Is the 23rd nuclear warhead unaffordable or needed? At each stage in the legislative or administrative process, only marginal questions are asked; these assume that many other related questions are unnecessary. This selective examination is the result of bias–some citizens accept poverty (especially that of others!) in their determination to have nuclear security. In the end, in this case, only concerted and determined intervention from political forces on the Left–which contain myriad contradictions of their own–as well as from knowledgeable activists forced compromise legislation through Parliament.

The media is to blame for the distorted nature of the Employment Guarantee Act debate in two ways. First, news organizations erred by leaving out of consideration some related questions. The legislators and others who were labelling the employment guarantee as 'unaffordable' were never challenged to prove that it was more unaffordable than anything else that the government was already spending money on. They were never told that other nations' pro-market economic policies are often accompanied by much greater unemployment protections when the system fails their citizens, even as our unprotected poorer citizens are already being thrust into the path of capital markets. Once the decision to focus only on matters closely related to the legislation itself was taken, the battle was already lost.

If the media had instead chosen to examine how the jobless rural poor could be provided succour as a priority of the government, then many other areas of spending–such as nuclear warheads–might have been brought under the lens too. At least the debate would have deepened an otherwise dissipative public sphere, absorbing some of the prevailing pessimism. The citizens would have witnessed that the poor matter too, and that the good society is a valid goal, a far more important one than the mere political victories of the parties passing or opposing the legislation.

Reality Demands Proportion in Reporting

But again, let us look at the fate of such a policy itself. Is all this talk of the 'good society' simply lofty rhetoric? Is it always likely that even when we are moved to respond to a desperate human condition–like starvation–we will end up asking whether the decent thing to do is affordable or necessary? Why do we not ask if suicides by the indigent are affordable? Why do we not ask in public, for all to see, that such a question is being asked–i.e., whether some other expenditure, say defence or a misdirected subsidy regime, is more necessary than keeping our people alive?

One answer lies in a key element of media reporting of issues and events, namely, proportion. Millions of literate Indians read newspapers and watch broadcast news in several languages every day, but how much of the reporting allows citizens to view our society's problems and stark disparities in the same proportion as the realities themselves? Roughly half our citizens–urban and rural together–are living in conditions that would be impossible for the privileged minority to describe as 'decent'. Yet, by and large, the image of our own society that the better-off among us get from the media does not reflect this imbalance in its true proportions.

As citizens in civil society, our recognition of and motivation to assert ourselves on the sheer immorality of some situations is based on our assessment of how important some things are. Proportionate reporting of society by media is the key to focusing our attention on difficult problems and building consensus around the solutions. Proportion offers media the opportunity to catalyse an informed citizenship. As we outlined earlier, it is also an original principle of journalism, offering balance to a public affairs discourse that is otherwise missing today. More significantly, it gives readers a more accurate (and hence navigable) map for the society we live in. Many media organizations miss this key point: no amount of investigation and detail in reporting can lead to accuracy if the material that is selected for coverage is not proportionately drawn from our society in the first place.

Media organizations do recognize the 'proportion' argument in principle. But many publishers argue that covering the concerns of the poor would simply be of no interest to their readers, and therefore such material cannot be included in their publications and programmes in the right proportion. This may particularly be the case in the English-language media; the 'targeted demographics' approach to revenues and growth distorts the attention to proportion that is needed to record society accurately. Moreover, what exactly is the right proportion in which to cover the issues? The answer is admittedly subjective–there are no media-wide standards for proportionate coverage in the communities that media outlets actually serve.

Still, the absence of such standards should not exempt the media from trying to maintain a proper proportion. Most alert citizens can spot under-reporting of the serious issues; they can tell when precious space and airtime is turned into infotainment while reporting space for serious questions is reduced.

Reflecting Delhi, Not the Neighbourhood

Another aspect of journalism that is inherently problematic when measured against the values we outlined earlier is also related to proportion; more specifically, the proportion of local news. This is particularly the case with the English-language press. English-language newspaper editors and publishers consider it unimportant to report critical local news at the same level or proportion as national news. From a general news perspective, English-language newspapers in India are far more culpable than the vernacular papers for the thin proportion of local news that reaches their reading citizenry. The extent of their national and regional coverage is proportionately more than local news coverage. Metro and local supplements of most English language newspapers do exist, indicating that publishers know that 'local news' is legitimate. But these supplements are typically only a few pages long; moreover they allocate only a portion of that space for city affairs, and even this is not done daily. When it does happen on a daily basis, city reports often insult the intelligence of their readers, who are otherwise expected to read serious national stories.

From records of researchers, this lacuna appears to have originally existed in both English-language as well as vernacular dailies from pre-Independence times to after 1947, but it has remained mostly in the English-language papers well into the 1990s. By the 1970s, several vernacular newspapers had already broken or were breaking the pattern, by becoming successful at local news coverage compared to their English language counterparts. But without a serious study of the quality of coverage in different language dailies, we cannot comment on their journalism in this chapter.

Why is local and community news in and of itself significant?

As citizens, most of our experiences and interaction with government departments and public officials happens where the rubber really meets the road—at the local level. In our developing society, citizens and officials alike are distraught over messy traffic management problems, water supply and sanitation, pollution, green zoning issues, slum development, fair wages and trading, real estate scams, and much more. Our cities and towns in particular are in a situation where local problems are growing faster than solutions are being found. There are plenty of interesting and relevant stories of struggle, courage and change as well as intransigence to tell readers concerned about their own local affairs and communities.

English-language newspaper editors and publishers often appear detached from city and district affairs. The best proof of this is that hardly any local dailies of the national papers regularly devote editorials to comment on and throw light on local affairs. They cannot, because they do not have a good grip on these matters and developments in the same way they do over the state capital and New Delhi politics, or even global politics. When locally focused editorials come out, they are usually on topics that have region-wide or national significance. In one sense, our English-language newspapers' assessment of citizen interest in public affairs mirrors our administrative legacy of power–i.e., it has been centralized to affairs at New Delhi and the state capitals, as opposed to more bottom-up growth, with the notable exceptions of 'juicy' matters like crime.

The problem with the step-motherly treatment of local news is that we cannot all be more aware of what is going on at the national and international levels but be locally disconnected at the same time, with little say over local decision-making. There is also an often forgotten connection between journalism and local reporting, one that is related to the original purpose of journalism we cited at the beginning of this chapter. We said that one original purpose of journalism itself is to provide information for citizens to be free and self-governing. If self-governance is the goal, the degree of local self-governance, as heralded in our Constitution and in that of many other democracies, is the most important indicator of our democratic health. More local journalism can only help, and therefore providing more local news in our coverage is a good value.

In arguing for more local reporting in the English-language dailies, we are not saying that national and international coverage must be significantly diluted or altogether dropped. We live in a society where there is already considerable apathy in one part of the country about implications of injustices in another part. Often, English-language papers–because of the status of English as a national link language–are bridging and bringing news from different regions of the country into the national editions; much of this reporting is necessary, and allows a connectedness that strengthens our common citizenship.

In sum, English language newspapers need to redress the current disproportionately low coverage of local affairs. Indeed, this may be necessary to build citizenship that develops a positive allegiance to our cities and towns, and a stronger political, but local, identity as well.

Multiple Public Spheres

We noted earlier that newspapers are accorded the power of creating and maintaining a public sphere. The presumption about 'the public' in this sphere is that citizens who read the same news on a given day know that everyone else reading that paper also reads the same news. Second, the readers are connected by at least the one language of the paper itself, in addition to any other languages that readers may speak in common. In the absence of any studies to show that the vast majority of news readers in the country read both an English-language paper and a vernacular paper each day, we think it is more likely that people usually read either an English-language paper or a vernacular paper. This leads to the conclusion that the reality portrayed in the media is not that of one public sphere, but of many–each composed of, and understood in, a dominant language.

Since Independence, English has retained an elevated status as a 'national' link language, and yet it is somewhat detached from the local culture and storytelling traditions of our diverse regions. Meanwhile, our native languages, including Hindi, have always been relegated to somewhat 'regional' status, despite their being the real carriers of our regional cultures and diversity. Still, because our languages are the carriers of our cultures, language reporters–especially those who are deeply in touch with culture– use idioms, metaphors, expressions and even cultural and religious symbols to frame, report and comment on news events in ways familiar to reading communities on the ground. English-language papers, on the other hand, matched as they are to the more culture-neutral style, are not as proximate in the coverage of society to their otherwise equally Indian readers.

This does not mean that regional-language papers have a better track record than English-language papers on the journalism values we have earlier outlined. (In fact, many studies have levelled as much criticism at the regional-language papers for their relative lack of journalistic independence from the confusing communal, religious and cultural factions in our society.) But the fundamental distinction between the approach of regional language newspapers and that of English language ones to society is itself a matter that needs clarification.

Our reading citizens could hence easily have different views and sensibilities—pre-existing, developed, sustained or nourished—about their society, depending on whether they rely largely on English-language papers or on the regional-language papers. This points to the presence of an Indian 'split public', or of distinct public spheres. That this may underlie the persistent disconnect in India between the small elite and the vast majority is a serious matter for journalists and citizens alike. And, in addition to all this, there is broadcast television, which, with its multilingual programming, is communicating across vastly different audiences.

It is not possible to say what is in store on this front, but we do not believe this is as intractable as it sounds. If both English- and regional-language papers strived to be close to the values and ideals of professional journalism that are widely agreed upon, it is even possible that, despite the cultural differences, the spheres may converge. But the current status of reporting does not portend this.

Promise of the Digital World

Cutting across the developing situation in the print media have been developments in technology, beginning in the 1990s and leading into the 21st century. The Internet has led to the opening of a new media for journalists and citizens alike to find a voice in, one that has growing implications for the public sphere(s) in India. The Internet—despite its rather modest user base in India—has brought more opportunities for journalism to be effective than may have been possible in print alone earlier.

First, length is not a serious constraint for online news reports, and as a result detailed reporting and investigative work are far lesser challenges for online editors than they are for print editors (holding readers' attention through such lengthy reports, however, remains a challenge). Second—and perhaps more significantly—online media allows easy organization of content in myriad different categories and sub-categories based on the taste and preferences of the readership. Readers of online news can find what they are looking for very quickly if the material is brought together in a well-organized news Website. Partly as a consequence of this, online media's informative reports—records of society as it is—and information-rich data can be permanently archived for citizens, and even updated for continuous reference and reading.

With these advantages, online journalism can serve as a dynamic (i.e., frequently updated), easily accessible (provided access is wide-spread) record of well proportioned reporting about society itself.

As natural homes for information and as vehicles for awareness, media organizations are ideally positioned to promote development through the use of information and communication technologies. But executing this requires us to imagine media too in a new way. Online spaces are terribly devoid of value if they are merely used to shoe-horn the daily print edition to be seen and read through a Web browser, which is the approach many newspapers continue to take. There is plenty more that can be done; in fact, news organizations may be able to serve the ideals of journalism online in ways that would actually boost their value to readers and advertisers.

Advocates of development within the media must see online media not only as conveyors of events and ideas but more importantly as their repositories, so that the information can be accessed by those seeking it at times of their convenience and need, not merely when the media choose to give it. As the Internet matures, the distinction between the reporting and repository roles of the media is becoming sharper. What has always been hailed is the power of online communication to create new ways of human interaction, and this is certainly to the good. But now there is growing awareness that the development potential lies not just in the information but equally in organizing it. Unfortunately, virtually all the big media organizations in history have prospered as daily deliverers of information, and only an insignificant part of their revenue has come from circulation figures built on anything other than transient news. In print, on television, and on the air, it is virtually impossible to find compelling programming and content that is already published or aired; indeed there is often a bias against these. But the Internet does not suffer this limitation; information has a lifespan online that is many times higher than its equivalent in the other media.

It should be stressed here that online media's potential role as a repository of public affairs material is complementary to the reporting role historically associated with the media. We must recognize that merely because content must first be created and developed before it can be archived, it does not necessarily follow that the former is the more important of the two tasks media can engage in. While the power of good reporting can be amplified by credibly organized repositories, we should note from this that there is much independent value in the organizing itself. There is plenty of good reporting that is unfortunately lost in voluminous and poorly organized structures online.

Moreover, the repository role is also potentially less bound by partisan purposes and expectations than the reporting role. Partisanship can filter out much information that is potentially good, but smart organizing could add this back so as to present things through a less coloured lens. Increasingly, we see this happening with blogs; individuals with no institutional or ideological axes to grind are more able to harness information that relates to their interest, and simply organize it as they see fit in their own online spaces.

An additional important distinction between the Internet and other media is that any presentation can be dynamically linked to others that are related, offering the audience the opportunity to spend additional time becoming informed. Already most online publishers provide links from their current material to other pages they have archived, and even to material outside their own domains. This certainly is a step in the right direction, but thus far it is only a small one. Development-focused media have taken this further, organizing content by topic more effectively than conventional media does. At *India Together*, we have pushed this categorization to an even deeper level, organizing content first into broad areas–agriculture, health, environment, and so on–and thereafter into sub-areas by further division (for instance, grouping material on environment by topics such as energy, water, waste management, etc.).

In the online world, this sort of detailed taxonomy is easier to maintain, because the medium offers nearly limitless space for content, and can therefore accommodate the information demands of some people without impinging on those from others. The binary selection common in other media–something is either published or not, something is either on the front page or not, and so on–does not apply as rigidly to the Internet, with its range of personalization and potential for targeted detail.

In sum, online media have capabilities that are not available to the print domain; when tapped, these offer value to readers of news and thus significantly enhance what the newspapers deliver. What is more, print and broadcast journalists themselves have their job becoming easier, as the 'public library' effect of credible online journals and newspapers has made their own research and reporting far easier than was the case before. In this manner alone, online media can contribute back to the public sphere that is still largely dominated by print, even as online audiences themselves grow. Whether in English or in any other language, online media can become a dimension to the public sphere, as opposed to becoming mere extensions of it.

Concluding Remarks

We began by arguing that a discussion on values, practices and morality in journalism is much needed today, and thereafter proceeded to identify the hurdles over which our media has stumbled. Let us recapitulate these here. First, the selection of material for inclusion in most news media is not proportionate to our realities. Publishers are placing commercial considerations above adequate emphasis on reporting the voices of underprivileged people and telling their stories. This sustains amoral policy-making in our public sphere. Second, an 'ivory tower' approach to English language news is depriving citizens of stories about their local affairs, and this again is a proportion problem. This does not help our evolution to better local self-governance. Third, our English and native language papers are serving out divergent views of society on critical matters and this may be sustaining the chasm between the 'well-connected elite' of the country and 'the others'.

Is it impossible to ground Indian journalism in a value-based framework in the future? Certainly not, and especially not when citizenship itself has begun to morally assert itself much more in recent times.

The last decade has seen the rise of informed local organizing by civil society organizations. Despite the choked space for participation in planning, larger groups of citizens are increasingly engaging with each other to seek solutions to problems in their cities, towns and villages; and their efforts, cutting across class and other divides, are forcing the administrative machinery to adopt a more responsive stance. The development of communication technologies too has increased manifold the potential for communities to organize their views and put them forth for legislators. Increasing automation of local government functions is likely to accelerate this trend.

In line with this, progressive trends in the print media may be emerging, at least on the local news front. Locally relevant, interesting and even gutsy stories do sell, because they, despite the massive social challenges facing us, are much more reflective of the progressive energy and the civic foundations from which we seek to build the good society. A few English-language newspapers have already started expanding their local editions and are noticing that circulation rises when their local affairs coverage is increased. We expect that this process will continue, forcing the many 'national' players in the industry to redefine how they select and report the news. The US experience suggests that broadsheet newspapers in India are vulnerable to competitors who take up local coverage earnestly. And, as a key driver of revenue—retail advertising—gains even further ground in the new economy, this will become inevitable.

We also identified the online world as one medium in which, despite the far fewer readers compared to print, some of the traditional obstacles to the value-based journalism can be overcome. In the past, the nature of media ownership and cost considerations have contrived to ensure that large and commercial media organizations would alone be informers of the public sphere. But, as we noted earlier, new technologies are already allowing credible online media to contribute to the public sphere in ways that are irreversible and positive for newsreaders.

Note

1. *India Together* editorials. A number of the key ideas referred to here are discussed specifically in separate editorials that the authors have written for India Together. A full list of these editorials is available from www.indiatogether.org/opinions/edits/.

23

Citizen Journalism and the New Media

Ethirajan Anbarasan

The media world witnessed a new phase in the aftermath of the 7 July 2005 bombings in London. Soon after the explosions, media organizations in the United Kingdom sent their journalists scrambling to the various blast sites in the city. But the initial information flow was restricted and confusing. The real picture was brought to light soon enough, not by television or radio journalists, but by eyewitnesses and those who were affected by the tragedy. In the first few hours following the event, the British Broadcasting Corporation (BBC), Sky News, ITN and other major media outlets started receiving pictures, videos and text messages from people who happened to be on the spot of the tragedy. People used mobile-phone cameras and video phones to tell the world about what they saw and what they experienced. Their photos were quickly uploaded to the Web, where bloggers passed them around. Their written accounts included moving stories of survival in horrendous situations.[1]

Within six hours, the BBC received more than 1,000 photographs, 20 pieces of amateur video, 4,000 text messages, and 20,000 e-mails. According to Richard Sambrook, the head of BBC's Global News Operations, 'our audiences had become involved in telling this story as they never had before.'[2] The next day BBC's flagship television news programme started with a package edited entirely from videos sent in by eyewitnesses. This was unparalleled in the history of BBC's news coverage. Unlike previous disasters and events, people's response in the aftermath of the 7 July bombings brought out a fundamental realignment of the relations between 'Big Media' and the public. While the traditional news outlets initially were struggling to make sense of conflicting reports in the minutes and hours that followed the four blasts, it was the eyewitness photos and videos which helped people around the globe to understand the gravity of the disaster.[3]

The collective action of eyewitnesses, victims and rescue teams added a new dimension to media coverage of the event, thereby announcing the arrival of 'citizen journalism' in a big way in the UK.[4] Citizen journalism has been described as individuals 'playing an active role in the process of collecting, reporting, analyzing and disseminating news and information.' The intent of this participation is 'to provide independent, reliable, accurate, wide ranging and relevant information that a democracy requires.'[5] It covers photos or video footage taken by a member of the public and published on a mainstream or personal news site; comment and opinion contributed to a news site or blog; and perhaps even a personal blog set up to cover a particular subject or location. Technology has helped citizen journalists or the person on the street, or at the scene of the tragedy, to be an eyewitness to breaking news and at the same time share it with others as the event unfolds.[6]

The phrase 'citizen journalist' became popular after the Asian tsunami in December 2004. Video footages shot by tourists and locals in Thailand, Indonesia and Sri Lanka dominated television coverage in the region. Video images taken during the tsunami captured the event as and when it happened. Soon after, this user-generated content, a new term for citizen involvement in the news, gained ground. More than 20,000 tsunami photos were posted on www.Flickr.com. Following their tsunami experience, global media outlets started separate sections to collect user-generated content. Emily Bell, the editor of the British online newspaper *Guardian Unlimited* explains what has changed now:

> What is new, I think, is the witnesses being able to now build a narrative around their own experiences, and so instead of just getting the immediate soundbite from the moment of crisis, you actually now have the opportunity to publish your ongoing feelings and thoughts, and this was completely unthought about, even two years ago.[7]

The London bombings were a tipping point for user-generated content. The response was instant and immediate. Citizen journalism is not just crisis-driven. It also involves proper journalistic initiatives in terms of blogs, discussion boards, community Web-sites or even people-dependent news Websites.

Traditionally, the print media used telephone responses or letters from their readers–either by telephone or letters–to act on a subject or even to get a tip-off. Radio and television broadcasts, with their phone-in programmes and live newscasts, increased this interactivity. But the growth of the World Wide Web in the 1990s opened up new avenues for citizen journalists or participatory journalists. The famous and oft-quoted example of participatory journalism was the South Korean Website, OhmyNews.com, launched in the year 2000, with the slogan, 'Every Citizen is a reporter'. It has more than 50 reporters and editors, but their work is supplemented by the contributions of approximately 41,000 registered citizen reporters. They post about 200 articles a day and the facts are checked before these are put on the Web. 'In six years, we have made Korean society different and many mainstream media have followed us,' says Oh Yeon Ho, the chief executive of OhmyNews.com.[8]

The other innovative Website is iTalkNews.com, based outside San Francisco. The aim of the founders is to create an interactive community, where people can read breaking news, discuss it, and post their own articles. This Website tries to distinguish be-tween blogging and citizen journalism. While blogging helps anyone to publish news and opinion, iTalkNews.com wants to use citizen journalism to preserve the accountability and factual accuracy of journalism. According to Elizabeth Lee, one of the Website's founders, 'Our site and others like it are changing the nature of news. Traditionally it's been a percolation from the top down. We want to see news that comes from the people, upwards.'[9]

Sharing Experiences

A devastating earthquake struck Pakistan and India in October 2005. Most of the affected areas were in rugged mountainous terrain and it was extremely difficult for the relief workers and journalists to reach them. The rest of the world did not realize the impact of the earthquake for many hours. Once again, the scale of the disaster was exposed from e-mails and texts sent to the BBC from that area which gave vivid descriptions of what happened. As during the tsunami, the BBC Website was once again used as a notice board for families trying to contact each other. As journalists could not reach many of the remote areas, it was up to some of the aid workers and eyewitnesses in the region to write their daily diaries using the BBC Website. 'Our focus is more on sharing people's experiences with others. We do not ask people to analyze the situation,' says Samanthi Dissanayake, working for the BBC's Interactivity division in London.[10] Now, according to the BBC managers, when major events occur, the public can offer as much new information as the corporation can broadcast. However, unlike other private channels, BBC does not pay its citizen contributors as a matter of policy.

Apart from inviting responses during calamities and natural disasters, the other form of participatory journalism is to involve the community in taking steps towards addressing issues of concern to them. The BBC's Action Network (formerly called iCan) was launched as a Website in November 2003 to help people get more involved in their community issues. Users find others who share their concerns, exchange information and advice, and organize campaigns. There is also material provided by the BBC, such as authoritative guides on how to negotiate civil life, briefings on issues, and a database of organizations covering about a thousand different issues. For example, when people heard about proposals to close special needs schools in Nottingham, UK, concerned citizens launched a campaign using the BBC's Action Network. Soon after, a survey was commissioned and the findings showed that local officials were contemplating closing the special needs schools. The campaign attracted the main news agenda of the BBC and the issue got into television news bulletins. The campaign still continues.

Apart from e-mails or text messages, photographs taken during a crisis are also in great demand. To exploit the potential, Scoopt.com, the first photo agency of this kind, was set up in 2005 'specifically and exclusively for citizen journalists'. The aim was to recruit a large pool of amateur photographers armed with camera phones and digital cameras. Members then hand their newsworthy images to Scoopt, which tries to sell them directly to newspapers and magazines, and splits the fee with the photographer.[11]

The online photo service, Flickr.com, has become the visual hub of amateur as well as professional photographers. The service lets people upload photos easily and 'tag' them with a description. For example, very quickly after the first London bombing, hundreds of relevant photos appeared on Flickr. While the collection was a bit haphazard, it visually brought the city to life on a day of chaos and tumult.

Citizen Journalism and Ethics

There are many advantages of citizen journalism, but it also raises issues like editorial balance, authenticity and fact checking. With modern gadgets, any individual without any proper journalistic training could become a reporter. While these citizen journalists give news organizations millions of eyes and ears on the ground, they present a host of challenges for media outlets. But beginning the process of getting citizen contributions poses a difficult, time-consuming and potentially risky process for publications. Facts have to be checked and unprofessional writing and reporting needs to be cleaned up.[12] During the Asian tsunami, fake photos made the online rounds. News outlets such as the BBC and MSNBC had to check the authenticity of what they received, before posting images and words online.

One of the proponents of citizen journalism, Dan Gillmor, says that the growth of grass-roots journalism has been accompanied by serious ethical problems, including dubious veracity and outright deception.[13] Any incorrect portrayal of a situation or an event or about an individual could possibly lead to libel or defamation against a citizen journalist and the media organization or the Internet site which published the narrative or pictures. 'If a citizen journalist commits something grossly libellous then I think there is a danger that they might be subject to libel. On the other hand, one would expect any experienced journalist in the desk to be aware of these dangers and also be very wary of publishing anything which could be libellous or defamatory,' says Bernard Gabony, editor of BBC News South Asia Online.[14]

In 2005, the *Los Angeles Times* announced the creation of a 'wikitorial', evoking the approach of the popular Wikipedia.com online encyclopaedia, which is written and refined endlessly by volunteer contributors. Writers on the left and right of the political spectrum battled ferociously over an editorial about the Iraq war, but the debate was cut short after only a few days, when the site shut down the experiment after vandals used the open forum to post pornographic images.[15] There is a danger that even citizen journalistic initiatives offered by others could be misused. Thus there is a need for journalistic gate keeping. As the BBC's Richard Sambrook says, 'There will always be a central place for editorial judgement to be applied. That judgement is the essential brand value of major news organizations.'[16] Citizen journalists often debate about the possibility of monitoring and editing every single post that comes in. The overwhelming response has been in the affirmative. As Steve Safran says, the contributions must be edited, just as any good news organization would do with their own staffers' contributions.[17]

Perils of Citizen Journalism

Not everybody agrees that citizen journalism can bring a new dimension to the news coverage. For example, News International chairman Les Hinton thinks that citizen journalists spell amateurism, misrepresentation and bad information. During the 2005 hurricane in New Orleans, he said bloggers were responsible for reports of unrest that were not later substantiated. With so much information out there, people needed journalists more than ever to put things into context, he added.[18]

Vincent Maher, one of the strong critics of citizen journalism, says that it is potentially devoid of any form of ethical accountability other than the legislative environment in which the individual operates. So, on the level of routine practice, there is very little control, especially in terms of accuracy.[19]

Now efforts are going on to regulate or introduce self-regulation in citizen journalism at various levels. Amid concern about standards, the National Union of Journalists in Britain has now launched a code of practice for so-called 'citizen journalists'. The union said the witness contributors' code of practice was aimed at maintaining 'the highest professional and ethical standards in the new media environment' and would cover concerns about accuracy and checking sources.[20]

But Maher agrees that traditional media will and should adopt and use the forms of the new media that work and assimilate them for better use within a structured environment, and bring some of that structure to them.

Will Citizen Reporters Replace Regular Journalists?

A recurring fear among journalists is that the coming of age of citizen journalism would signal the end of journalism as a serious profession. Bertrand Pecquerie, the director of the World Editor's Forum, told a conference on citizen journalism in Doha, Qatar, in 2006 that citizen journalists and bloggers are not credible or reliable, and the phenomenon will therefore disappear. 'Citizen Journalists will be part of journalism, but just a small part,' he said.[21] But others, like Jean K Min, argue that the OhmyNews experience showed that trained journalists will be in greater demand as an increasing number of citizen journalists start to produce explosive amounts of news themselves. Alas, if only journalists would understand how to re-invent themselves in this age of citizen journalism.[22]

Will citizen journalists threaten the existence of traditional journalists? No, says, Bernard Gabony. 'Citizen journalists do report occasionally when they happen to be at the right place at the right time. I don't think any citizen journalist can make a living out of citizen journalism alone. In my opinion, they'll grow to complement each other.'[23]

On the contrary, Dan Gillmor argues that the rise of participation from ordinary people means that traditional media should stop lecturing and be in a real dialogue with its readership. 'It has a big meaning for traditional journalists ... who have to shift from lecture mode into something more like a conversation. The "former audience" know more than we do and once we embrace that, we can get in to some powerful journalism.'[24]

Convergence?

Some of the supporters of citizen journalism like Steve Outing claim that only a few news organizations have the staff or manpower to cover everything that their readers are interested in, but by tapping the volunteer resources of the citizenry, a news organization can potentially provide coverage down to the little league team and church group level, as well as offer better and more diverse coverage of larger issues by bringing in more voices and perspectives.[25]

After the tsunami, contributions of citizen reporters will at last be taken more seriously by editors of mainstream media. In the coming years, it will be routine for news consumers to find the best of citizen reporting mixed with the work of professional journalists.[26]

Citizen journalists may attract sceptics; nevertheless they seem to have changed the way news is being perceived. As BBC's Richard Sambrook says, news organizations do not own the news anymore. They can validate information, analyse it and explain it, and they can also help the public find what they need to know. But they no longer control or decide what the public know. 'It is a major restructuring of the relationship between public and media.'[27]

Citizen journalism is made possible by what is new in technology. By effectively utilizing the technology and journalistic skills, as Dan Gillmor says, it could be made excellent. The most creative work probably lies ahead.[28] In addition, he says,

> The democratisation of media creation, distribution and access does not necessarily foretell that traditional media are dinosaurs of a new variety. If we are fortunate, we'll end up with a more diverse media ecosystem in which many forms including the traditional organisations can thrive. It's fair to say, though, that the challenges to existing businesses will be enormous.[29]

Notes

1. Mark Glaser, 'Citizen Fight back with Cell phones and Blogs', Yale global online, http://yaleglobal.yale.edu/display.article?id=6075, 28 July 2005.
2. Richard Sambrook, 'Citizen Journalism and the BBC', Nieman Reports, *Harvard University Quarterly*, The Nieman Foundation for Journalism at Harvard University. http://www.nieman.harvard.edu, 22 December 2005.
3. *The Guardian*, 'We had 50 images within an hour', Media Guardian section, London, 11 July 2005.

4. Sambrook, 'Citizen Journalism and the BBC'.
5. Shayne Broman and Chris Willis, http://www.hypergene.net/wemedia/weblog.php?id=P36.
6. Glaser, 'Citizen Fight back'.
7. Emily Bell, interviewed in 'Citizen Journalism' by Ed Butler, in Analysis, BBC World Service Radio Programme, 9 March 2006.
8. Julia Day, 'Citizen journalists divide delegates', *The Guardian*, 1 February 2006, London.
9. David Marti, 'We are changing the nature of news', *The Guardian*, 15 August 2005, London.
10. BBC News Interactive, 'Interview with Samanthi Dissanayake', February 2006, London.
11. Graham Holliday, 'Citizen Scoops: a new online photo agency wants to sell your amateur snaps to the mainstream media', *The Guardian*, 4 August 2005, London.
12. Ahmed ElAmin, 'Ready or not, here come citizen journalists', *The Royal Gazette*, 10 February 2006. Available at: http://www.theroyalgazette.com/apps/pbcs.dll/article?AID=/20060201/BUSINESS/102010107.
13. A Dan Gillmor, *We the Media: Grassroots Journalism by the People, for the People* (Sebastopol, CA, O'Reilly Media, 2004), p. 173.
14. Interview with Bernard Gabony, Editor, BBC News South Asia Online, February 2006, London.
15. Simon Houpt, 'Citizens of the world report', *Globe and Mail*, 9 July 2005.
16. Sambrook, *Citizen Journalism and the BBC*.
17. Steve Safran, 'How Participatory Journalism Works: A Journalist Describes Why and How', Nieman Reports, 22 December 2005.
18. Media Guardian, *The Guardian*, London, 17 October 2005.
19. Vincent Maher, 'Citizen Journalism is Dead: Misnomers and False Witness', Menthol:the blog, http://nml.ru.ac.za/mentol/?p=32.
20. *The Guardian*, London, 24 January 2006.
21. Julia Day, 'Citizen journalists divide delegates'.
22. Jean K Min, 'Journalism as a conversation', Nieman Reports, 22 December 2005.
23. Interview with Bernard Gabony, Editor, BBC News, South Asia Online, February 2006.
24. Julia Day, 'Citizen journalists divide delegates'.
25. Steve Outing, 'The 11 Layers of Citizen Journalism', *Poynter Online*, 15 June 2005. http://www.poynter.org/content/content_view.asp?id=83126.
26. Jemima Kiss, 'Citizen Journalism: Dealing with Dinosaurs', *Online Journalism News*, 26 July 2005. Available at: http://www.journalism.co.uk/news/story1458.shtml.

27. Richard Sambrook, 'How the net is transforming news', BBC News Online, 20 January 2006. Available at: http://news.bbc.co.uk/2/hi/technology/4630890.stm.
28. Dan Gillmor, 'Where citizens and journalists intersect', Nieman Reports, *Harvard University Quarterly*, 22 December 2005.
29. Dan Dillmor, 'Technology feeds grassroots media', BBC News Online, 9 March 2006. Available at: http://news.bbc.co.uk/2/hi/technology/4789852.stm.

24

Online Journalism in India: 2000 to 2005 and Beyond

Sunil Saxena

Online journalism in India continues to be dominated by the traditional media, which not only generates news but also shapes the online perspectives. The heartening feature is the effort of New Media to carve an identity for itself. Most would dismiss this effort as too small and too limited. But the truth is that the online media continues to experiment, using the tools that technology has placed at its command, in its brave effort to develop a new news model.

The Indian media sites that are in the forefront of this revolution are Timesofindia.com, Hindustantimes.com, Indianexpress.com and Newindpress.com. There are also two pure play sites that have made their presence felt. These are Rediff.com and Sify.com. Interestingly, the two Indian news agencies, Press Trust of India and United News of India, have also set up Websites, though they seem to be wary of putting all their stories on the net.

Unfortunately, the media sites are still a prisoner of non-resident or NRI traffic, which accounts for 50–75 per cent of all traffic. This traffic was a great bonus in the initial years of the Internet in India, when very few Indians had access to the net, and the sites could tout these figures to show their popularity.

Today, however, the sites want the traffic to flow from within India. But this is not happening, at least not in the numbers that the advertisers want. The result is that media sites are still not a favoured property as far as Indian advertisers are concerned. Their reluctance to include New Media in their campaign plans means less revenue for media sites and continued dependence on parent companies.

It is no wonder that the online media continues to live in the shadows of the traditional media. Three quarters of content on any newspaper site is content generated for newspapers. The remaining quarter is content that has been sourced from news agencies. There is virtually no content that is generated by the media sites.

This dependence on traditional media stems from the absence of Web reporting teams. The media sites are yet to appoint Web reporters to generate real-time news reports. There have, of course, been occasions when the newspapers have bailed out their Web team by feeding reports of major news breaks. But such occasions have been few and far between.

It is ironical that it was a non-media site, Rediff.com, that was the first to put up the photographs of Veerappan, the slain sandalwood smuggler. For the media sites this lapse was inexcusable. Veerappan was killed in an encounter around 9 PM, and his body was brought to the morgue early in the morning. Still, it took newspapers the best part of the day to get pictures live from the site.

In fact, the media sites would look stale and old without agency feed. All of them use PTI and UNI and their international feeds to run breaking news and bring freshness to their home pages. But this also makes them faceless when it comes to breaking news. A user finds the same story on the home page of all Indian news sites. It is only in the night that the news sites redo the home pages to include special and exclusive stories generated by their print teams.

One area where media sites have broken away from traditional media is news selection. They focus more on people, crime, fashion, entertainment, sports and human interest stories. They also play up stories that are likely to interest NRIs. There is a clear move away from political stories and the shenanigans of politicians, which have traditionally formed the bulk of newspaper content.

The news mix has been arrived at after studying the log files. These files indicate which stories are being read most. Interestingly, the verdict is the same: online readers are not interested in what the politicians are saying.

Another interesting trend is the hunger for news from smaller districts. This is especially evident on the sites of language newspapers. For instance, readers of Kannadaprabha.com, the Website of *Kannada Prabha*, want to read more and more news from Shimoga, Belgaum, Hubli, Davangere or Hampi, which are small towns of Karnataka and rarely figure on the news map of metro newspapers. The same is true of readers visiting Dinamani.com, a Tamil media Website. They want to read reports emanating from Salem, Erode, Tirupur and Tirunelveli.

This shows the reach of the net and the way it is redefining news priorities. Most of these news reports are not published in the Chennai edition of *Dinamani* or the Bangalore edition of *Kannada Prabha*, because these areas are beyond the distribution basin of these newspapers. However, the Websites of these newspapers go to great lengths to access and host these reports. If they don't, they will be flooded by complaints from Internet users who hail from these small towns and are now settled in bigger Indian cities or abroad.

There is also a great hunger for photographs. In fact, a fourth of all downloads on most sites are celebrity pictures. Traffic spurts on the days when there is a major event involving the film industry. The launch of a Rajnikant starrer will invariably cause a spurt in traffic on Tamil sites while a photo feature on Aishwarya Rai will cause an increase across all sites, irrespective of language.

The obsession with photographs has also created an aberration. Respectable media sites have started using photographs of half-nude women to attract traffic. These photographs are mostly sourced from international photo services like AP, Reuters or AFP, and comprise young women catwalking in western and Latin American countries. The booming fashion industry in India and the Page 3 culture are other sources of these photographs.

The popularity of slide shows or photo features, as they are known in Website parlance, can be gauged from the ratio of site visitors to page downloads. An average site visitor on an Indian news site opens 3–4 news pages during a single session. In contrast, 10–11 pages are opened by an average site visitor on news sites that run photo features. In other words, net users spend more time on photographs than on text.

Another reality is that even today the Websites are reluctant to charge for content. They cite the example of Newspapertoday. com, a Website set up by the Living Media group, which had introduced a subscription fee in the heady days of the Internet. The site, which was doing very well, had to close down because the traffic moved away. The other media sites don't want to go the same way. That is why they continue to provide news content for free.

What is interesting is the flexing of muscles by news agencies. PTI has served a notice on newspapers asking them to pay for the text and photographs that they use on the Web. This notice was served in the second half of 2005. UNI had done the same in 2000, though it did not enforce its fiat. The news agencies are clearly looking at the net as a useful revenue source. Apart from media sites, they are targeting non-media dotcoms too.

Extra revenue may also lead to an improvement in the Web-sites of PTI and UNI. Currently, Reuters is the only major world news agency that has a well-defined Web strategy. It posts news reports and videos in real time, and charges for its financial content. The Indian news agencies post the stories late. Even their number is limited. The same is true of photographs. Clearly, the Indian wire services are still experimenting with the Web, and are not sure how to exploit it fully.

One area where the Indian news sites have moved ahead is technology. The days of static HTML-based sites, where six to seven stories were crammed on a single page, are over. Even the age of ASP (active server pages) is over. The sites today, like the rest of the world, have either moved or are in the process of moving to the more dynamic and versatile XML pages.

The site speeds have also gone up. Most newspapers are now using multiple servers with high processing power to serve pages. Earlier, these servers were located primarily in the US. Now, Indian sites have started hosting content on servers based in India. This has improved the experience of Indian surfers, because they now spend less time opening pages. An added advantage is the stemming of dollar outgo. Earlier, all media sites were paying huge sums in dollars. Now, they are paying in rupees to Indian companies.

Another major development on the technology front is the stress on self-sufficiency. Major media sites now have their own development teams that design, code and maintain sites. The outsourcing is limited to building applications like auction engines or e-paper software. This has not only cut costs, but also brought in greater flexibility in site management.

E-paper is another fine innovation. The *Times of India* was the first to host an e-paper. It was followed by the *Hindustan Times*, *Deccan Chronicle*, *Vijay Times* and *Vijay Karnataka*. The e-paper is an advancement on the pdf newspaper, whose format was quite cumbersome and tedious, where the reader had to struggle to locate stories of interest.

The e-paper is the digital version of the physical newspaper, and comes with three major advantages. First, the e-paper is the exact replica of the physical newspaper, and can be easily archived; second, the e-paper has all the interactive features that an Internet edition can provide; and, third, it extends the reach of the advertisements, giving the newspaper the opportunity to increase advertisement tariffs.

However, despite these advantages the e-paper has not been as successful as was anticipated. One reason is that the first e-papers asked for subscriptions. This trend is now being reversed, because newspapers realize that the Internet customer is not willing to pay for news content, however good and valuable it may be.

But there are many areas where the Indian sites have not kept pace with their Western counterparts. Blogging is one key area. The *Times of India* site is the only news site that has its own blogging section; the *Hindustan Times* site is using blogging software provided by Sulekha.com; the remaining media sites are yet to set up their blogging software. Once again, it is Rediff.com and Sify.com that have taken a lead on their media counterparts. Both these sites provide blogging as a useful interactive interface on their sites.

Rediff.com is also a leader in the field of mobile content, though Indiatimes with its 8,888 service and the India Today group with its 2,424 short code are also doing well. Initially, the short codes were limited to providing news updates, forecasts and cricket scores. Later, services like contests, dating, film clips, and ringtones were added.

Ironically, it was the addition of non-news content that made the mobile forays of these sites profitable. But this does not mean that mobile content is not an important part of New Media. Every major telecom operator has tied up with content providers to provide breaking news. However, from the media point of view the mobile foray is largely limited to these three sites. The other media houses are yet to wake up to the full potential of mobile content.

Another area which is yet to catch the fancy of Indian media sites is audio-visual content. There was a brief phase when ANI, a television agency, provided audio-visual clips of major news events. These multi-media files were hosted next to the text, and added value to the news. However, most sites stopped subscribing to ANI video feeds on account of low bandwidth and the absence of revenue.

Now, Sify.com has set up Sifymax, a broadband offering, and is trying to promote both news and entertainment videos. Indiatimes too has hosted several entertainment video and audio files, but they are yet to make a mark in the news space.

Another area where Indian sites need to catch up is in the area of citizen journalism. The net today provides the possibility of involving ordinary citizens in the news creation process. A few American newspapers are experimenting with this idea. They have created sections on their sites where the citizens can report news developments. This facility provides more than blogs, which are like personal diaries on the net. A few newspapers publish selected postings after careful vetting. Indian newspapers too are looking with interest at the idea of citizen journalism, but are yet to take any concrete steps in this regard.

A hobbling reality for Indian sites is lack of revenue. Almost every site is struggling to generate revenue. The irony is that this is not the classic vicious circle where revenue generation is directly dependent on the number of readers. The number of unique visitors grows every day—and with it the attendant costs of server upgrades—but the advertiser refuses to embrace the net.

The few advertisers who use the Indian media sites insist on performance advertising. They want to pay for actual sales or for leads generated by a campaign. For instance, a couple of banks who advertise on the net pay Rs 150 for every application form that is filled by a prospective NRI customer. This means that a site that has served 100,000 advertisements may earn only Rs 1,500 at the end of the month if the campaign has generated only 10 leads.

The pay for clicks or CTR (click-through) campaigns is even more exploitative. The advertiser pays only for the number of times a customer has clicked on the advertisements. Since the click-through rate varies from a low of 0.1 per cent to a high of 0.3 per cent, it means that a Website will earn money for only three of the 10 banners that it has served for a high-performing campaign. In contrast, a newspaper or television advertisement is based on the reach of the media vehicle, not on the ad results.

It is because of this lopsided revenue model that a few media sites have started building revenue streams that are radically different from the traditional advertising and subscription revenue models. Indiatimes has undoubtedly been the torchbearer in this regard, and is followed by the Websites of the *Hindustan Times* and the *New Indian Express*. Some of the revenue streams that have been developed are e-commerce, mobile content, job portals, money transfer, Website development, auctions, etc.

The arrival of broadband and the hype about wireless access have raised hopes in most New Media newsrooms. Adding to the optimism is the continued drop in the prices of computers and the penetration of the Internet in Class C and D towns. The launch of cable net is expected to further revolutionize this access. There is therefore a sense of anticipation and excitement. Everyone realizes that the first Web battle was fought for NRI eyeballs. The victors of this battle now stand on the threshold of a bigger war: the war for domestic eyeballs.

The winners of this war will be the true net barons. But before this happens several existing media practices are likely to change. The most important change will occur in the way news is processed. When the Internet arrived in India, media houses set up separate teams to look after web operations. This was more or less on the lines of the American and European response.

However, it did not take long for American newspapers to realize the folly of having two media teams, one for the newspaper and one for the Web. They have already started dismantling the walls. It is interesting to read a memo issued by Executive Editor Bill Keller and Vice president of Digital Operations Martin Nisenholtz of the *New York Times*. The two point out: 'By integrating the newsrooms we plan to diminish and eventually eliminate the difference between newspaper journalists and Web journalists–to reorganize our structures and our minds ....'

These are words that are echoing across all American newsrooms. There is growing acceptance that Web teams need not sit in different buildings and chart separate agendas; they need to share the newsroom. This way the duplication of work will become a story of the past. There will be better integration and a greater sense of purpose in news processing and news delivery.

In India too we can expect a similar integration to happen, especially in newspapers, because editing for print is very much like editing for the Web. The publishing software developed by companies like Adobe and Quark provides for this integration. It allows a story to be tracked from the idea to the destination stage, which may be print or net or wireless devices.

In the coming years, we can expect Indian media companies too to treat content as a single resource, to be tailored—by a single team—to meet the needs of newspapers, mobile devices and Websites. There will also be a fresh appraisal of news value and news priorities. Stories will not be held back for being published the next day; they will instead be run on mobile and Web channels the same day. Of course, for this to happen, wireless technology will have to take a quantum leap.

A heartening factor is the money that is being invested in this field by mobile phone companies like Nokia, Motorola and Samsung. These companies realize that the only way they can retain their market share is to come up with more value-added services. They are therefore in a hurry to develop tools that will make mobile publishing a reality. The telecom giants too realize the value of wireless, and are investing heavily in research.

In contrast, traditional print companies, especially newspapers, arc doing precious little to take the product forward. There is certainly research being done to build faster and more efficient printing machines, but it is not easy for newspapers to change their printing machines every time a new product hits the market.

The dice are clearly loaded in favour of New Media.

25

Caught in the Net

Frederick Noronha

'Don't fall sick ... and don't die on us,' the lady, an expatriate Goan, told me, as we were winding up our meeting. 'We do need you.' She was referring to the writing work I put in on the Web. Rather, the volunteer part of it.

Should one feel offended? Or flattered? As one evaluates the so-virtual contribution of an online life, that half-in-jest comment meant a lot. A lot more than promotions, designations or bylines in my 22 years in mainstream journalism.

As journalism searches for ways to re-invent itself, for means to become more relevant to its readers, is the online world a large untapped domain which most of us have been guilty of ignoring till now? For many years now, one's faith has remained intact that there indeed is vast space within the online world. We shoot ourselves in the foot by prematurely asking questions like whether journalists can earn from the net. Or we get instantly put off that the net mostly does not deal with us as the main-stream media does, with the clear promise of a fixed monthly salary, designation and job expectations. But there's a great jour-ney awaiting the willing, if only we have the patience to try and the willingness to experiment.

Some time in 1995, a 17 year-old college kid launched a cyber venture called Goanet (www.goanet.org). Unlike the high-profile dollar-promising Websites that came in the dot-bomb avalanche half-a-decade later, this venture was simple and lacked the lure of money. It was unelaborated, and almost rudimentary, in the technology it used. *Goanet* was a mailing list. Thanks to ventures like Yahoogroups.com, almost anyone can start a mailing list. To maintain it is a bit tougher. And the technology it deployed was hardly cutting-edge, even then. But that was a powerful idea from Herman Carneiro, who is now in his late 1920s. It has since served my home state of Goa, and her people, particularly those overseas, in a significant manner. But the past years have left many lessons for us to learn from.

When UK-based engineering librarian Eddie Fernandes visited Goa and broached the idea with local newspapers, he was greeted with disdain. There was clearly no money-earning potential involved. So why even bother? Eleven years and 8,000 daily readers later, Goanet is about one-third the size of the largest newspaper in Goa. But the miracle lies elsewhere: it has been running all this while without any money involved (apart from some pocket-money spent on server space, list-hosting charges or the occasional Web-design fees). Nobody is charged to 'subscribe', and no writer gets paid to write. Yet it works!

Also significantly, this small experiment in collaborative functioning taught us a lot. In turn, some of us in Goa adapted the idea to build communication and share news with other groups. It may emerge as a surprise that India's smallest state has one of the largest online presence in terms of citizens' journalism, when one excludes the commercial media.

After taking part in a UNESCO-sponsored workshop in Hyderabad to highlight the potential of community radio broadcasting, some of us decided not to let the meeting end after the workshop ended. So, a mailing list has continued that theme for nearly half a decade. If India's unhelpful restrictions on low-power, low-cost alternative broadcasting are removed one day (campus radio is currently being permitted), then this cyber initiative could claim some small credit, in some small way.

Today, Yahoogroups.com makes it very easy for anyone to set up their own mailing list. But in times when even e-mail addresses were largely unheard of, this was hardly widespread. Goanet gave some of us the inspiration to start mailing lists on a range of issues, discussing journalism in Goa, issues in Chattisgarh, technical software trends, or even alternative themes from across India.

Writing in the July 2005 issue of the Delhi-based *i4d* magazine, Alfonso Gumucio-Dagron of the Communication for Social Change Consortium in the USA[1] makes some very interesting points that we seem to have mostly forgotten. A quarter century after the MacBride Report on communication and information was sidelined and subverted by the Western interests that dominate global news flows, Gumucio-Dagron hints that a subtle and little-noticed change has taken place. He writes that the 'control of information by multinational companies goes much further today than three decades back, largely thanks to the advances in technology, which allows concentrating mass media in the hands of multinational companies.'

But there are also two 'encouraging elements' that have emerged in the last 25 years. First, there is the emergence of new technologies of information and communication (or ICTs). Besides, there has also been 'the renewed participation of civil society, which keeps a watchful attitude on the way our future is being designed.' It is time to closely look at how new ICT tools can democratize the media, a goal that earlier seemed elusive.

It seems as if most of us in the media do not realize the true potential of ICTs. Sometimes we are technophobic, and simply negate the possibilities even before starting off. This writer should know, having bought the union line that 'computers equal unemployment' before going in for a computer himself circa 1990. At other times, we actually see the computer and its democratizing potential as a threat to the clout we currently wield.

There may actually be a justifiable case to be made out for 'de-professionalizing' the media, to ensure that free speech does not get reduced and equated to merely taking care of the interests of a handful of media barons and 'journos' with a stake in maintaining the status quo and their earnings.

Recently, the SAJA (South Asian Journalists Association, http://saja.org/) mailing list, largely made up of *desi* journalists in North America, showed signs of this. While discussing the issue of blogs, at least some taking part in the discussion laughed off their potential, and went on the question the credibility of bloggers. If you search hard enough, you could find any number of dishonest and inefficient journalists, as well as any number of insightful and hard-working bloggers. But are we willing to create space where it is needed?

Journalists, with a few exceptions, seem to be still fighting shy of the new media. In one case, this writer was involved with a mailing list for a couple of years before anyone else started getting involved in the discussion. This, mind you, was a journalists' mailing list made up of people who are meant to be communicators! If we take almost all the Indian journalism and journalist-related mailing lists today, we would find very low levels of participation. Sites like thehoot.org manage to survive only because of the determined initiatives of a small core team.

Sometimes, the attitude of the scribe is too much of on the lines of 'what's-in-it-for-me'. At other times, journalists simply do not appreciate the potential that more efficient communications could bring into any society. Or, after a tiring day at the 'real' job, who has the energy to dabble in such initiatives?

In a so-called 'developing' society like India, the media person does have a key role to play when it comes to enhancing communication. Online options offer the scribe a chance as never before to do so.

There are some positive signs. In the world of blogging, for instance, a number of journalists have made their entry. It was interesting, for instance, to read the story-behind-the-story that appeared in one journalist's blog during the International Film Festival of India in 2005, held in Goa.

In January 2006, Indibloggies announced the results of its competition for the best *desi* blogs.[2] Some 1,278 people registered for the poll, and 892 of these actually cast their vote. Amit Varma, a Mumbai-based journalist and author of *India Uncut*, bagged the highest votes in any category. Other winners were journalist Sonia Faleiro (best topical *IndiBlog*), and another Delhi-based journo Jai Arjun (best humanities *IndiBlog*), among others.

Here is what one online comment says: 'Bloggers are independent publishers, and the best bloggers are successful and effective because they do what the best Old Media publishers do—consistently provide quality content that is interesting and useful to their readers, and by passing along scoops from other media sources.'[3]

But can media persons make the transition fast enough to also understand the requirements of the new media? Unfortunately, when we journos, who have grown grey in the profession, take to the new media, our approach is controlled by old approaches.

Blogs need not simply be online versions of traditional news reporting (or editorial) styles. The cage is now open. One has a lot more freedom to experiment with writing styles. But are we willing to take the plunge?

Journalists actually have a key role to play in all this, for several reasons. First, we no longer have an alibi. We cannot point to the management's disinterest as an excuse for not taking up an issue that has critical implications for hundreds of millions in our country. Second, given our ability to cull out facts or edit a story into shape, ours is one community that can smoothly transplant itself on the new ICT tools. Third, communication is itself the middle name of ICTs. Yet, it is strange that as a profession we stand-by watching ICTs getting reduced to mere IT (information technology). That too, we are often dominated by technology with little or no locally relevant information involved.

Finally, for all our claims of heading towards superpower status, we need to recognize that India is still a very information-starved country. For a country of India's diversity, we are still very poor in creating content relevant to the majority of our citizens. This is true for most parts of India, and even the 'information' generated by the metros is not quite of the kind that could really make a difference to the lives of the majority of its people. This is a yawning chasm, waiting to be filled.

But before that happens, it is necessary that we recognize the potential of ICTs, and weed out the hype that goes with them. These new tools can become workable only if we are ready to involve the citizen in an up-from-the-grassroots approach. Top-down paradigms that we are so used to in the media are unlikely to be of much use.

India needs many more journalists who will venture out into cyberspace, work their way through uncharted waters, and deploy the Internet as a tool to meet society's needs.

Much is expected of us. Globally, interesting initiatives are underway to make this happen. Two recent guides, available online, try to make the transition easier by offering various tips. One useful text is the Reporters Without Borders' *Handbook for Bloggers and Cyber-Dissidents*.[4] The other is Martin Huckerby's very useful book, *The Net for Journalists: A Practical Guide for the Internet for Journalists in Developing Countries*. It says in its introduction: 'Imagine a giant buffet, a great array of dishes, stretching further than the eye can see. Most of it is free—all you have to do is help yourself. This feast of information is almost too good to be true. For a journalist, it is hard to believe anyone could invent something quite so useful, and then give most of it away.'[5]

Why the delay in deploying this tool, and also in contributing to its riches ourselves? A lot is possible if only we try.

Notes

1. Available at: http://www.i4donline.net/articles/current-article.asp?articleid=374&typ=Features.
2. http://indibloggies.org/results-2005.
3. http://publishing2.com/2006/03/03/web-20-and-media-20-are-still-in-the-11-phase/.
4. RSF: Reporters Without Borders, *Handbook for Bloggers and Cyber-Dissidents*, September 2005. Available at: http://www.rsf.org/rubrique.php3?id_rubrique=542.
5. Martin Huckerby, *The Net for Journalists: A Practical Guide for the Internet for Journalists in Developing Countries* (UNESCO, The Thompson Foundation, Commonwealth Broadcasting Association, 2005), p. 6. Available at: http://portal.unesco.org/ci/en/file_download.php/5733565b43a86e9408818f66ef2742b3net_for_journalists.pdf.

26

Blogging—A New Paradigm in Journalism

Subhash Rai

Much of the literature on journalism speaks of flaws in the way the profession is practiced and on how the situation could be remedied. Prime among these flaws is the apparent disconnect between the editorial and commercial functions of a publication. There is an inherent discrepancy in practicing journalism as a social responsibility while at the same time running a news organization as a business proposition. New media, and then blogs, were touted as the answer to this crisis.

In the early 1990s a solution—the new media—was conjured up by 'media entrepreneurs' to resolve all that ailed old media. With its 'non-linearity', 'interactivity' and 'multimodality', the new media gave voice to the consumer. It heralded the brand new world of dotcoms. But soon the words 'bubble', 'boom' and 'bust' came to be used ad nauseum during that sorry chapter in journalism. 'Sorry' because many journalists who wrote the stories about the boom actually began to believe in them and joined the rush to become 'dotcom journalists', only to be badly mauled by the cruel virtual world, or, should we say, the market. It was not that the money did not come in, but that the operatives in the market pulled the plug after making a killing. And down fell the dotcoms.

But the new media, it is still hoped, will bring in the moolah. Only the 'how' of it is to be figured out. Some journalists too seem overly concerned about this. Online media mergers and acquisitions have again become the subject of online news discussion forums. The takeover of About.com by the *New York Times*, and the purchase of Slate by the *Washington Post*, to name a couple, indicate another bull run on the new media—or do they?

Much of the present crisis in journalism lies in accepting news media as a business—a business with a public service component. That is a strange contradiction, but it is almost universally accepted—and it is the only estate of democracy that is private.

Corporate journalism is capable of doing away with 'effective journalism' as it is expensive. 'Dumbing down' acquires various hues, such as soft stories and syndicated material liberally used as fillers by anchors, to name just a couple. While profit remains the overwhelming concern of the owners of media organizations, the crisis manifests itself not necessarily in terms of falling circulation figures or competition from 'dumber' newspapers but as a general disconnect with the readers or users of media products. This indubitably results in the depoliticization of the readers. Blogging seems to provide one way out of this impasse.

For those reading this book the word 'blog' might not be a strange one. But for the uninitiated, a blog, according to the BBC, is a Website written by an individual or group, typically using free and easy-to-use tools, consisting of periodic articles, normally in reverse chronological order.

The first blog apparently came up on 17 December 1997, and it was started by a 'techie'. Blogging's meteoric rise since is evident from the fact that in about five years' time, in 2003, the word 'blog' entered the *Oxford English Dictionary*.

Any discussion on journalism and blogs needs to examine what one's views on journalism are. If journalism is to be restricted to only those select 'professionals' trained in selecting, packaging and distributing 'stories' in an appropriate format for the 'consumption' of 'users', then this article cannot go too far.

Blogging is increasingly being used by mainstream media practitioners as well as citizens as part of their professional tasks and private initiatives. This grand conversation has become the topic of heated debates. The mainstream media's approach to blogs has been ambivalent. In the initial days of the Iraq war, for instance, Kevin Sites, who was an embedded journalist for CNN, set up a Weblog or blog, which quickly became popular for the un-embedded US public. But Sites was asked by CNN to shut the Weblog down, despite his willingness to make it a publication from the CNN stable.

The writer of Mediaah Weblog,[1] Pradyuman Maheshwari, acquired international fame when the *Times of India* slapped him with a threat for libel, ostensibly for attacking the publication in his blog. Maheshwari's plight was noted by many media watchdogs all over the world.

Andrew Sullivan, the conservative journalist in the United States, has become a brand in his own right by using his blog, now part of the *Time* magazine Website, effectively.

But more than individuals there are some new corporate stars of this 'revolution'. Undoubtedly the search engine behemoth Google has turned out to be the largest player in the blog market. Google purchased the entire archive of Usenet,[2] and then bought Blogger.com; as a result, Google now owns hundreds and thousands of blogs that attract about 15 million visitors a month. The site can now boast of as many visitors as those going to the Websites of the *New York Times, USA Today* and the *Washington Post*.

One view goes as follows: Journalism, as we have known it—be warned—is in for a shock from this weird monster called a blog, which is about to render the task of the professional journalist tough. No more can the expert journalist produce something that an amateur with a blog has not already spelt out. No more can a journalist take the news consumer for granted by putting out what he or she considers newsworthy. Every issue can be, and is, contested, ripped threadbare and digested. Take the case of Dan Rather, the erstwhile anchorperson of CBS' 60 Minutes in the US. Rather's 'mistake in judgment' in reporting a story challenging President Bush's military service cost him his job in 2004. Rather had based his story on documents that he had reproduced using a word processor, but claimed were original. His illustrious career came to an unfortunate end, with bloggers going after him for claiming he was in the right, and that he was sure of it. That George W Bush's military service was, indeed, a matter of controversy, did not matter. Dan Rather had to go, no matter what justification he offered to prove that his claim was merely flawed, whereas Bush, he claimed, was morally wrong.

Blogging is clearly journalism as practiced in the mainstream, if measured by the standards of what Bill Kovach and Tom Rosenstiel enumerate in *The Elements of Journalism*: (*a*) Journalism's first obligation is to the truth; (*b*) Its first loyalty is to citizens; (*c*) Its essence is a discipline of verification; (*d*) Its practitioners must maintain an independence from those they cover; (*e*) It must serve as an independent monitor of power; (*f*) It must provide a forum for public criticism and compromise; (*g*) It must strive to make the significant interesting and relevant; (*h*) It must keep the news comprehensive and proportional; and (*i*) Its practitioners must be allowed to exercise their personal conscience.[3] Points of view such as 'Blogs are cheap, easily updated, and can focus on a niche market with passionate followers–an advertiser's dream,'[4] are merely worth taking note of, nothing more.

The *Guardian*, which has used blogs very effectively, is an example of the trend of mainstream news organizations finally coming to terms with this new form of publishing. It probably also signals the arrival of blogging as a form of 'making money online'. This is a concern that, not surprisingly in the age of the market, is common in discussions on online journalism. Advertising, especially context-sensitive advertising, made popular by Google AdSense, where advertisements appear on Webpages that can potentially be of interest to the user of the content on the page, has made it possible for bloggers and small publishers to generate revenue.

News blogs have become popular destinations for users of mainstream publications because they tend to publish the 'juicy' bits of the story a reporter could not get into the article published in the main edition. They have also become forums for eliciting information from expert users and generally keeping in touch with users. In a thought-provoking paper, 'How "The News" Becomes News in Everyday Life', Vivian B Martin, Assistant Professor of Journalism, Central Connecticut State University, says that readers 'reference news in everyday conversation, writing letters to the editor, and participating in public affairs online discussions.'[5] Crucially, she says,

> People determine news reports to be newsworthy or not newsworthy, hence relevant or irrelevant, or they may focus on some of the particulars of a news report as irrelevant, an assessment that can have consequences for further attending.... Relevance construction is both straightforward and nuanced; people often concede some items are newsworthy and relevant to other people, but not to them personally.[6]

Indeed, Martin thinks:

News articles can become vehicles for any number of discussions not immediately related to the subject, taking decisions about relevancy out of the hands
of news producers as commentary on news presentations becomes part of the
news. It also illustrates the role socio-cultural context plays in how people
direct their attention. As interviews, letters to the editor, group discussions,
Internet interactions and other data illustrated, affiliations, particularly group
identities and political ideologies, can explain a significant amount of the
variation in how people assess media relevance and credibility, and frame the
issues or events that are the subject of media reports. Depending on context,
some identities are more active than others during news attending.[7]

If journalistic products hold such an important part in the
worldview of news consumers, the task is to keep the interest
and even extend it. The Internet offers a way out for traditional
media to connect with the citizens in an interactive way.

But for journalists, the words of Robert McChesney are
more relevant. He says, 'The Internet has opened up a very important space for progressive and democratic communication....'[8]
Blogs, discussions forums and other forms of community building
tools online could be deployed effectively to further the democratic dialogue. For journalists, it is less important whether blogs
or other forms of the new media can turn 'profitable' than
whether they offer news consumers and journalists attractive ways
to interact. Indeed, from Martin's paper one can surmise that all
forms of media are equally important to reach out to news consumers. Blogs ought to be viewed merely as another tool of
communication.

Any tool of communication, however, has the potential to be
compromised. Blogging, while it had its moments of glory such
as when the Baghdad blogger Salam Pax wrote about the other
side of the picture in the US–Iraq war, was compromised when
Pax was quickly roped in to perform the bidding of the established
media.

In India, the entire mainstream media, save *Frontline* magazine,
declared unanimously in the last Lok Sabha elections that India
was indeed 'shining' under the Bharatiya Janata Party-led dis-
pensation. The people thought otherwise when they voted the
BJP-led National Democratic Alliance out of power. But the mainstream media got away with its flawed views. Significantly, it was

only bloggers that hauled up a management institute for its false claims about the programme it offered. Despite the institute going after the bloggers, the latter were able to bring the issue to the notice of the mainstream media.[9] In addition, Indian bloggers helped in organizing relief to victims during the 2004 tsunami that hit South Asia. But these are relatively small achievements. Any viable online alternative to emerge could be in the form of, say, The NewStandard.

The NewStandard vows: 'Rather than hide behind the label of "objectivity" while serving the interests of investors and advertisers, our mission is to portray the world from the perspective of people who view it and are impacted by it.'[10]

Noam Chomsky acknowledges the independent hard-news Website's role. He says, 'It is hard to exaggerate the significance these days of independent, careful, probing and thoughtful news reporting. The NewStandard has set a very high standard in that regard. It has already won an important place among those who want to understand the world, and to act to change it. And the prospects ahead are exciting.'[11] The reader-funded publication helped sponsor Dahr Jamail, a journalist from Alaska, United States, to do independent journalism from Iraq. Jamail was able to do some real journalism as a result. He now has his own Website with a Weblog at http://dahrjamailiraq.com/index.php. The NewStandard also uses blogs effectively.

Another online success story that has gained a lot of attention is the South Korean site OhMyNews.[12] It epitomises a citizen journalism site. The site has a core staff to ensure editorial quality, but beyond that it also pays contributors for news items. It relies on the readers to rank the stories on the Website according to importance.

The NewStandard model is encouraging. It needs special mention because it has used ways to reach out to its readers effectively. That is the promise of the new media, but not exclusively so. Can we have media outlets that, on the lines of The NewStandard, are independent and anti-commercial and wedded 'to portray the world from the perspective of people who view it and are impacted by it'?[13]

In the final analysis, whether it be blogs or Websites or any other method of reaching citizens, the bottom-line is that we need more independent, democratic media. McChesney made a crucial point when he said, 'If the Internet becomes a viable commercial medium, there is a good chance that many of the media giants will be among the firms capable of capitalizing upon it.'[14] Thus the democratic media needs to be fought for and preserved zealously, to ensure that information in the public domain is uncorrupted by commercial considerations.

At the very least, as Ken Layne, editor of Sploid, says: 'Journalists should blog to make Weblogs better. Too many of these sites are poorly written, rarely updated and of no real interest to anyone but the author. Your Weblog should at least amuse or educate your friends and colleagues. And too many of them are terribly designed—unreadable fonts, headache-inducing backgrounds and huge graphic files are the most common sins.'[15]

Journalism in its pristine manifestation should be democratic and non-commercial. If the battle to keep the Internet democratic and non-commercial is winnable, then journalism's marriage with the Internet can herald a refreshing and essential direction for democracy.

Notes

1. Mediaah.com (http://mediaah.blogspot.com/). Accessed on 9 March 2006.
2. Wikipedia defines Usenet as a distributed Internet discussion system that evolved from a general purpose UUCP network of the same name. Users read and post e-mail-like messages (called 'articles') to a number of distributed newsgroups, categories that resemble bulletin board systems in most respects. See http://en.wikipedia.org/wiki/Usenet. Accessed on 9 March 2006.
3. B Kovach and T Rosestiel, *The Elements of Journalism* (New York, Three Rivers Press, 2001), p. 12.
4. Stephen Baker, 'Big Media, Little Blogosphere', *BusinessWeek*, 24 October 2005.
5. V B Martin, 'How "The News" Becomes News in Everyday Life' (Paper presented at the Association for Education in Journalism and Mass Communication in Toronto, Canada, August 2004), p. 3.
6. Ibid., p. 9.
7. Ibid., p. 11.
8. Robert McChesney, *Capitalism and the Information Age* (India, Cornerstone Publications, with Monthly Review Press, New York, 2001), p. 21.

9. Gaurav Sabnis, 'Vantage Point', http://gauravsabnis.blogspot.com/2005/08/fraud-that-is-iipm.html. Accessed on 9 March 2006.
10. http://newstandardnews.net/about/index.cfm/page/faq_tns. Accessed on 9 March 2006.
11. http://newstandardnews.net/promo2/index.cfm?action=show_special-testimonials. Accessed on 9 March 2006.
12. http://english.ohmynews.com/. Accessed on 9 March 2006.
13. http://newstandardnews.net/about/index.cfm/page/faq_tns. Accessed on 9 March 2006.
14. McChesney, *Capitalism and the Information Age*, p. 22.
15. K Layne, 'Media Web Logs For Fun and No Profit', *Online Journalism Review*, 7 December 2000, http://www.ojr.org/ojr/workplace/index.cfm. Accessed on 9 March 2006.

27

Tell Me a Story: Writing and Teaching Narrative

Robin Reisig

The phrase 'narrative writing' is very much in vogue now in American journalism. The Nieman Foundation for Journalism at Harvard University even runs an annual conference on narrative writing; the first was in 2001.[1] The conference, aimed at newspaper reporters, is so popular that it was recently moved out of a more genteel setting into a convention hall with rooms so vast that former *Los Angeles Times* editor John Carroll began his remarks by thanking Joseph Stalin for inspiring the architecture.

'Narrative' is a hot buzzword, as though it's the new *new* thing. Newspaper editors, eager to retain dwindling readers, are willing to experiment with it. The *LA Times* even won a Pulitzer Prize after re-creating–with copious footnotes–the journey of a Latino teenager who crossed the border illegally into the United States! While the plump middle-aged reporter didn't jump onto moving trains, as the teenager did, she did her best to retrace his steps to check out his story and add verisimilitude to a breathtaking account that she did not in fact witness. The story broke many of the conventional rules of journalism, yet still met ethical standards.

Of course the narrative form is older than the *Iliad* or the Bible, which reminds us that 'there is nothing new under the sun'.

'Tell me a story!' That childhood refrain can apply to journalism too. But a reporter typing an article on deadline can easily forget, as political writer Matt Bai put it, that 'There is a reason why they call it a "story".'

Newspaper journalism too once told stories in chronological order. In the United States, the conventional newspaper form of the 'inverted pyramid'–where the most important information is at the top of the story, and the rest of the information is placed in descending order of importance–was a result of unreliable technology. During America's great Civil War, in the 19th century, reporters would send home gripping accounts of battles, but if the telegraph wires went down, the editors in New York would find that the story lacked the most important element: Who won?

Some modern writers–notably Truman Capote, who talked about creating a non-fiction novel with *In Cold Blood*–talk as though they had invented something new. But the *New Yorker* magazine was publishing narrative long before Capote made his discovery that crimes make good stories, and terrible crimes make bestsellers. John Hersey's *Hiroshima* put us there the day the bomb dropped.

'Magazine articles are about ideas,' some magazine writers and teachers of magazine writing say (I've even occasionally lapsed into repeating this myself). There are sub-divisions of this thinking, such as the useful SINI (for 'a Subject Is Not an Idea'), that remind reporters to find an angle.

A *New Yorker* editor, talking to my class, put all this in a useful context when he observed that the reason many magazine editors say their articles are about ideas is that most magazines don't give writers enough time to report the story well.

New Yorker writers have regularly done narrative writing where they witness everything they report. At the Nieman convention, some speakers paid tribute to Jon Franklin. In his book *Writing for Story* (Penguin), Franklin explained how he transformed himself into an accomplished writer. 'As a young man desperately committed to literature,' he explains, he would scour local libraries for books that would reveal the secret of writing. The books he found 'would often make a point of saying that while writing was a craft, it was also an art– and ultimately one either had it (whatever "it" was) or one didn't. The clear implication was that if you didn't understand what they were driving at, you didn't have it. By that measure, I sure didn't.'[2]

'I still don't have "it",' he adds. But Franklin has won two Pulitzer Prizes, including the first ever awarded (in 1979) for feature writing. His secret: he decided that a good story should have a complication and a resolution. The pitfall for young writers, he explained, is that they find stories that may have interesting complications but that lack resolutions. He had many more tips, including a suggestion that the resolution should be positive or upbeat. But Franklin's definition of upbeat might be viewed as elastic. In his Pulitzer-winning 'Mrs Kelly's Monster', a woman undergoing brain surgery dies during the story.[3] Franklin said that he therefore focused more on the surgeon, who accepted defeat and moved on.

As a young *Village Voice* writer, I too often fell into the trap that Franklin mentioned. For my slice-of-life narratives, I would go out with a group of people and tell of their adventures. The group might be women drinking at chic restaurants where unescorted women were not served drinks (on the theory that they might be prostitutes); or women whistling at construction workers; or feminists trying to have a convention about prostitution only to get beat up during the proceedings by the prostitutes they wanted to help; or demonstrators against the Vietnam War, including John Kerry, camping out in Washington; or young white unemployed men in a working-class Boston neighbourhood acting restless as the local high school is integrated. But if I look back at the stories that worked best, they were the ones that—by chance—ended in some stunning victory or surprising defeat. The feminists going from bar to bar were served so often that they became inebriated by their success. The conference about prostitution ended with a fistfight.

Stories. Surprises. The stories worked best when luck was with me and the story had a natural ending, and was in fact a story.

I would look at what I considered my best stories with astonishment. Half were written quickly and easily, in a day or two (or as I progressed to longer stories, a few weeks) and the writing flowed easily; the other half were written with great agony and often over a considerable period of time. The narrative ones were the easy ones.

When Gene Roberts turned the *Philadelphia Inquirer* from the number two paper in Philly into a winner of Pulitzers for investigative reporting, he also remembered the storyteller. As a tribute to him, his reporters wrote about an imaginary Eugene Roberts prize, a tribute

> to the story they'll be talking about in the coffee shop on Main Street;
> to efforts at portraying real life itself;
> to journalism that 'wakes me up and makes me see';
> to the revival of the disappearing storyteller.

Here are two exercises that readers who are young writers or who teach journalism might want to use. I created the second one and learned the first from Jonathan Mandell, a former adjunct professor at Columbia University's Graduate School of Journalism, who spent most of his career as a feature writer for many newspapers including the New York-based *Daily News*'s magazine and *New York Newsday*. He is now the editor-in-chief of the fine public-spirited Website www.gothamgazette.com.

Mandell learned the story from his mother, who taught the third grade. I will explain more about that—and why the exercises can be useful—after the exercises themselves. I'd urge readers who want to try the first exercise themselves not to read the explanation after it until they have tried writing the assignment.

The assignment (do not read on unless you are prepared to do this now and have a pen or pencil handy; this is to be written by hand):

> For the next 15 minutes, write about the neighbourhood where you grew up (other topics can be substituted). If you grew up in more than one neighbourhood, just quickly pick one. You can tell about something that happened in the neighbourhood, or describe the neighbourhood or people you know. You can take a moment (no more!) to pick your neighbourhood or idea, but once you start writing, you cannot stop writing. You cannot pause or lift your pen from the page. Even if all you can think to write is 'I can't decide what to write next,' write that; but keep writing!

Read the following *after* you tried this exercise:
You probably wrote a simple, powerful narrative. Perhaps it had vivid descriptions: If you mentioned trees or flowers, for example, you probably mentioned the kind or at least let us see what the tree looked like. If you described a scene, you probably wrote so vividly that we could see it.

Most important: Your writing was very likely to be free from flowery language, purple passages or what George Orwell called 'humbug' generally.

The secret is that when people don't have time to think or to do things that they consider writerly, they write simply, directly, powerfully. In short, they write well. It helps, too, that they have a story to tell, something to say.

Mandell expected this exercise to be of great use to our Columbia students when we taught a class together. But Columbia students tend to be experienced journalists and quite sophisticated, so it is only the rare student who falls into the trap of flowery writing.

However, the exercise is still extraordinarily useful for a few students. For the rare students unexcited by journalism or bored with their assignments (luckily, these are few), this helps remind the students about what they care about—and that they can find similar things to write about as journalists. A student who pulled pranks in high school ('low level juvenile delinquency') and was constantly in trouble as an adolescent might find that he can find stories he cares deeply about—and has a special gift for telling—by going to alternative high schools filled with problem students. A student who went to a religious school might find that the closing of Catholic schools (even though he is not a Catholic) will touch his imagination. Students realize that they can write about what they care about.

Interestingly, I found the exercise had its intended purpose in two very different places in my teaching career. One was teaching journalism in India to students who had, for the most part, graduated from college only the previous year and had little or no journalism experience. The other group—where some students found the exercise transforming—was one with more, not less, experienced students than most of my Columbia students: experienced Portuguese journalists who had won a fellowship and come to Columbia for a few weeks of classes. Like many Europeans, Portuguese journalists seemed to write with opinion in the news columns; to write for what is now coming to be known as viewspapers. I knew that I wasn't going to change Portuguese journalism in a few classes, and I'd have to figure out a way to teach the writers something useful. What to do? The answer was easy. The articles I had seen, while rich in opinion, were lamentably short on facts that supported that opinion and that could make the writers' point of view more persuasive.

It was only after we did the exercise that the brightest of the group, an editor in his 30s, exclaimed happily: 'Now I get it!'

In the second exercise, students enact a courtroom scene where they sob, hug, bury their heads in their hands and do their best to look upset, but they don't talk except for one student who cries out, 'Oh, no! Oh, no!' Their classmates write up the scene, as though it is the moment when a verdict was announced in a murder trial. The lesson is easy. Every high-school fiction-writing class taught it: 'Show, don't tell.' Don't say the mother comforted her son; show her hugging him. Don't say the son was distraught; show him burying his head in his hands. Or as Mark Twain put it: 'Don't say the old lady screamed; bring her on, and let her scream.'

Afterword

Tips from the Nieman Website (http://www.nieman.harvard.edu/ narrative/ is the main Website):

Nieman Program on Narrative JournalismDirector's Corner Nieman Foundation > Nieman Program on Narrative Journalism > Director's Corner > What Is Narrative?

At a minimum, narrative denotes writing with (A) set scenes, (B) characters, (C) action that unfolds over time, (D) the interpretable voice of a teller–a narrator with a somewhat discernable personality–and (E) some sense of relationship to the reader, viewer or listener, which, all arrayed, (F) lead the audience toward a point, realization or destination. To comment on each of these: (A) Set Scenes: Lots of unpractised narrative writing simply is haphazard or naive about painting physical location: Objects fly about, are near and far, we're inside and outside. I call it 'Chagall-like description.' Narrative–engaging narrative–sets the reader down in a scene. (B) Characters: The standard newsvoice is the voice of a beneficent bureaucracy–the speech of informative sentinels on the walls of the city, issuing heads-ups to citizens ('A fire yesterday at 145 Elm St. destroyed ... damage is estimated at ...'). It is a voice that eschews investigations of character. In the world of news-voice, people are citizens, not characters, and they have 'civic traits': addresses, ages, arrest records, voting district and precinct locations, official hospital conditions and military statuses. Narrative is about people doing stuff and, to some extent and in the right places, must reach past civic traits if it is to cover real folks' real stories well. (C) Action that unfolds over time: This is the very essence of narrative construction: the I-beams of narrative on which all else leans. Action also offers a non-topical way of organizing material–arraying it chronologically as it's experienced by a character in a setting, crossing outline categories but following experiential ones. (D) Voice: Most narrative articles, books and documentaries represent a sensible truce in the struggle between chronological and topical organizational principles. This is possible only (1) if readers, viewers or listeners are so engaged by the strong voice of the teller that.... (E) Relationship with audience: ... they willingly follow the teller through unset topical digressions, shift gladly and interestedly to other settings and characters and back; and (2) if readers then start assembling in mind a sequence of sub-textual comprehensions that works toward their engineered discovery that .... (F) Destination: ... the story has a theme, purpose, reason, destination and that it's worthwhile to ingest.

Notes

1. See http://www.nieman.harvard.edu/narrative/.
2. Jon Franklin, *Writing for Story: Craft Secrets of Dramatic Nonfiction* (USA, Penguin Group, 1994).
3. http://www.bylinefranklin.com/bylinefranklin/drama-monster.html.

28

India: A Billion Testimonies Now

Robert Brown

Maximum City, Suketu Mehta's breathtaking tapestry of stories about the beauty and brutality of modern Mumbai, has been hailed by critics around the globe as one of the best non-fiction works to emerge from India in recent years. It undoubtedly is, as the blurb on the back-cover says, 'a book as vast, diverse and rich in experience, incident and sensation as the city itself'. But what does this book about Bombay (as Mehta still prefers to call the city of his upbringing) have to teach experienced and aspiring journalists about how to set about covering the sub-continent at the start of the 21st century? Quite a lot, according to a couple of the most astute and self-critical critics. Adam Hochschild, an American magazine writer-turned-teacher and author, stated in his review for a leading American monthly: 'Mehta makes virtually any other reporting on India look pallid by comparison.'[1] Reviewing the book for an Indian audience, Debashish Mukerji surmised: '*Maximum City* is journalism at its best. It is journalism of a kind never seen in India before. For us hacks it ought to become a beacon, a model, a guide book.'[2]

In this chapter, I want to explore these two assertions, asking first how and why Mehta's observations put in the shade the vast majority of journalism which rolls off India's presses. Second, I want to question to what extent this book can serve as a source of inspiration and instruction for journalists who cover the sub-continent. My central argument will be that *Maximum City* does impressively demonstrate the rich potential for literary reportage in India but a critical reading of this text also points up some of the potential pitfalls awaiting those who stray into this demanding genre.

Maximum City, it must be stated from the outset, is a fusion of genres: part memoir, part travelogue and part journalism, a rich alchemy all researched and written with the precision and elegance of a fact-based novel. The author's vivid documentary-like prose captures and conveys the teeming metropolis of Mumbai, where the desperate and the sadly deluded flood in from the surrounding countryside to either make it or be maimed and crushed. He shines an especially revealing spotlight into the dark corners of the city where skimpily skirted bar-girls dream of becoming Bollywood stars, those who have made it onto Page 3 indulge their perverse sexual appetites, and disillusioned police officials routinely torture suspects. Amazingly, Mehta managed to observe some of these brutal interrogations, which he describes in one of the most gripping, and gruesome, passages in the book:

> The constable comes back with a thick leather strap, about six inches wide, attached to a wooden handle. One of the cops takes it and brings it savagely down across the fat man's face. The sound of leather hitting bare human flesh is impossible to describe unless you've heard it. The man screams. The cop brings it down again. Meanwhile, the cousin is getting blows in his back with the other policeman's elbow. Both men are bending, cringing, to avoid the blows, with the strap, the belts, and the policeman's bare hands, which are landing all over their face and bodies....
>
> 'Bring in his wife and child. We'll beat his child in front of him if he doesn't talk.'
>
> 'No, sir! I'll tell you everything. I've told you everything.'[3]

Observe how, in the midst of this manically brutal assault, Mehta notices that the counterfeiters never forget India's deep consciousness of rank: 'As they are being beaten, they address their tormentors as "sir". Thus we addressed our teachers in school.... Not once do they fly out; not once do they scream an obscenity.'

This is journalism that reads like fiction with the ring of truth of reported fact, what has been variously labelled literary journalism, intimate reporting, the journalism of immersion, the art of reportage, the new journalism or even the new, new journalism. The book was short-listed for a Pulitzer Prize, US journalism's equivalent of the Oscars, and it collected an accolade at the annual

Ulysses Lettres awards for the Art of Reportage, which are distributed each October at a glittering ceremony in Berlin. It was at one such ceremony that Ryszard Kapuscinski, the legendary Polish-born foreign correspondent and non-fiction writer, voiced his criticism of the standard coverage of developments across the developing world. Kapuscinski told the Berlin audience:

> Working in Third World countries as a correspondent for a press agency for quite a long time, I often felt dissatisfied,' Kapuscinski told the Berlin audience. 'This arose from the paucity of the language of conventional journalism when confronting the rich, varied, colourful, ineffable reality of those cultures, customs and beliefs. The everyday language of information that we use in the media is very poor, stereotypical and formulaic. For this reason, huge areas of reality are rendered beyond the sphere of description.[4]

Traditional print journalism is plainly struggling to capture and convey the full enormity of the contemporary Indian experience and the captivating dramas being played out across the subcontinent on a daily basis. This failing is not unique to India. It is—and always has been—a constant frustration for people who ply this trade the world over. In the words of an Australian journalism educator: 'Journalists with more than a few years newsroom experience start to chafe against the limitations of daily news; they realise that the form of the standard news story may be tailor-made for conveying information but flounders under the weight of emotion or subtlety.'[5]

Isn't it unfair, even absurd, to compare quotidian news features knocked out under the frantic pressure of fast-looming deadlines with an acclaimed work of creative non-fiction, meticulously and lovingly moulded by a master craftsman of this particular literary genre over a much longer time period through countless drafts and redrafts?

Of course, Mehta's 542-page epic (trimmed down from a truly Himalayan first draft measuring 1,667 pages) took several years to complete. In fact, there was a gap of seven years between the day this book was commissioned by Knopf and the day of its worldwide publicity launch in Bombay. No magazine or newspaper could afford to indulge even its most gifted writers to that degree. Apart from anything else, their stories would be out of date by the time they appeared.

But, make no mistake, even journalists tied to a topical news agenda can raise their game and rise above the ordinary. Every so often, when scanning Indian news-stands or surfing the Internet, one can come across pieces of inspired journalism which really distinguish themselves with their evocative power, penetrating insights and narrative drive. Raj Kamal Jha, fiction writer and executive editor of the *Indian Express*, has encouraged his most gifted correspondents to engage in narrative journalism, as did the editor of news portal rediff.com, Nikhill Lakshman, during the heady days of the dotcom boom. Executive editor of *Tehelka*, Sankarshan Thakur, has done the same since *Tehelka* metamorphosed from a Website into a weekly paper.

Basharat Peer, a young Kashmiri-born journalist who cut his reporting teeth on rediff.com before transferring to *Tehelka*, has been keenly endeavouring to develop his writing talents in this direction. 'The essence of narrative journalism for me is to represent people as complex, multi-layered human beings and not as simply statistics and names as in the traditional inverted pyramid,' he enthused. Peer's own particular engagement with this genre stemmed from growing up in Kashmir during the most violent phase of the conflict in that state. 'Almost every day since 1990 I would sit with my family huddled around a radio at night and hear the news about the conflict,' he remembers. 'News was always all about how many more had been killed. Later, when I left Kashmir to study law at college in Delhi, I struggled to keep up with the conflict through reading the newspapers. But all most newspapers told me was: 31 killed, 41 injured. People were reduced to mere statistics.' Literary reportage has the power to bring such bare facts alive and tell the real stories behind statistics, Peer is convinced. 'But, sadly, narrative journalism is an orphan, living on the margins of newspaper society in India.'[6]

Even in the few publishing outlets which are prepared to give literary reportage a try, one finds that the vast majority of the journalism remains hastily composed hackery. There is a slowly growing band of journalists dotted around India's newsrooms who are devoted to this more demanding form of journalism, but there has been no magazine likewise devoted to publishing it since the closure some years back of Kai Friese's *India Magazine*. India simply has nothing on par with the *New Yorker, Atlantic Monthly*, the *New York Times'* Sunday magazine or the *London*

Review of Books, Granta or the *Guardian* weekend supplements. It is to these outlets that one of the most talented Indian literary journalists of these times, Pankaj Mishra, has turned in order to practice literary journalism on a sustained basis.

To tell their true stories more powerfully, some of the most acclaimed journalists in America and Britain, and to a lesser extent those in other advanced industrialized countries, have long deployed a range of techniques normally associated with novelists. Significantly, Mehta's book began its life as an article in a British magazine. It was bought on spec by the publisher, Knopf, on the basis of a feature which Mehta wrote for Granta in 1997, reflecting upon the malign legacy of modern India's most vicious Hindu–Muslim riots in Bombay 1993. Founded by Cambridge students in the late 19th century but based for the last quarter century in the heart of literary London, Granta is a promoter of new writing and has always published as much non-fiction as fiction. Literary journalism in Britain can trace its lineage all the way to Daniel Defoe back in the 18th century and the tradition is still proudly upheld to this day, not just on the pages of Granta but also by the *London Review of Books* and *The Guardian Saturday Review and Magazine*. However, the centre of gravity for literary journalism long ago shifted across the Atlantic.

The American tradition of writing in this genre can be traced back to Mark Twain in the 19th century, although most scholars would commence a little later with famous muckrakers such as Lincoln Steffens and fast forward to John Steinbeck in the 1930s or Ernest Hemingway around the time of the Second World War. Others would say it was Truman Capote who most masterfully demonstrated the true potential for blending reportage with creative writing techniques in his controversial 1965 book *In Cold Blood*, about the murder of a respected local family in rural west Kansas. Capote, a hungry, still youngish talent in search of a great theme, was sent out by the editor of the *New Yorker* to chronicle the impact of the killing on the local community, but he consciously set out to yield what he called 'a serious new art-form: the non-fiction novel'. Although some questioned the authenticity of his 'true account' of the murders and their aftermath, he was enthusiastically embraced by the New Journalism movement being spearheaded in the late 1960s by Tom Wolfe.

Wolfe, an east coast author, applied a 'technicolour vernacular' to writing about California's drug and car cultures in *The Electric Kool-Aid Acid Test* and *The Kandy-Kolored Tangerine-Flake Streamline Baby*. In his oft-cited introduction to the book that became a self-promoting manifesto, he argued that non-fiction had surpassed the novel as 'the most important literature being written in America today'.[7] New Journalism, from his perspective, injected four fictional devices into conventional coverage: dramatic scenes, extensive passages of dialogue, status details and point of view or attitude. Accounts of real events and true stories were to be supplemented by the writer's personal opinions and reactions, which the writer could only gather by putting himself into the story:

> They had to gather all the material the conventional journalist was after–and keep going. It seemed all-important to *be there* when the dramatic scenes took place, to get the dialogue, the gestures, the facial expressions, the details of the environment. The idea was to give the full objective description, plus something that readers had always had to go to novels and short stories for: namely, the subjective or emotional life of the characters.[8]

Suketu Mehta must have encountered the leading luminaries of American literary journalism–Wolfe, Norman Mailer, Joan Didion, Hunter S Thompson, Gay Talese and the rest–when he studied at New York University and the Iowa Writers' Workshop. The person he cites as his role model was, however, supremely engaged in this genre before Capote or Wolfe was even in diapers. Described by one admirer as 'the paragon of reporters', Joseph Mitchell joined the *New Yorker* as a feature writer in 1938 and spent the next 58 years on America's most august magazine, chronicling the quirky characters he encountered on the streets, the waterfront and in the saloons. Mitchell's keen powers of observation combined with his wit, empathy and spare, elegant style helped set a standard for writers of non-fiction, a standard more than upheld on the pages of *Maximum City*.

A boyish-looking 41-year-old when his masterpiece appeared, Mehta set out to respond to what he perceives as 'a global hunger for learning about megacities, Bombay in particular'. He could have approached this task by penning a standard city portrait or even a sombre urban history, but he was eager to engage the maximum possible audience, and, like Mitchell, he chose to do so by the most tried and trusted method–the ancient and eternal art of storytelling.

The power of narrative has been apparent from the days when primitive people sat around campfires and told each other stories. Mary Lawrence, a journalism professor at the University of Missouri, explains:

> People have had their stories from the beginning, whether they're fables or teaching lessons great and small, or histories that tell us where we came from or big stories that help us cope with the world.... We're fooling ourselves if we think we communicate primarily by bursts of information. We live for stories– whether they're movies or TV shows or plays or poems or even newspaper pieces. We want stories to hold us over and over again.... They comfort us, arouse us, they excite us and educate us, and when they touch our hearts we embrace them and keep them with us.... Why else would we need VCRs?[9]

Suketu Mehta's biography of Bombay is, as he expresses it, 'a group of interrelated stories and what links them all is my story and my quest to go home again.' He consciously set out to insert himself into the narrative, to inhabit the story he recounts. Born in Calcutta, and bred in Bombay until the age of 14 when his father migrated to New York, Mehta moved his own family back to Mumbai for two years in order to undertake intensive research. This is another essential defining element of narrative journalism: the writers quite literally get themselves inside a story, sometimes inflicting upon themselves a degree of discomfort, if not danger.

This requires massive investment of time and that can be a real turn-off for the vast majority of writers, editors and publishers, who tend to favour a fast turnaround of news stories and features. In the words of Robin Gaby Fisher, a two-time Pulitzer finalist, 'Narrative is the private story behind the public story and it takes time to get that.' John Hersey interviewed almost 40 A-bomb survivors in Japan before settling upon six whose stories he would tell in a *New Yorker* article. Another New York writer, Adrian Nicole Blanc, devoted two years of his working life to chronicling the chaotic life of a teenage drug-addicted prostitute for a single magazine piece in *The Village Voice*. Ian Jack took almost a year to write and research for Granta his 20,000 word account of the killing of three Irish Republican Army terrorists by the British Army in Gibraltar in 1987. The finest literary journalists have always expended as much mental and physical energy as the most

committed investigative reporters do in following up every available lead and trawling through reams of background notes, government documents and interview transcripts. They have also
deployed an additional weapon which few of the aforementioned
journalistic detectives are capable of deploying: their powers of
personal observation.

Tom French, a Pulitzer Prize-winning feature writer at the
St. Petersburg Times in Florida, has stressed the need for narrative
journalists to 'zoom in' with cinematic detail on a key moment
in every story. *Maximum City* is teeming with pure cinematic
moments, which isn't surprising when you consider that Suketu
Mehta is not just a journalist but also a Bollywood screenplay
writer. With a moviemaker's eye, Mehta tightens his lens on a
mini-skirted Bombay bar-girl and her suitor having sex for the
first time in a taxi as they bat away six fluttering love birds, which
are slaughtered for titillation in the course of copulating, their
carcasses hurled out of the cab after the couple climax. (The sexual rituals of gangsters and their hit men become a source of recurring fascination for him—and for us, his readers.) In order to
sketch the dark shadow that the 1993 communal violence has
left in some quarters of Bombay, he persuades a Shiv Sena activist to walk him through a quarter of the city and point out the
exact spots where he and his fellow Hindutva fanatics set fire to
a mosque, looted shops and raped and murdered Muslims. The
man even tells him: 'It was like a movie!'

Movies move us in many different ways, not all of which may
be unsettling. Mehta appreciates this. One of the most oft-quoted
passages from *Maximum City* is his uplifting description of the
choreography of early morning commuter trains:

> If you are late for work in the morning in Bombay, and you reach the station
> just as the train is leaving the platform, you can run up to the packed compart-
> ment and find many hands reaching out to grab you on board, unfolding
> outwards from the train like petals ... and at the moment of contact they
> know not if the hand that is reaching for theirs belongs to a Hindu or Muslim
> or Christian or Brahmin or untouchable or whether you were born in this city
> or only arrived this morning.... All they know is that you're trying to get to the
> city of gold, and that's enough. Come aboard, they say. We'll adjust.[10]

This joyful scene captures the spirit of *insaniyat* (humanity),
which is one of the many redeeming qualities of modern Mumbai,
a city which may strike some as a completely insane place to live

and work until they realize that this city can also be surprisingly warm. Narrative journalists should never forget that the world is not just packed with pain and misery but is also bursting with scenes of joy. French urges his fellow practitioners: 'You need to open yourself simply to the things around you that spark your attention or that penetrate you and hang with you and the things that make you smile or just make you gasp. I am a very, very big fan of joy.'[11]

Along with scenes and characters which arouse the entire gamut of human emotions, literary journalism is also jam-packed with sensory detail. Mehta makes us smell the diesel exhaust, rotting fruit, sweat and perfume throughout 'a city in heat' which is 'humid with sex'. Above all, there is the smell of shit (human waste and where to put it is an ever-present issue).

This genre is sometimes called intimate journalism or immersion reporting because its practitioners immerse themselves so that they inhabit the story. By taking up residence in the story, their presence in the unfolding plots seems to affect everything, including choice of language and, most of all, the sense of authority that a good narrative has. Total immersion was plainly Suketu Mehta's approach to capturing and conveying the teeming metropolis of Mumbai. 'The book became an obsession,' he has reflected.

> Every day, I'd take my laptop bag with me and go out to the Bombay streets. I mostly just watched people and what they did. I was like a kid in a candy store. People opened up to me on incredibly personal, private matters.... The police invited me to watch them torture suspects; the biggest Bollywood film stars were telling me about their sex lives.[12]

The critic who reviewed *Maximum City* for the *Economist* in London was struck by how astoundingly open and co-operative so many of his subjects proved to be. 'Throughout much of this drama, Mr Mehta, it seems, is just sitting there, tapping it all straight on to the keyboard of his laptop. Many of those he writes about obviously no longer see him as a reporter or writer, but as a confessor and friend.'[13]

Mehta manages to become incredibly intimate with a smorgasbord of characters, winning their trust and gently winkling out of them their stories. In the course of his research, he developed an especially close bond with a bar-girl called Monalisa, who performs for gangsters and businessmen who shower her with rupees as she writhes seductively on the dance floor. In fact, he devotes a whole 50 pages to the life she leads at the Sapphire 'ladies bar'. Monalisa shares with him stories of her childhood, her fights with her family, her frequent attempts to kill herself, her clients and how she lures them.

> 'Every person wants me,' Monalisa had said. People in Bombay think I want her too, and when they see how I am received at the bar, they think that she has given in to my want. I know what colour and type of underwear she wears. I know how she likes to make love. I know when she is sad, when she is suicidal, when she is exuberant. What is sex after such vast intimate knowledge? ... At some point the Monalisa that I'm writing in these pages will become more real, more alluring, than the Monalisa that is flesh and blood. One more *ulloo*, Monalisa will think, but imagine her surprise when she sees what I am adoring, what I am obsessed with, is a girl beyond herself, larger than herself in the mirror beyond her, and it is her that I'm blowing all my money on, it is her that I'm getting to spin and twirl under the confetti of my words. The more I write, the faster my Monalisa dances.[14]

Actually, the more Mehta writes about Monalisa—and, as already noted, he writes an immense amount about her—the more uncomfortable his relationship with her starts to appear from an ethical standpoint. In an interview to promote his book, Mehta divulged: 'With Monalisa, I became involved with her in a way that was more intimate than sex. I never did sleep with her. I realized if I had slept with her, all the stories would have been cut off. Then I would have been just another customer. I was at once a voyeur and her best friend.'[15]

This practice of 'befriending' his subjects left one American critic distinctly uncomfortable. In an otherwise gushing review, Adam Hochschild posed the question:

> I wonder how this woman, and the other people who readily confide their stories to him, may feel when these are read by family and friends ... most of the others who opened their souls to Mehta probably have no sense of what it means to speak to a writer.... Such insatiable curiosity about people's lives carries a greater burden for journalists, whose subjects are real and vulnerable, than it does for novelists, and Mehta seems oblivious to this.[16]

Mehta's modus operandi is that of the fly-on-the-wall documentary-maker, and he faces the same ethical dilemmas as those who make such films. Documentary-makers might fade into the background when they are observing their subjects, but they face flak if it is later alleged, or felt, that they lulled their subjects into a false sense of security, exploiting their innocence or naivete. Mehta has himself acknowledged that some of new-found 'friends' never seemed to quite grasp the true purpose of his research: 'They thought I was writing a novel but I always said I wasn't,' he stated in an interview, adding: 'I would hope that they will find that I've been fair to them, presenting them as fully rounded humans.'[17]

Whether this explanation would satisfy those who insist on adherence to the highest ethical standards in literary journalism is debatable. Mark Kramer, Director of the Nieman Program in Narrative Journalism at Harvard, believes that the writer should be a writer, not a friend to the source from the very beginning, and make sure that the subject has an accurate impression of this relationship at the outset. Advocating that narrative reporters should uphold a key element of the Hippocratic oath–'Above all, do no harm'–Kramer also insists that writer-reader contract is just as important as the writer-subject contract. The former, he feels, should include a disclosure clause stating 'If you take any liberties, tell the reader.'

Mehta did take steps to disguise the identity of some of his subjects. 'I've changed the names of most–probably they won't be identified,' he says. 'But there's potential for really serious violence or lawsuits.'[18] The veteran police official who allows him to observe the torture of a suspect is granted a protective pseudonym (although any reader of Indian newspapers will instantly recognize that the man in question is Rakesh Maria). A senior police official is presumably sufficiently versed at handling the media to realize the exact nature of the relationship into which he is engaging with any reporter. He also presumably weighed up the pros and cons of ceding to Mehta's request to sit in on a few interrogation sessions.

American practitioners of the New Journalism did take liberties–inserting themselves relentlessly into their copy, describing and quoting people who were actually composite characters, even claiming to get inside the heads of these characters to tell us what they were thinking–an exercise of artistic license which left some readers feeling confused if not downright suspicious.

'Entertaining though it was, this school of journalism left a persistent public perception that journalists are about as trustworthy as second-hand car salesmen,' noted one critic of the movement recently.[19] The tendency for Wolfe and his associates to strut around like literary rock stars also proved a turn-off for many.

There have been journalists who have been too creative in their pursuit of this category of creative writing. Although *In Cold Blood* was hailed as a masterpiece of literary journalism by many critics, two subsequent biographies of Truman Capote revealed that he either massaged or even made up some key events. Another account of an American murder case, this time set in Savannah and penned by a former editor of *Esquire* magazine– John Berendt's *Midnight in the Garden of Good and Evil*, which was described in 1994 by the famous critic Edmund White as 'the best non-fiction novel since *In Cold Blood* and a lot more entertaining'–was denied an award by the Pulitzer Prize non-fiction committee because of concerns about some of the fictional devices deployed. Berendt placed himself in the narrative of events which occurred *years before he set foot in Savannah to commence his investigations.* More recently, a young writer called Stephen Glass was sacked by the prestigious Washington-based political weekly *New Republic* because he totally fabricated many of the features he wrote for that publication–a tale of deception and downfall which has been portrayed in the film *Shattered Glass.* The temptation for some writers to cheat and take shortcuts when confronted with the messiness of finding and filing the truth is one of the chief pitfalls of literary journalism, according to an Australian professor who has studied the genre:

> If the reporting work earns literary journalists the freedom to borrow fictional techniques to write the story, there is just one problem: how does the reader know that the events described are real? The simple answer is they do not; they trust the writer. But some writers are not trustworthy. They envisage all those months of research, of gaining people's trust, hanging around waiting for things to happen, recording minute details, asking endless questions and they start to think: *Why don't I simply make it up?* Or else, they amass all the material and are horrified by all the gaps and lumps and mess of real life. They are tempted: *Why don't I make this read better?*[20]

The freedom of literary journalists to borrow from fiction to tell their stories imposes upon them, according to this educator, a duty to keep faith with their readers. If–and only if–they can uphold that duty, literary journalism 'offers readers much more than they customarily get and the best literary journalists create pieces that, unlike most daily journalism, stand the test of time.'[21]

There is plainly a demand for such long-form, long-life journalism in the United States, and journalists are rising to the challenge of providing it in impressive quantities. Today the leading exponents of what has been termed the 'new, new journalism' are to be found not in the bohemian quarters of the Big Apple but further up the east coast in Cambridge, Massachusetts. In the leafy groves of Harvard University you'll find the richly endowed Nieman Foundation promoting narrative journalism with almost evangelical zeal. Each December writers and editors from around the world are drawn to its snow-covered campus to participate in a series of seminars aimed at equipping them with the tools for powerful storytelling.

Literary journalism has not just survived in the United States but is arguably enjoying a new golden age. 'Rigorously reported, psychologically astute, sociologically sophisticated and politically aware, the new "New Journalism" may well be the most popular and influential development in the history of American literary nonfiction,' according to one recent celebrant of the art form.[22]

Former *Los Angeles Times* editor John Carroll told the most recent Nieman conference on narrative journalism that this genre is 'never needed more than today, when we're bombarded with fact and no context. We need to gratify the readers' emotions and intelligence to help make sense of the world.'

This is not just in the public interest. There is an urgent commercial imperative behind this cultural phenomenon: newspapers are struggling for survival in the US as young people forsake print media–indeed the very concept of squirting ink on dead trees–in favour of electronic information and entertainment. In the words of a key advocate and practitioner of this genre, Isabel Wilkerson,

> Narrative hugs and holds readers, which is just what is wanted in these times of dropping newspaper circulation and wandering audience attention. With well-developed craft skills, good narratives have kept readers glued to sagas about crucial education issues, electoral issues, race issues, and oil regulation and pollution deregulation issues. Narrative is remarkably well-suited to transforming tedious topics by offering revealing moments in the lives of people involved and affected.[23]

As American editors and proprietors struggle to supply a more appetizing and nutritious alternative to News McNuggets on the Internet, they have been embracing what might be considered the news media's equivalent of the slow-food movement.

Literary reportage has been slow to catch on elsewhere. In the words of Jane Kramer, who has spent much of her career writing in and about Europe, 'People have tried to imitate the genre and somehow can't. It's really only in America–and in a different way England–that this experiment has developed.' One reason it may not have taken off so rapidly in India is because newspaper and magazine publishers in this country are under no real pressure to review and revitalize their products at a time when readerships are soaring anyway due to record rates of economic growth and expanding literacy levels. In this highly favourable climate Indian editors are in the enviable, and indeed almost unique, position of notching circulation gains almost irrespective of what they serve up on the news-stands. The standard fare is selling, so why invest in the time or training that journalists would require to engage in a far more demanding form of journalism? India isn't England or America, after all.

Some have suggested that the popularity of literary journalism is 'inextricably connected with the effort to express the force and magnitude of the American experience'.[24] Traditional journalism, others have argued, is simply not vivid enough to render the extraordinary changes in American life. With Vietnam, political assassinations, rock, drugs, hippies, yahoos and Nixon, America in the 1960s and early 1970s was going through a time of extraordinary upheaval. As he later wrote in his book *Dispatches*, Michael Herr embraced New Journalism in his reportage from Vietnam, because 'conventional journalism could no more reveal this war than conventional firepower could win it'.

But aren't the tumultuous changes which India is currently undergoing–economic liberalization, rapid technological advances, recurring bouts of communal violence, periodic nuclear showdowns with Pakistan across the Line of Control–every bit as extraordinary as anything America has experienced? Could anyone conceive of a larger, richer canvas for literary reportage than this always fascinating, and sometimes frightening, subcontinent at the start of the 21st century? *Tehelka*'s Basharat Peer cannot think of a better place to be a literary journalist than this point in history. 'Pakistanis and Indians both love telling stories and spend many hours socially doing precisely that,' says this young Kashmiri scribe. 'If a magazine that tells important stories and tells them well were to emerge, I am sure it would succeed.'[25] As Debashish Mukerji noted in his review of *Maximum City*, quoted at the start of this essay, 'There are treasure troves of fascinating stories all around us in this country and Mehta has shown how, with effort and patience, they can be unearthed and presented.'[26] It is a tantalizing prospect for those journalists who do want to escape from the inverted pyramid in order that they might not only chronicle but challenge and change the subcontinent. Never mind a million mutinies, India is a billion testimonies now.

Notes

1. Adam Hochschild, 'Capturing India's impossible city', *Harper's*, February 2005.
2. Debashish Mukerji, 'Journalism at its best', *The Week*, 5 January 2003.
3. Suketu Mehta, *Maximum City: Bombay Lost and Found* (London, Review, 2004).
4. Ryszard Kapuscinski, Keynote speech at the Lettres Ulysses award ceremony, Berlin, 4 October 2003.
5. Matthew Ricketson, 'True Stories: The power and pitfalls of literary journalism', in Suen Tapsall and Carolyn Varley (eds), *Journalism: Theory in Practice* (Melbourne, Oxford University Press, 2001), p. 152
6. Interview with the author, conducted at *Tehelka* office, Delhi, January 2006.
7. Tom Wolfe, *The New Journalism* (New York, Harper and Row, 1973), 'Preface'.
8. Ibid., p. 41
9. Jacqui Banaszynski, 'Why We Need Stories', *Nieman Reports*, Spring 2002, p. 41.
10. Mehta, *Maximum City*.
11. 'Sharing the Secrets of Fine Narrative Journalism', *Nieman Reports*, vol. 56, no. 1, Spring 2002.
12. Q&A with Suketu Mehta from the *New Jersey Star Ledger*, 10 October 2004.
13. Review in *The Economist*, 7 April 2005.
14. Mehta, *Maximum City*, p. 343.

15. Q&A with Suketu Mehta from the *New Jersey Star Ledger*, 10 October 2004.

16. Adam Hochschild, 'Capturing India's impossible city', *Harper's*, February 2005.

17. Q&A with Suketu Mehta from the *Wall Street Journal Europe*, 8 October 2004.

18. Ibid.

19. Christopher Parkes, 'Cry Wolfe', *FT Weekend Magazine*, 17 September 2005.

20. Ricketson, 'True Stories', p. 158.

21. Ibid., p. 161.

22. Robert S Boynton, *The New New Journalism* (New York, Vintage, 2005), 'Introduction', p. xi.

23. 'Sharing the Secrets of Fine Narrative Journalism', *Nieman Reports*, Spring 2002.

24. Chris Anderson, *Style as Argument* (Carbondale, Southern Illinois Press, 1987), p. 2.

25. Interview with author, conducted at offices of *Tehelka*, January 2006.

26. Mukerji, 'Journalism at its best'.

About the Editor and Contributors

Editor

Nalini Rajan is presently Associate Professor at the Asian College of Journalism in Chennai. She obtained her Ph.D. in Social Communications, specializing in Political Philosophy, at the Catholic University of Louvain, Belgium. Her thesis, 'Within the Fragments–A Non-Holistic Approach to Indian Culture', was published the same year. She has been a Homi Bhabha Fellow (1991–93), a Fellow of the Indian Council for Social Science Research (1993–95), and has held visitng fellowships at the Hastings Centre, New York (1996), and at the universities of Oxford and Edinburgh (1997), among others. She has also worked for the *Economic Times*, Mumbai.

Dr Rajan has previously publsihed two books with Sage, entitled *Secularism, Democracy, Justice: Implications of Rawlsian Principles in India* (1998) and *Democracy and the Limits of Minority Rights* (2002).

Contributors

Ethirajan Anbarasan is a BBC World Service journalist based in London. He writes regularly for BBC News Online. His academic interests include new media and its impact.

Mustafa K Anuar is Associate Professor at the School of Communication, Universiti Sains Malaysia. He is also a joint coordinator of Charter2000–Aliran, a citizens' media initiative that is dedicated to media reform. Through Charter2000–Aliran, Dr Mustafa helps manage the *Malaysian Media Monitors' Diary*, a Weblog that monitors developments in Malaysia's media industry.

Robert Brown is senior lecturer in journalism at Napier University in Edinburgh. He has taught at the University of Westminster in London and has been a visiting professor at the Asian College of Journalism in Chennai. Before entering academia he was media editor of the *Independent* in London and deputy editor of a Sunday newspaper in his native Scotland.

Subarno Chattarji is Reader, Department of English, University of Delhi. He has a D.Phil degree from Oxford University on American poetry and the Vietnam War. He was a Fulbright Senior Research Fellow, 2004–05. His research interests include media and conflict, globalization and identity politics, and Vietnamese representations of the Vietnam conflict.

Aditi De is currently a Bangalore-based freelance writer and editor. Cultural journalism has been her forte since her stints at *Indian Express*, Chennai, and *Deccan Herald*, Bangalore. Her passions in life include travel, interacting with creative people engaged in the arts, crafts and textiles, and sharing special time with children.

Subhashini Dinesh started her career as a trainee journalist on the political news-desk of the *Telegraph*, Kolkata, and worked her way up to becoming the chief sub-editor of the newspaper. Her masters' degree in political science helped her write analytical articles for the editorial pages. She has also worked in the *New Indian Express* and *Business Line*. Presently she is Associate Professor at the Asian College of Journalism, where she teaches editing, news writing, newspaper production and design.

Geeta Doctor is a well-known freelance writer and critic on art and literature who lives in Chennai. She contributes to a number of magazines and newspapers in India and outside and is known for her acerbic style and forthright manner of expressing her views.

V Geetha is a writer, teacher and translator and has been involved with the women's movement for over a decade. She has written in English and Tamil on caste, gender and popular culture. Her current interests include education and religion. She is an editor with Tara Publishing, Chennai.

Amanda Harper has been a journalist for more than 20 years. After a career in print journalism, she joined the BBC as a radio reporter and producer, before moving into television as a reporter, producer and documentary film-maker. She currently teaches broadcast journalism.

India Together (**IT**) is an electronic publication devoted to coverage of public affairs, policy, and development in India, providing news in proportion to the country's broad development experiences. The publication is edited and published from Bangalore by two lead editors, **Subramaniam Vincent** and **Ashwin Mahesh**, who are also the co-founders. Mahesh and Vincent work with a team of 35–40 freelance writers, who range from reporters and commentators to development professionals and scholars. *India Together* has been in publication since 1998. Over 1,700 articles have been published as of year-end 2005.

Ammu Joseph is a journalist and media watcher based in Bangalore, writing mainly on issues concerning gender, human development and the media. Among her publications are *Whose News? The Media and Women's Issues* (with Kalpana Sharma, Sage 1994 and 2006) and *Making News: Women in Journalism* (Konark 2000 and Penguin 2005).

K Kalpana is a social activist and doctoral student at the Madras Institute of Development Studies. Her research and activism interests include issues of community health, gender and microcredit.

Anjali Kamat is a freelance writer, radio journalist and activist based in New York. She has an MA in Near Eastern Studies from New York University and works with the NGO, Coalition for the International Criminal Court.

Desikan Krishnan teaches photojournalism at the Asian College of Journalism, Chennai, and has worked for Associated Press, and is presently with the *Hindu* group of publications.

Sashi Kumar is Chairman, *Media Development Foundation*, and has wide experience in the print and broadcast media. He headed the first south Indian satellite channel, Asianet, for several years.

Shonali Muthalaly graduated from the Asian College of Journalism, Chennai, in 2001, and is currently working as senior reporter in the Metro section of the *Hindu*, Chennai. Her job involves tracking city trends, nosing out quirky stories and co-writing a humour column on the battle of the sexes. She has just completed work on a book on Chennai's restaurant scene for the *Hindu*, which involved a lot of eating out and many hours on the treadmill.

Siddharth Narrain has been a journalist with the *Hindu* in New Delhi, and has earlier worked for *Frontline* magazine. He has covered issues related to law and human rights. He is a part of the campaign for the repeal of Section 377 of the Indian Penal Code, the law that criminalizes homosexuality in India.

V K Natraj, former director of the Madras Institute of Development Studies, has been registrar and head, Institute of Development Studies, at Mysore University. His interests include development economics and devolution.

Frederick Noronha, or FN, is Goa's most active journalist in cyberspace. He mostly writes on developmental issues, the environment, information technology for development, the media, and related themes. He runs *Docuwallahs2*, a network for documentary film-makers in India, and *IndiaEJ*, a list for environmental journalists. See http://fn.goa-india.org.

A S Panneerselvan is Executive Director of Panos South Asia. A bilingual journalist and writer, he was Managing Editor of Sun TV, India, between May 2001 and June 2004. He was in the founding team of *Outlook* magazine and was its bureau chief in South India since the magazine's inception in 1995 to May 2001. Earlier he had worked for the *Business India* group. He has written extensively on neighbourhood relations and the nuclear issue.

Subhash Rai is chief sub-editor, *Frontline*. He started his online journalistic career with *Economic Times Online*. He was a founding member of indya.com's news channel. He then joined the Indian Institute of Journalism and New Media, Bangalore, as Assistant Professor and Director, Centre for New Media. He edits a blog on online journalism and moderates a discussion forum.

Geeta Ramaseshan is an advocate practising in the Madras High Court and a legal scholar, working on women's issues and human rights. She is also adjunct faculty at the Asian College of Journalism, Chennai.

Baradwaj Rangan is film critic for the *New Sunday Express* and a freelance writer whose articles on the arts, entertainment and humour are archived at http://brangan.easyjournal.com/.

Sandhya Rao gave up a satisfying career in mainstream journalism to work on books for children. For the last 10 years, she has been an editor with Tulika Publishers, a leading children's book publisher based in Chennai. She is a writer and translator. Her *My Friend, the Sea* won a special prize at the Berlin Children's and Youth Literature Festival, 2005, and she has translated Astrid Lindgren's *Pippi Longstrump* into Hindi.

D Ravikumar is a Pondicherry-based activist and theoretican of the Dalit movement in Tamil Nadu. Along with S Anand of *Outlook* magazine, Ravikumar launched the *Navayana* publishing house in November 2003.

Robin Reisig is a lecturer at Columbia University's Graduate School of Journalism. She has written for many newspapers and magazines, including the *Village Voice* and the *Washington Post*, and was a feature and opinion-page editor at *Newsday*. In 2006, she won the Columbia Journalism School's alumni award.

Sunil Saxena is the vice-president of Express Network Private Limited, the Internet company of the New Indian Express group. In this capacity he has set up nine news sites in five languages. He has worked for 16 years as a print journalist, seven years as an Internet journalist and six years as a journalism educator. He is also the author of two books: *Breaking News*, the first book on Internet journalism in India, and *Headline Writing*.

Vijaya Swaminath is an adjunct faculty at the Asian College of Journalism, Chennai, India. She has a Ph.D. in Astrophysics from the University of Wisconsin, Madison. She has written a book, *The Science of Sights and Sounds*, published by McGraw-Hill. She is a freelance science writer contributing to *Frontline*.